Cry Havoc

Cry Havoc

W. Redvers Dent

Edited, introduced, and restored to the original text
by Bruce Meyer

Rock's Mills Press
Oakville, Ontario
2017

Published by
ROCK'S MILLS PRESS
www.rocksmillspress.com

Copyright © 2017 by The Estate of W. Redvers Dent
Introduction and editorial arrangements copyright © 2017 by Bruce Meyer
Published by arrangement with the Estate and the Editor. All rights reserved.

Cry Havoc was originally published in substantially different form by the Macmillan Company of Canada in 1930 under the title *Show Me Death*. Editions were also published in 1930 by Harper & Bros., New York, and Constable & Co., London.

For information contact:
Rock's Mills Press, 2645 Castle Hill Crescent, Oakville, ON L6H 6J1
customer.service@rocksmillspress.com

Introduction

W. Redvers Dent's novel, *Cry Havoc*, was published in 1930, almost twelve years following the end of World War One. Written by an ex-soldier more than a decade after his experience of war, the novel depicts a young man named Lionel Thor surviving an incomparable sequence of tragedies and misadventures, almost in the form of a *bildungsroman*. We witness the growth of Thor's mind and his evolving grasp of theology and philosophy in a novel whose depiction of the war is unsparing.

Few novels about World War One rival *Cry Havoc*. Those novels that come close are arguably Charles Yale Harrison's *Generals Die in Bed* (1930) and *All Quiet on the Western Front* (1929) by German writer Erich Marie Remarque. (Remarque's detached journalistic prose was a strong influence on Dent's own novel.) Both *All Quiet* and *Generals* were considered to be definitive statements about the war, benchmarks of a new perception that spawned Modernism and a public awareness of the brutal realities of a violent century. Where Dent's book differs from other World War One novels is his embrace of the humanity of his characters, their philosophies, their spiritual perceptions of the war, and the cost not only to the body or the mind of those who suffer through the horrors, but the cost to their souls. In the end, what emerges is not merely a parable of the pity of war, but a vision of redemption that overcomes the madness and hatred that the war engendered. The incredible journey from despair to redemption forms the narrative of Dent's under-age protagonist, Lionel Thor.

The circumstances surrounding the publication of *Cry Havoc*, however, have led to the near-erasure of this unique and haunting work from Canadian literary history. Dent's original manuscript was rewritten as a much weaker novel by another writer, and was nearly misattributed to that writer when the Dent family intervened, requesting the republication of the novel in its original form.

Cry Havoc has now been restored in this edition to the original text as composed by Dent in the late 1920s. The book itself, however, has a curious publishing history. For many years, it was attributed to Raymond Knister (1899–1932), an author known for short stories as well as the novel *White Narcissus* (1929). Hugh S. Eayr, the publisher of Macmillan of Canada, asked Knister to make editorial changes to Dent's manuscript. But the manuscript only needed a copy edit, not a rewrite. Knister went overboard, changing far more than spelling errors. Knister needed employment and Eayr sought to help by creating a make-work project for a Macmillan author (whose own books were not selling).

At the time he wrote the book, Dent was an Anglican minister in Limerick, Saskatchewan. Between parish duties and suffering from lingering effects of lung damage, Dent composed the first draft of his novel with his wife, Olive Butcher Dent.

The manuscript Dent originally submitted to Macmillan was untitled, but he had envisioned "Why Smitest Thou Me?" as the title. Both Eayr and Knister felt this proposed title was too "Biblical" to sell successfully. In the letter of March 15, 1929, Dent responds to various suggestions and criticisms from both Macmillan and Knister, especially with regard to the book's title:

> Just the other day I had a letter suggesting several new titles for the book but I am afraid I am not satisfied with any of them and in turn suggested *Travail* from "The souls of individuals, as the souls of nations, are born in travail."

In the ensuing correspondence, Dent was persuaded that neither a political title nor a Biblical title was appropriate. Instead, he turned to Shakespeare, to the concluding portion of Mark Antony's funeral oration for Julius Caesar in Act III, Scene I of the play by that name. A separate title page was appended to the original manuscript and the title *Cry Havoc* became Dent's choice. The new title had not been among the suggestions offered by either Eayrs or Knister, and appears to be Dent's work. Though *Cry Havoc* was arguably the most apropos title for the book, Knister and the publisher won out with their rather sensational choice: *Show Me Death!* The choice of the book's title stems from the fact that the protagonist, Lionel Thor, feels that he is a bad omen to those people who he encounters, and that to know him is to be cursed. In many ways, the phrase from Shakespeare is far more fitting. *Cry Havoc* is a study of the ways in which a world can be seized with violence when the rhetoric of society, government, and religion takes hold. Not only does Thor lose almost everyone he has loved during the war, but he also becomes a tragic metaphor for both lost youth and broken youth.

In Dent's mind, the book was "meant to be a message to [his fellow] parsons and to show that man is to be pitied more than condemned, as both Sinclair Lewis and parsons do condemn him [Man]" (Letter to Raymond Knister, March 15, 1929). To Dent, sin was comprised of actions committed by mankind against God, and foremost among those actions was murder—the murder of war. His arguments against war were met with derision to the point that he was relieved of his charge as a minister of an Anglican church in Orillia, Ontario, not for having spoken out against war, but for having used cuss words in *Cry Havoc*'s text. The absurdity of counting swearing and raw language as a greater sin than murder was too much for the author. For Dent, there was the larger issue of Man's inhumanity to Man that needed to be addressed. The reading public missed the point. The battle to change hearts and minds, cussing aside, was not going to be won by a solitary author who

Introduction

was simply attempting to tell the truth of war.

Much of the middle portions of the book, especially the stories of Lionel's adventures with Allen, are a part of a larger theological debate about the origins of war and the destructiveness of mankind. The scenes of debate are reminiscent of Jane Eyre's discussions with schoolmate Helen Burns in Charlotte Brontë's *Jane Eyre*. What Dent was attempting to work out was more than a theological question of why man goes to war: he was struggling to understand how a society could blindly believe in a God that would permit such suffering and slaughter as an expression of divine consciousness. Dent argues that God is a force in things; this argument goes back to fifth-century Christian theologian St. Augustine. Dent denies God's meddling in human affairs and, in an answer that seems right out of the mouth of John Milton, answers the question "where was God?" with the question "where was Man?"

In Knister's rewrites, the theological questions take a back seat to the relationships between the characters. Dent's conclusion was that mankind still possesses a sense of good; Knister removed this conclusion, along with the theological leap taken by Dent to avoid a sappy, melodramatic ending. For a man who had witnessed the full horrors of the war, Dent's theological conclusion is both miraculous yet redeeming, not only for the character but also for the reader (who has experienced Lionel Thor's torments). For Dent, the ability for survivors to find redemption of some kind from the war's horror was more precious than any happy ending could possibly offer. Knister, who himself had no firsthand experience of the war, arguably ruined a novel that spoke to the triumph of the human spirit. For Knister, the literary ending, expected by readers who (like him) were far removed from the trenches, took precedence. The original ending—a soldier's hard-won philosophical insight that the war had not been fought for a happy ending but for a spiritually deeper understanding of good and evil—was lost in Knister's simplistic rewrite.

In Knister's hands, Lionel's school chum, Hartley, with whom he enlists in the Canadian Mounted Rifles, becomes a figure of an almost homoerotic relationship. Even the encounters with Allen are rife with innuendo about male-male relationships. Dent was unequivocal about such relationships, and he describes the Lionel/Allen relationship as a Platonic bond between understanding minds with no hint of physicality. It was Knister who transformed Hartley into a male love object, inserting a scene into the novel where Lionel and Hartley go swimming in the Humber River and Hartley's naked body becomes an object of attraction.

In addition to giving the book a new title, Knister effectively poeticized the plot by overwriting Dent's blunt and unsparing narrative prose. He also blurred the realities of life in the trenches of the First World War that Dent had sought to chronicle so meticulously. Dent's language was toned down for fear that readers might find the soldiers "uncouth." In fact, Dent had explained in the March 15, 1929 letter that:

Profanity—Every other word in the army was a curse, and no army character would be proper without it, just as their grammar was rotten and meant to be so. You can take my word for it that the profanity in it is mild compared to the reality. Sex also was as natural in the conversation as cursing. Any soldier would recognize the authenticity of the episode with Luella. It was made purposely blunt, so that there would be nothing romantic attached to it. I didn't want anybody to get the idea that petting was nice, and at that, is it any worse than *Elmer Gantry*?

Knister saw little purpose in Dent's determined sense of authenticity. How could he? After leaving Victoria College with a case of pneumonia, Knister spent the war years working on his father's farm on the north shore of Lake Erie. For Knister, the war was about as far from the Talbot Trail as the moon. Dent, on the other hand, had been there. He had tasted the cordite, he had been gassed in the trenches and was told that he would not live beyond his thirtieth birthday as a result of the damage to his lungs (though he lived to the age of sixty-three). As was the case with his protagonist, Dent had survived some of worst battles in history. When he speaks of suffering he speaks from experience. Lionel Thor, although far more wounded than Dent, was not merely a shadow of his author; Lionel Thor is a metaphor for an entire generation that was murdered and broken in all but spirit. Dent knew what he was talking about.

Knister, it must be said, can be forgiven (in some part, though not completely) for poeticizing Dent's novel. The reading public in the late 1920s did not want to hear about the realities of the war. Harrison's *Generals Die in Bed* had been voted the best novel of 1928 by *The New York Post*, well ahead of Hemingway's *The Sun Also Rises* (1926) and Morley Callaghan's gangster novel, *Strange Fugitive* (1928); yet like Dent's book, it too went largely unnoticed in Canada. Critics of the time, such as E.K. Brown (who in his turn taught a whole generation of major Canadian literary critics including Northrop Frye) argued that "nothing of significance was written during the war years" (*On Canadian Poetry* [1943]). Brown, along with many other critics, dismissed the war poets and novelists. What Brown did not realize—and what history has shown—is that Modernism was born in the trenches of Ypres, the Somme, Passchendaele, and the slope of Vimy Ridge. Knister's language, the language of acceptable story-telling of the time, is a long way from Dent's gritty, often harsh prose. Dent captures the nuances of accent, from the Americans (his friend the Yank and the Nurse who is also known as "the Yank") to the cockney slang of an east-end Londoner, to the subtle slurring of a New Zealander. The point that Dent was making was simple: the war was not merely a struggle between men but a melding of all the dimensions of the English language into a new consciousness.

Dent believed that this new consciousness would emerge in the war's aftermath. Lionel embraces the philosophy of Allen on his road to a view of God

Introduction

that ultimately becomes the expression of redemption in the face of nihilism and horror. Dent believed that another war was inevitable—and this he believed as early as 1929—and that the military machine that had drawn his era into total armed conflict would drive the next generation into a similar disaster. In this Dent was profoundly prophetic.

This Rock's Mills Press edition restores Dent's original prologue to *Cry Havoc* (Knister had deleted it). To contemporary readers, Dent's rage might seem misogynistic. The war, at least as he saw it, was not merely driven by male behaviour but by the women who encouraged and played off that behaviour. For mothers, such as Mrs. Thor, the loss of two sons and a husband, to say nothing of the horrific bodily harm caused to her remaining son, was ennobling. Here, Dent attempted to explain that the lives of the men of his generation—the lives that were wasted and scattered across the battlefields of France and Belgium—were shaped by misperceptions of three things: God, women, and war. This trio of 'powers,' as Dent perceived them, were the cornerstones of Victorian society. The social rebellions of the Victorian era had been largely attempts to liberate the first two from the societal strictures that had tempered them for centuries, while the final element in the trio, war, had been long idealized during the Pax Victoriana, the one hundred years of peace between Waterloo and the Battle of Ypres, that had dulled the harsh realities of armed conflict. Dent, in *Cry Havoc*, finds himself fighting two wars: the actual, violent battles of the Western Front, and the psychological strangle-hold of the archaic virtues that dictated the structure of society in 1914. He noted that the book was a psychological journey out of himself and out of his world—even out of the boundaries of humanity—in which he understood that his experiences had brought him to the threshold of a new vision and a new purpose for post-war man.

> And I have grown to love and hate of at least two of them and from the other learned many things pertaining to life and death. I did not actually find God until I sat down to write my life, and then I found Him at my shoulder.... War supplied the scenery to my life, a scenery that lived and moved and had its being, but after all—was just scenery.

In some ways, Lionel Thor is Walter Redvers Dent. Dent, of course, denied that the work was autobiographical in his letter to Knister and tried to convince the poet-editor that the work was almost "entirely fictitious, and yet built on characters I have met...." The repeated hospital stays in England, the acute description of the wards, the convalescences, the dreaded returns to the front carry too much of a sense of verity to be fictional. Where *Cry Havoc* tells the story of a young man who went to war to prove himself worthy of his own life, the reality of Dent's own biography suggests an uncanny similitude between author and character. The novel goes far beyond what a fiction-writer could have conceived in 1929. The careful detailing of the war suggests that at the heart of the work there is a profound sense of a memoir that borders on a record of a living nightmare.

Walter Redvers Dent was born on May 3, 1900, though his enlistment papers indicate that his date of birth was four years earlier. His father, Lionel Dent, had fought in the Northwest Rebellion; the name of the protagonist is partly a tribute to Dent's respect had for his father. Walter Dent enlisted and was accepted into the Canadian Expeditionary Force on August 31, 1915. It may have been his height, if not his weight, that helped him navigate through the recruitment process. Like his father, he was over six feet tall. He served through the Salient (the soldier's name for Flanders) for over three years. He was wounded during his service on the Western Front. Following his recovery he volunteered and was accepted into the Siberian Contingent of the Canadian Overseas Expeditionary Force in August of 1918, a force sent to Russia to assist the Czar and the White Russians in their efforts against the Bolsheviks. The tour of duty to Russia was possibly the worst assignment Dent could have accepted. The extreme cold likely exacerbated the damage to his lungs. But he survived the experience.

On his return to Canada in 1920, he studied at the University of Saskatchewan in Yorkton, and married Edith Olive Butcher in 1921. He became an Anglican clergyman, holding parishes in Burnaby, British Columbia and Limerick, Saskatchewan. While in Limerick, he suffered from the gas-inflicted damage to his lungs; he also went through a nervous breakdown, which may have been a result of his re-visitation of his war experiences as he wrote *Cry Havoc*.

The novel—as rewritten by Knister—was published in the early spring of 1930 to positive reviews, just as Dent assumed a parish in Orillia, Ontario. *The Toronto Star* hailed the book for its "vivid realism." *The Winnipeg Free Press* called the novel a work of "outstanding features." At the same time, there were recriminations against Dent's theology. The *Regina Post* wrote, "there are arguments presented that would no doubt arouse the wrath of staid old theologians, but as Mr. Dent has passed through hell on earth there is reason for allowing him latitude in this respect." The parishioners in Orillia were not nearly as forgiving or understanding. On May 3, 1930, an article datelined "Orillia" and published in the *Lethbridge Herald* quoted a prominent, though unnamed, member of the community:

> "He is a dangerous man," said a prominent Orillia businessman two weeks ago at Y's men's club banquet. "He said he was ashamed to be a Canadian, and decried pacificism. He said that was absolutely necessary in the world and should be taken as meat and drink. Talk like that is what starts wars."

The article also mentions how the women of the town also disliked Dent's

Introduction

novel. His parishioners boycotted his church, and he was dismissed from his post. In an article published in *The Toronto Telegram* within days of the Lethbridge column, Dent's church superior denied that the book was the reason for Dent's dismissal from his charge. When Dent was asked by *The Toronto Star* on June 7, 1930 if he would agree to preach again (should he be invited to do so), he replied that he would rather fish. Dent recognized that in speaking out against the war, his ideas were falling on deaf ears. As far as Canadian society was concerned, the war had been fought on principles of honour for the empire (God, King, and Country), and that nothing of lasting human value had been learned from the four years of agony. The Germans had been defeated. God, King and Country had been vindicated. There was nothing more to be said. Public opinion steadfastly stood behind the idea that war was moral, not matter how immoral it seemed from the perspective of those who had endured the suffering of the trenches. Yet for all the abuse he suffered from those who had no idea about what war did to human beings, Dent was not alone in his belief that the insanity of killing had to cease. In a preface to one of his books of poetry, Wilfred Owen, the great British war poet, wrote that the purpose of poetry was to warn (Owen, sadly, would not live to see this book of poetry in print). Canada would have to suffer more before it learned that it was caught up in an ever-repeating cycle of self-destruction.

Throughout the 1930s, Dent lived in Muskoka and worked at a series of odd jobs from a road work foreman to a fishing guide. He continued to write short stories that appeared in various publications, though these have never been collected. He joined the Canadian Air Force in 1940, but was found unfit to serve in an air crew, and instead was stationed in his native city of Toronto with stops in Brantford, Belleville and Trenton. Following the war, he moved to Vancouver, worked as a writer for the *Vancouver Sun* and other publications, ran and was defeated for a seat as a Progressive Conservative candidate in 1953, and died in 1963.

The book that appeared in 1930 and that caused Walter Dent such grief in his vocation as a clergyman, was almost republished several years ago under Knister's name as *Show Me Death!* But, as noted above, this re-publication was halted by the editor of this edition along with the support of the Dent family. This current edition, restored to its original text as the author wrote it, is a powerful testament to an experience that could not have been imagined, either by a poet/short story writer or by the readers who could not come to grips with its ground-breaking theology and the stark actuality of its content and language. *Cry Havoc* is arguably one of the finest, most complex novels of World War One. It is more than just a description of fighters in trenches; it is a focussed examination of an entire society at war, both on the front and behind the lines. It speaks to lives of those who were touched by the war: the nurses, the mothers, the fathers, the families, and the lonely soldiers who tried their best, against all the prevailing odds of societal norms and beliefs, to make sense of the senselessness in which they found themselves. Their experiences, their beliefs, their insights, were crucial to shaping the world we now live in. It is only fitting that almost one hundred years later, after decades of dismissal, neglect, and silence, Dent should finally be heard. Walter Dent was one of the millions who experienced "the war to end all wars" from a myriad of perspectives, and it is that scope that makes *Cry Havoc* not merely a rediscovery, but a recovery. This edition has returned to Dent his original voice, and has returned to Canadian literature a classic novel that should have been available more than eighty years ago.

DR. BRUCE MEYER
Professor, University Studies, Georgian College, Barrie
Visiting Professor, Literature, Victoria College, University of Toronto
December 2016

To Hartley—killed at the capture of
Passchendale Ridge, 1917.
Good Friend.

Prologue

God, Women and War—each one of them bound and fettered in a haze of dreams, so that no man can reach unto them. This is my story of all three, and of how I found them, not as they are painted but just as they are. And I have grown from hate to love of at least two of them and from the other learned many things pertaining to life and death. I did not actually find God until I sat down to write my life, and then I found Him at my shoulder. Women found me, put themselves in my stumbling way, until at last I came to recognize them, not as some dream, but made of flesh and blood, just as you and I, and War supplied the scenery to my life, a scenery that lived and moved and had its being, but after all—was just scenery. There is a sermon here for you somewhere. Find it.

One

My mother was not like other mothers—the kind you read about—for to begin with I wasn't wanted. Her words, repeated in my presence from the time I was able to understand them, still ring in my ears: "Two children are enough for any woman to look after." I was the third. It didn't take me long to find out how I got into this mortal sphere—accidents will happen. There were two brothers older than I, enough older to seem grown up. Gordon was tall, fair, handsome, suave, like his mother, and could charm any girl into obedience. Bob was like Gordon, except that where Gordon displayed only a momentary interest, he displayed a heat of passion, and won his way. Mother loved him too, but not so much as Gordon, who was the first and in her image. I was different, —an Ishmael, tall and dark with dark eyes, and an awkwardness in her presence because I knew she hated me. She was very entertaining to strangers and could be kind to my brothers, but to my father and me she seemed a devil incarnate who plagued and tore at us for the sheer enjoyment of it. Dad and I were much closer to one another as a result. He—God bless him—took me in the real sporting spirit of his family, a line of Empire Loyalists, being proud of them, yet ashamed of himself for not living up to the glorious heritage.

But I found a mother at last. I was a long gangling boy with the propitiatory, ingratiating look of a half-starved mongrel dog. I did want to be loved and petted and mothered like other boys, though I only half realized it. And I found her in this way; I wanted spending money and an excuse to keep out of the way of my own mother, and as the local butcher needed a boy to run messages after school and on Saturdays for the magnificent sum of $1.50 per week, I applied for the job. The butcher himself was out, but his wife was there looking after the shop, a woman still in her thirties who had guessed wrong in husbands. She was clever, probably lonely, and we liked each other at once. Perhaps she scarcely knew at first that she was becoming my mother, but I worshipped her, adored her. She was to be my star, my guide, my life; I would have died for her. She had two children, little tots whom I loved because of her, just as I hated the husband, a blonde, rather good-looking man with the manners and outlook of a motor salesman. He was the sort of man whom women hate and yet in some cases, for some reason, admit to their homes when their husbands are away. Women know the kind I mean. Mrs. Braithwaite knew, but greater love hath no woman than she who lays down her life for her children. She took me to her, made me hers. We were both lonely, both not wanted very much in the world. We talked a lot, and carefully, day by day, she implanted seeds, nursed and guided me, and kept me clean from the influence of other boys. She *made* me clean, *made* me respect women, and taught me to look for beauty in the midst of ugliness.

My home became a place to eat and sleep.

One day Dad came to fetch me from the store for some reason. We were both standing looking out of the window when he came. Mrs. Braithwaite had not met him, and I awkwardly introduced them. Dad lingered, and I stood by Mrs. Brathwaite, her hand on my head ruffling my hair, while she gazed out of the window.

I faced Dad a little defiantly but didn't move. I loved to have her ruffle my hair. They talked casually, then suddenly Dad said, "Lionel seems to have found both home and a mother here." She half turned to him, and for a minute was silent, then she said lightly, "No, not a mother. Lionel and I are just children of the storm who get along fine, don't we, Lionel?" I heard no word, but they must have spoken, for Dad asked, "I am accepted then, into the company?" and turned to me: "Come on Lionel, we must go. We have to go."

I looked back when we were outside, and saw Mrs. Braithwaite watching me. When we reached home, on the porch Dad stopped suddenly to stoop and kiss me, as he said, "Poor kid, life is sure some storm for you." He seemed to be happy. I had never seen him so happy as he was that night, whistling and content. We were good friends after that. Dad and I.

When I was fourteen we moved from our old home. For a year, Mother had nagged, stormed and cried, till we moved over to the west end of the city. The boys liked it because we were nearer to the park, and the lake for swimming. She claimed that it was a more pleasant, a more refined district. For me the important thing was that I was a long way from my star. But I still managed to see her. I would take the street car by myself, and wait patiently at the transfer corners, looking at the strange people. And when I reached her place she welcomed me just the same as before.

One day I found her looking very tired. She told me that her husband had been away all day, and she had had to do all the work of the shop. It was a summer evening, the sun was setting, and she leaned wearily against the back door watching it. I waited for her to speak, and she said, "Oh, Lionel, I would give anything to die like that, just like that, in one great triumphant burst of radiance." I realized dimly then, and more keenly long afterward, how she suffered and was sad, so that she no longer thought of *life*, but of *death*. Of dying. Such words seemed like rain that falls on your hand, made by destiny to plunge into my spirit and tincture its essence.

Two

It is a peculiar thing that time and memory soften the harsh and brutal circumstances of life. If I were to give a detailed description, a story of my early years, I would find myself dwelling on the experience which we all have in youth, and which give to our memories of it an aroma of beauty, a haze of romance. Therefore, and for other reasons, since it is of my life as a soldier that I wish to tell, I shall skip lightly over these first years, and give only salient incidents and traits of the people with whom I found myself growing up: the things which made me different, an individual separate from my fellows.

Today some of that same romance hangs over the days of the Great War, when millions of men went forward bravely, brilliantly, to die. It has assumed the character of a play for the edification of mankind, if only we could forget the enthralling nature and the awesome sweep of its portents, and remember the moral. But the lesson seems to be generally forgotten. We still mouth of the survival of the fittest, when our civilization is denying the theory. Ever since the dawn of history one kind of man has died before his time, and that type is the strongest and ablest among men. Why did they die? For the protection of the weak, once somebody had started the conflict. We make special efforts to prolong the lives of the unfit, and then send the strongest men out to die for their protection. It is a farce, a burlesque. Who survived the Great War? Was it the strong? Most certainly not, the men who survived were those left behind, who were not healthy enough to die. Is it any wonder we have post-war troubles? Why the very children being born are from those not counted fit to die. Such a joke, such a tragedy!

And Toronto, the city of Tories and United Empire Loyalists, the city of Imperialism handed down from father to son, the city that has seen war once when the Americans burned it, and which in turn organised a few companies of militia and marched through the whole American army to burn Washington. The city that could be roused like a fighting, snarling pack of wolves at the cry of "No truck nor trade with the Yankees." This city, the city of my birth, the city that I loved, and still love for its peace and serenity and hominess—went mad, stark, staring rabidly mad. Gangs of University students and civilians marched up and down the thoroughfares looking for Germans, demolished a German club on King Street, raided the German consul, finally ending at the Armouries where they shouted for a chance to get at the Germans. Then they went home, home to their wives, who pricked them down to normal like the gas bags they were.

My brothers were men by this time, and came and went as they pleased. Once in a while, I would hear my mother give some girl a dressing down for phoning for her boys. Bob seemingly was very popular with the girls, with his devil-may-care air. He could plead the virtue out of any girl, or so I overheard my mother say once, with pride in her voice. Gordon was more cool, more suave, planned campaigns to gain his objective, and, I gathered, usually won it. At least, one night a girl came to the house, went into the sitting room with mother, and I heard sobs alternating with mother's strident voice loudly upholding her sons. "Why, my boys would never think of such a thing. And if it is true, why did you give in? No girl who is decent would ever give in to any man. You are nothing but a common streetwalker, get out of my house before I call the police."

The sobs grew farther apart, the street door slammed, and Mother came back to where I was sitting, puffing, looking virtuous, and snorting, "Humph, indeed, indeed! Mothers are a sex to themselves, there are not just two sexes but three, men, women, and mothers. For the last, the sons and daughters they favor cast out all consideration for anyone else in the world."

The girl's father came that night, and he and dad were closeted together for a long time. When Dad came out into the kitchen once he was clenching and unclenching his hands, his brown eyes were black, with pin points of light. He didn't speak, didn't see me, but just stood there for a moment. The decision was finally made, and he went back. When I went to bed, Mother was listening at the head of the stairs to their talking. She did not seem to see me either, and I went into my room. Then complete silence settled upon the house for hours, a silence that fairly shrieked. I couldn't sleep. The girl's father hadn't left.

Then, steps on the veranda, shouts, laughs, a girl's laughter too. The door opened. Bob, Gordon, and a girl were there, I could tell by the voices. Then Bob's voice: "Hello Dad old scout, what do you think; Gord and I enlisted in the army, and I married Edith. Meet *my wife*, Mr. Thor." A shriek from Mother, patter, patter down the stairs.

"Oh, oh, my boys, my boys, surely you haven't joined the army? And married, married. Oh my poor boy, she must have tempted you, why you are only a child. Oh, oh, oh!"

Cry Havoc

Then Dad's voice, very quiet, yet so distinct it made me shiver. "Gordon, I want to see you, come in here."

"Sure, Dad, what do you want?" A door slammed, Mother talked loudly, excitedly, telling Bob about the girl. Bob laughed and said, "I always warned the kid, he'd be having a shotgun wedding, why he's a regular Mormon. What? Oh, shucks, listen, Mother, don't kid yourself." And in a tone of admiration, "Why, say, that kid of yours could get a statue into life once he—"

The study door opened, mother's voice in a babble of crying, started after Dad, harsh, strident, making me grit my teeth. Then Gordon's voice, quiet, but with a new tone in it that I couldn't place. "Oh for God's sake, Mother, shut up. It wasn't her fault. I'll marry her tomorrow. Now for heaven's sake let me go to bed in peace. Good-night, Dad, good-night, Mr. Davidson. I'll surely be at your house in the morning. *And* tell her—tell her I do like her and am only too glad to have her accept me. Tell her that. Now, Mother, go to bed and keep quiet." Gordon is a man.

Then Bob spoke up. "Well, Mother, you will have to put the wife up tonight. This is our honeymoon." Mother pattered upstairs with Gordon following slowly, dragging his feet. Dad followed Gordon. Bob and his wife went into the living-room. At the top of the stairs Gordon stopped for Dad to catch up, and after a moment's silence he said quietly and, respectfully, "Don't worry, Dad, honest to God, I will make her a good husband. And I will be going away next week in the army, anyway."

Dad's voice came in reply, understandingly. "I know you will, son. You are going to marry her, and you may have to pay, pay daily, hourly, for this. You will be tied to her always, it won't matter what she becomes, careless, dirty, dowdy, shrewish. And if you are ambitious she may hold you back and now I almost feel like telling you to take the first train out. I *know*. My own Dad taught and practised one thing, and that was, that a man must play the game, and play by the rules and you are expected to marry her. What are you going to do?"

"I'll marry her, Dad. I honestly think I'll never come back from overseas, so it won't matter anyway. I am almost glad this happened, in a way. I've found you out. Why, Mother always told us to stay away from you, that you were a brute, and so on. I guess she had us frightened of you." He laughing, added, "That's why we have acted so brave in your presence lately. We wanted to show you we were grown up, and not afraid of you. But I understand a little better now. Women are darn queer creatures, aren't they? I wonder what makes mother that way?"

Dad said nothing in answer except, "Oh, well, son. It doesn't matter. I guess I'll go to bed." Gordon's steps were brisk in contrast to his, as he went to bed. When I went to sleep an amazing jumble of things remained in my mind, but I seemed to hear and see these words: Gordon expected to get killed, *killed*.

Three

The next week was one of hysterics on Mother's part, and continuous denunciation of Dad. "Why don't you stop them from going?" "Oh, I wish you were young enough to go," or, "If my boys are killed you will be a murderer for allowing them to go." "Oh, I hate you for looking on so complacently, you actually think they should go. I hate you, hate you!" And she put me in my place with:

"It's a pity you are not old enough to go in their places, you are no good anyway, it would be a pleasure to be rid of you." Her pose to strangers was:

"Yes, my boys are going, you can't stop them, and I know my duty. I am terribly wounded to see them go, but still they are brave and gallant lads. And that is the cross mothers have to bear. I *am* proud of them."

There was a great bustle for Gordon's marriage, and both boys were away for three short days' honeymoon. Then preparation for the day of departure. One afternoon Dad and I were downtown and met Mrs. Braithwaite shopping. She looked tired and unhappy, and dad looked worn and older. She saw me, came up and said to us, "Well, Lionel, your dad and you both look as though you have been in the storm. Let's go and have a cup of tea, and you can tell me your troubles." So we dropped into a tea shop on Yonge Street, but curiously, neither of them talked about their troubles. They seemed almost lighthearted, Dad smiled and talked, and I was glad to listen. I was at peace, and so were they, our spirits just resting.

But it had to end, Dad finally rose to go, and awkwardly I rose too. He motioned me back, and said, "Stay in harbor, son, stay in harbor. See Mrs. Braithwaite home. I am the only one who has to go." Mrs. Braithwaite stood up at his words, and for almost a minute they stared at each other with never a word spoken, and at length each slowly smiled at the other, but there was a tear in Mrs. Braithwaite's eye, which ran down her cheek. Suddenly Dad said, "The joke's on me, isn't it, and on you, too? And I never did think much of anybody who could not take a joke." With that he left.

We remained motionless and watched him go, then with a start we turned to our chairs. "Well, Lionel, I think the best thing you can do is to go to the movies. I would rather be alone anyway, and you would like it, I am sure." I did not want to leave her, but sat watching her tap with her spoon, tap, tap, tap. I felt somehow as though someone were drowning before my eyes, and I could do nothing.

I went to the movies, saw Charlie Chaplin, forgot everything, and enjoyed myself.

Then came the day when my brothers left on their picnic trip for the old country. That is how they regarded it. Time and again, I heard them tell of the fun they would have in England. They figured the war would be over and nicely settled in six months. Bob's exact words were, "Darn it, I wish the war wouldn't be over. I would like to get a crack at it." Gordon, while agreeing with Bob, seemed quieter since his marriage. When some neighbors complimented him on his patriotism, he said:

"Patriotism, bunk. If we're Canadians, we are going for a holiday and a little adventure. If we are English, we enlisted to get a trip 'ome to the old land. If this war lasts three years as Kitchener says it will, it will be the guys who enlist next year, who will be doing it out of patriotism. Bob thinks we are going to have a swell holiday, but I'm a little doubtful."

And so, regarding it as a great lark, did the Canadian Contingent entrain for the war. Mother and Dad and I went to the station to see them off. Mother made me go. I hate crowds, especially at such things as weddings or funerals, and it seemed that this was going to be like that. There would be crying, as at a wedding. Mother would carry on terribly, though the boys were off for a good time. I envied them, and wished I were a man and that I could go along.

My brothers were dressed hodge-podge, part old militia uniforms of the Q.O.R., part civilian. They looked funny. At the station, all I can remember is frantic cheers, catcalls, chalk-marks all over the coaches, "On to Berlin" etc. Shouts of "Give 'em one for me." "Bring home the German sausage." Mother was crying and waving her handkerchief, while the two brides were silent, with veils over their faces, and Dad stood with a face like stone. I was curious. I had never seen people so frantically boisterous before.

The train began to move, which was the signal for more and louder shouts, as heads appeared again at the windows of the cars, waving good-bye, some throwing kisses, and even crying. Then the train took the bend, went out of sight, and for a moment there was absolute silence. Not a person moved, time seemed to have stopped. The angel of death or some grim presence hovered over all, and shouted something in our ears. I heard him distinctly saying,

"Never forget, this is your last sight of them, never forget, your last sight." A woman sobbed and sobbed. We sneaked away, the whole multitude shuffling furtively from the station while each looked at the other to see if anyone besides himself had heard the dread words.

Dad went down to business while I took Mother home. The street cars were jammed to suffocation. We had to stand for one solid hour in a sweltering, gasping, jostling mass of people. To make matters worse, women were crying, and men were trying to look as if they didn't notice. So as soon as I had delivered Mother at our house (she had not spoken one word since Dad had gone) I hurried off to the lake for a swim, and came home feeling soothed and at peace with the world. I hunted up my favorite book, *Twenty Thousand Leagues under the Sea* by Verne, and settled myself to read. Mother, I thought, was either out or upstairs, for I had not seen her since I came home. I grew interested, enthralled, unconscious of my surroundings. Suddenly a hand reached over my shoulder, snatched the book and tore it before I could even turn to look.

It was Mother. My body was rigid. My eyes spoke murder if they spoke what I felt. Mother stopped tearing the book, while we stared at each other. She threw the book on the chair, and went away, while I sat still, my hands trembling. My book, my book, my book! I gathered it up, fondled it, petted it. I went out, and walked and walked, coming home at dark. Dad was home, and looked like a wounded dog, as he shook the fire, his eyes liquid. But it was my turn again, and as soon as Mother saw me she started.

"What do you think of that heartless, cold-blooded son of yours now? What do you think he did as soon as he came home? Went swimming, *swimming*. And then he sat down and read, as if nothing had happened, as if my sons had not gone to be killed. He has no heart, he is a devil. He would kill me, I can see it in his eyes."

Poor Dad said nothing, but shook the fire a little harder. Oh, Dad, now you are up there with God, *I* hope He gives you a little nook with your pipe and detective stories, just to rest. When I think of all we went through and how we got it, day and night, at meals, bed-time, and in the morning, I think that all I went through in the war was nothing to that. Whenever Dad would sit back at night for a quiet smoke and read, she would begin:

"Oh, if only my poor boys could have comforts like you. There they are on the hard cold ground with nothing over them. Sniff, sniff, sniff." Dad would go down to the cellar.

Or at meal times. I was a growing boy of sixteen, just coming into manhood. I needed lots of food, but whenever I asked for a second helping, it would be, "There you are, you big, lazy lout, gorging yourself, and your poor brothers starving. Sniff, sniff." It promptly killed my appetite. Or she would say to Dad, "Oh, how I wish you were young enough to go, you would feel more sympathy for the boys."

Never a word did Dad speak but of comfort and sympathy. He took it all. But he suffered; one night I saw him just sitting and staring, tears rolling down his cheeks, though he did not seem to know it. My hate grew, hate of her, hate of war, hate of life, hate of men, hate of my brothers, though I knew it wasn't their fault. Sometimes I prayed that God would strike her dead.

We received news fitfully from the old country, most of it through the newspapers. From Bob and Gordon we received little besides demands for parcels of food, clothes and money. The papers reported an outbreak of spinal meningitis. Bob said in one letter that his impressions of England consisted of three things; mud, rain, and more mud. Neither squealed when they found that the war and the army were not a joke after all. They were like Dad. They found that the picnic trip was not just what they had anticipated, but took it like men. News in the papers was never reliable, but the day came when they announced the arrival in France of the Canadians.

They were in France. Mother became even worse. Nag, nag, nag, morning, noon, and night. Bedlam struck our house one morning. I was in bed, when I heard Mother scream for Dad. He came out of the cellar, where he had been cleaning the furnace. "Oh, God, oh, God, oh God! My boys are gone, killed! Oh, God, my Bob, my Gordon, my Bob, killed! How can I stand it! Oh, if it were only you or Lionel, or somebody of no use!"

She kept it up, and I heard Dad's voice, soothing, quiet. I had to go down into that. I will never forget it. In the kitchen was a newspaper on the table, Mother sobbing and wringing her hands, and Dad comforting her.

I looked at the paper. Huge red headlines: CANADIANS IN BATTLE. Save the situation. Hold the Line Against Terrific Odds. GAS USED BY GERMANS. HEAVY CASUALTIES. I looked around. Dad was still trying to soothe Mother. I did not see her. He was dying a hundred deaths, and I was the lone mourner. Fury filled me suddenly.

"Damn you. Mother. Shut up. Shut up, for Heaven's sake. You are not hurt. Shut up and think of somebody else for a while. Think about the boys. You don't care whether they're killed or not, you just want to show off. Shut up, I say!"

She quieted as though I had struck her, and looked at me with eyes of pure hate. My mother.

Dad tried to remonstrate with me, but I was roused. She gave in finally, and started to get breakfast, and Dad went back to the cellar. That day passed and the next and the next. Her silence was not so bad as her shrewish shrieks, but it did become the kind that jars your nervous system.

The papers were very cautious, and published lists of casualties. Then the family across the street received a telegram. Their son was killed. I heard the news from the daughter, who went to school with me. I said nothing to Mother, but she found out by telephone. She had thought so much about it that she really began to suffer. She became a wraith flitting across the street, out for walks, anywhere. Dad and I got our own meals, made the beds, and did the housework. He seemed to be a little happy in a quiet sort of way. Once in a while, he would take my hand in his, and look at me, or say, "I will have a lot to answer to God for in you." That was Dad, always thinking of somebody else. I would have died for him.

One night, when Mother was across the street, and Dad and I had just finished the dishes and he sat smoking and reading the paper, while I read another book of Jules Verne's, the doorbell rang, like the first screaming shell in a battle. Mother never would answer the bell. We both started, and Dad looked at me as though to say, "You go," then slowly dragged himself to his feet, and went marching out.

I heard the door open, Dad speak, and a boy's voice answer some pleas-

antry. The door closed, then silence again, dead silence, as if the heart of the world had stopped beating. I heard the rip of an envelope, one and then another. *Two*. I stood up, bracing myself, watching the door. Then in the doorway I saw him. As God is my judge, he was dead. He walked and moved, but he was dead. He stared at me, recognized me, then a struggle began. That poor soul that had taken so much, came back, and he lived, lived again. I ran toward him, fell on my knees before him. His hand moved over my head.
Then his voice, sounding far away.

"Lionel, I want you to go down to your aunt's, my sister's to-night, and stay there. Don't come back for two days, anyway. Hurry now, and get ready." His voice sounded very tired, and went over and sat down.

I was bewildered at this, but obediently went and packed. At the door, leaving, I asked him, "Is it both, Dad?" His eyes grew soft. "Yes, kid, it is both, both."

Twenty-five years to educate them both. Bob was going to take over the business soon. Gordon was going to be a doctor. Both, both. "Hurry, son!" He looked across the street.

And I left, deserted my post. To this day I castigate myself for it. I left Dad to stand it alone. But I did not know then why he sent me away. I was hurt, if anything. But I understand now.

Four

Several times Dad tried to enlist, but he was turned down time after time. He sold his business and concentrated his efforts on getting a commission as officer. But he was too old. He had had experience in the Riel Rebellion of Western Canada, back in 1885, and one day he met an old friend who had been with him in that campaign. They had a long talk after dinner one evening. I think he scented the situation, anyway, and he was a military man with influence. Dad finally was accepted and sent to take charge of a concentration camp for aliens. Mother had to stay behind, so at last Dad got a little peace. The first shock was wearing off Mother by this time, and woman-like, I believe, she even enjoyed her role of martyred mother. She became active in recruiting meetings, and was one of a group of silly women who went around the streets or wherever men congregated, looking for cannon fodder, and sticking white feathers on men who had tried to enlist and failed. I would hear her say to some woman or a group of them, "I gave my two boys and I am ready to give my last one. I am glad they died for their country. We are patriotic. Our family is noted for serving its country."

While Dad was away she left me alone, after a certain day at meal time when she started the same old story. I spoke slowly, quietly, in a strange sounding voice, and I told her what I thought of her doings and ways. She had never thought that Dad was far more hurt than she could ever hope to be, for their sake, not for his own. He had built for them, and lost them, but she had talked about them to get a little cheap notoriety and sympathy. I stood over her and talked for a long time. I told her the reason she hated me from birth was that I had kept her from going out for a few months. I told her it wasn't my fault I was her son, that she could rest assured that if I had had any choice I would rather have been born of a cow. And I was putting up with her, it wasn't a case of her putting up with me, but just the reverse.

I was sorry, I felt like a beast when it was over, yet I felt relieved. I went upstairs to pack my things. I knew we wouldn't be able to stand the sight of each other after that. She came upstairs and watched me. To get out of the room I had to pass her, and she put out her arm and said, "Where are you going?"

"Oh, what the devil do you care where I go. I am sick of this. I am just going."

She appeared to be struggling against something, but finally said, "Please don't go, Lionel, I will go. It should be me. You stay, I will go."

That put me in an awkward position, I didn't want her to go, it would worry Dad. So I said, "No, I will go. I am all ready, anyway." It sounded foolish. But she was quite determined that if I left, so would she. I gave in, and there followed days of armed neutrality. She never mentioned France, didn't go out with white feathers, and took an unusual interest in seeing that my clothes were repaired. Finally she bought me my first suit with long trousers. I felt grown up and a man. I almost looked it, I was so tall and dark. Some days after that Dad remarked in one of his letters that Mother seemed a lot more cheerful.

The fall came round, and I was starting in Second Form in High School. I had found my first friend, Hartley McKenna, a splendid looking boy a year older than myself. Tall and fair, with quiet blue eyes in a beautiful well-shaped head set on the slim graceful body of an athlete. He never seemed to pay any attention to his studies, yet was always first. He was a philosopher in a way, with an increasing disregard for girls, who because of that, worshipped *him*. He was the school hero.

We were strange chums. I was reckless, quick-tempered, a born gambler; the teachers said I had a brilliant mind for composition, philosophy, and I was even at this age dogmatic and quick in decision. Hartley was just the reverse. Yet whatever mischief I would plan he would execute. Outside of school, there were occasional parties, an occasional dance, though boys and girls of high school age did not try so hard then to behave as men and women of the world. We used to hang around pool rooms a little, for something to do, but not so much as plenty of others. The girls did not pay me any noticeable attention as they did Hartley. I gathered even that they were afraid of being alone with me. I asked one why. The one I asked was a modern. Her answer puzzled me at the time, "It isn't what you might do, it's what I am afraid I would want you to do."

Hartley and I often talked of sneaking into the army, but never seriously until one day we attended Toronto's Canadian National Exhibition. We went to the evening performance before the Grand Stand. The searchlights, fireworks, massed bands, the tattoo, the Scarlet Riders, the huge number of people singing "God Save The King" and "O Canada" made me wish that I was a soldier and could die for my country, die gloriously, spectacularly, bravely, with the flag in my hand, and my face to the foe. Then the end came, the lights all came on, and everybody began to move. In the crowd ahead of us we heard a woman's shrill voice addressing some men, "Why don't you enlist? You are young enough, are you cowards? If you are, take this." The crowd laughed, Hartley grinned at me, I grinned back. The crowd moved on. We gradually neared the group of women.

We were before them, the world became one huge eye. "Here are two yellow slackers! Why don't you enlist, you shirkers, hiding behind the other men. Shirkers, cowards, slackers!" White feathers were stuck in our caps. I was dumfounded, amazed. Were the women crazy? Somebody laughed, everybody laughed, all except one, a soldier. He pushed his way to us, and said, "For God's sake, women, can't you see they are only kids? Are you crazy? They will try to enlist now. You are fools. Go home and look after your own kids, if you ever had guts to have any. Leave the boys alone." He turned to us and said, "Don't pay any attention to those old fools, kids, go home and for God's sake don't try to enlist, I have boys your age." He pushed the women aside. The crowd was silent, till somebody shouted, "That's the boy, soldier, if the women had to go they wouldn't be so damned anxious."

We passed through the entrance gate in silence, walked in silence, each looking at the other furtively to see how he had taken it. The soldier had saved our faces, or as we might have felt then, our souls, for there is nothing worse than to be accused of cowardice and be laughed at. Finally, Hartley spoke. "Well, Slim, it looks as if we can enlist after all. If that woman mistook us for men, I'll bet the army doctors would. Let us try anyway; at the very least we will get a rejected button."

I said, "Oh, gosh, join the army? They will never take us, but sure, let's try anyway."

So, we arranged it. We were to meet next morning and as school had not started we could go down in the morning and enlist. We shook hands on it and parted.

We were up bright and early next morning. I met Hartley and we immediately set forth. We were both excited by this time at the prospect of enlisting.

Hartley suggested that we might be taken on as buglers, but I objected. I wanted to go into the cavalry. Why? By George, didn't they have nifty uniforms and horses to ride? The cavalry for me. Finally, we arrived at the Armories, and duly applied. We got as far as the doctor, but when we stripped for examination he only laughed, and said, "Go home, you kids can't get in here."

So, we dressed ourselves and departed despondently. Outside the Armories we stopped to argue the question, when whom should we see but another fellow belonging to our school, in the complete outfit of a cavalry man. We hailed him excitedly, and as we knew him to be under the age limit asked at once how he got in. And in a very patronizing manner he told us. He had gone down and joined an out-of-town unit, the C.M.R.s. He didn't have to strip, but underwent only a chest examination. It was easy, he said, and offered to show us the place. So, we went to a dirty little office near York Street, and there faced a very fat, cold-eyed doctor who only examined us in the chest and then passed us as fit. We signed the papers and were in the army. Just as easy as that, no trouble, no fuss, nothing. Hartley had given his age as twenty, I gave mine as nineteen. No questions were asked, we were simply told to report back next day to take the train to camp. And so we became soldiers of the King.

I am not going to bother giving all the details of how we sneaked away next day, and took the train to Kingston, lost to our relatives and friends as completely as though the earth had swallowed us. Nor describe the various further examinations. Suffice to say that Barriefield Camp was located just outside of Kingston, a huge plain covered with tents and army equipment. There was a total army population of some ten thousand, divided into infantry, cavalry, and artillery, with various machine gun and hospital corps units. There were six men to each tent, and our group was a fair average of the types found in the army. Hartley was there, and myself, and besides there were, first, a man by the name of Coles, a cheerful ruffian with a mind like a sewer and a face pitted with blackheads.

Then there was the Methodist, that was the name applied to men of his type, very virtuous, soft spoken, and sneaky, with all the outward appearance of a soldier and without the qualities of a fighter. He was held in general contempt, or in contempt on general grounds. He later got an orderly room job and stayed with it, never going to France. Then the Yank, a young man who had come from the States to enlist, a soulful young man, romantic, who spoke like a girl. He was liked. Later he earned the V.C. honestly. Then there was Knight, the tallest man and the eldest, a South African veteran, with a voice like a bull, who held us, by sheer bluff, under his domination till we got to France. All of these men contributed their share to the making of that individual, Lionel Thor. Some for good, some for bad.

The weeks were filled with drills, inoculations, vaccinations, and worry on

Hartley's part about his relatives. I was never, happier, full and overflowing with life. Then came the day when we applied for leave. It was granted. I shall never forget our swaggering down to the train like hardened soldiers, flirting with the girls on the train, trying to act, speak, and think like men. Then Toronto again, and Hartley began to lose his nerve about going home. So we took our first drink to give us courage. More swagger, more boasting, and then *home.*

It was the same old house, nothing had changed, and as I walked up the long footpath, there slowly boiled and seethed all the things I had taken from the woman who sat waiting within. I was fighting drunk. I was going to tell her, she would get an earful all right, all right. I opened the door with a bang. I knew where she would be, there in the sitting room, and she was, sitting in an easy chair, slumped out with a sort of lost look. She started when she saw me, but I gave her no chance to say anything.

"Well, here I am, in the bloody army where you wanted me to be. Here is one more son for you to tell your cackling friends about. And if I am, you will know who did it. You can't blame it on Dad, oh, no, it isn't Dad's fault. It is yours, YOURS, and every time you eat or go to bed, you won't have me to preach at. Oh, no. You are the only one left, so preach at yourself about your boys. I hate you. See? Hate you. And don't forget that."

I noticed then that she was looking queerly at me, her mouth open, her eyes staring. I was held for a moment by some power, and then I cried, yes cried, went down on my knees, chafing her hands and crying, "Mother, I'm sorry. Oh Mother, I'm sorry, don't look like that, Mother." The hour that I had dreamed about, gloated over, turned to ashes in my mouth. Presently she seemed to come to herself, and began to fondle me, kiss me, and babble about what a fool she had been, the torture she had undergone at not hearing from me, and how sorry she had been.

After a time, we had supper and not wanting to stay there, I suggested the theatre. On the way, we met a friend of Mother's, one who went with her on the white feather expeditions. I will never forget it. She came up smirking and said, "Why how do you do, Mrs. Thor, and who is this gallant young man off to fight for King and country?"

Mother gave one look and said. "This is my third and last son. Damn king and country." I could have cheered. And on the way home she said in a voice that did not sound a bit like her old one. "Well, I have certainly made a mess of things. I have made your and Dad's life a hell. But from now on I intend—" She said no more, and what could I say?

I saw Hartley next day, and he and his parents had argued far into the night, but Hartley of course had won. We were off for the world's greatest war at the ages of seventeen and eighteen. The babes in the woods were nothing to us. Mother was at the station when we left, as were several other relatives. Her face was pale and grim, but her eyes were shining. She kissed my hand instead of my mouth. I felt foolish. On the train going back I remembered Mrs. Braithwaite. Her eyes followed me. I *was* a rotter. I had forgotten her altogether!

Five

One of the curses of modern war is the fact that a citizen must merge, or is supposed to merge his own individuality with that of his army unit. It is the battalions that have personalities, not the men. The man of spirit naturally resents this and strives in a sort of blind rage to realize and assert his individuality, sometimes adopting very queer methods. At Barriefield Camp we became numbers. We were no longer known by name; I was 51934. I resented being ordered around like a horse. I rebelled at standing in line for meals and because of this I became a mark for N.C.O.s and officers, and was considered, in company with Hartley, as hardboiled. We were more often before the commanding officer than not. He was just as determined to break us into patient truck horses as we were not to be broken. Curiously our companion in revolt was the Yank. He too resented authority. We grew hard inwardly, took to drink, and while in our cups found expression. Once in a while, we beat the army at its own game.

Our section sergeant was an old English army man, who like many others, could stand neither riches nor authority. He abused his power in little ways that hurt, and lashed you into a furor. In drill, he would make sarcastic remarks about us—safe behind the shield of his authority. The penalty for striking a superior was a Court Martial.

We brooded and bided our time. Then one night a brilliant idea occurred to me, which we immediately put into action. We arranged with another man to take the sergeant downtown for a drink and to get him into the darker part of the town. This other fellow was to have a midnight pass, and to stay in the saloon until closing time, while the sergeant would have to leave around 9:30 for roll call and then we would get him on the way home. Later we would hop a taxi that would be waiting to take us back to camp where we would then make ourselves conspicuous for an alibi, even seeing our lieutenant if necessary. The plan was carried out. The sergeant was duly waylaid and served by the Yank while we watched to prevent interference. (The Yank was the eldest, besides having taken boxing lessons). Inside ten minutes we were back at camp, had hidden our bandoliers and town equipment in the tent, and immediately dawdled around the orderly room tent and guard tent, and even went so far as to borrow money from our lieutenant, to make everything complete.

After lights out a guard appeared and we were put under arrest, arrest meaning we had to sleep in the guard tent. I won ten dollars from the guards at poker and then in the morning we were duly presented at the orderly room. The charge was read to the three of us at once. We were amazed. "Did the sergeant definitely accuse us?" He did. A badly mauled and bruised sergeant whom even the O.C. had to grin at a little, gave his version. Yes, he could definitely identify us. The O.C. asked him if it was as bright as that, that he could see us clearly. The sergeant said no, it wasn't very light, but he could recognize our figures. He gave the time as approximately 9:15. Praise be, his watch was fast. The Yank was asked if he had anything to say, and with a very injured air he gave a big story of petty persecution and ended up by definitely denying the charges, saying he could call witnesses. The O.C. smiled at this, for anybody could get witnesses for any purpose as long as it would get anybody higher up in the eye.

Very daringly the Yank went out to make a counter accusation and said the sergeant must have been drunk and in a fight and was now trying to cover it up by charging us. He then said, "And now sir, I would like you to ask the sergeant if he had been drinking, and who he was with last night." The O.C. thought this a reasonable request (although the adjutant with a copy of the King's rules and orders said it was absolutely out of order) and said, "Sergeant, can you give an account of your actions previous to the alleged attack?" The sergeant looked, and probably felt, troubled at this question, and said, "Well sir, Private McIver asked me to go down for a drink." But before he could say anything further the O.C. interrupted, "Do you mean to tell me that you, an old soldier, went out drinking with a private?" The sergeant was alarmed now and said, "Well sir, I didn't see any harm in it."

The Yank chimed in again, "Please sir, could we call Private McIver as a witness?" The O.C. granted the request and court was adjourned till Private McIver was called back from drill. On the way out, I noticed that our Lieutenant was eyeing us very curiously. We were grinning and with my last side glance at him I saw a smile at the edges of his mouth. Orderly room re-opened about one hour afterwards with Private McIver in the place of honour. He was a tall gawky chap with an ugly but humorous face and a grin that was irresistible. The O.C. had been primed in the meantime by the adjutant and looked very stern. "Now Pte. McIver, what do you know about this? Was the sergeant with you last night?" Pte. McIver looked the picture of injured innocence. "Well sir, I just thought I would take the sergeant down for a drink, sir, I thought, he being an old soldier he could hold liquor sir." The O.C.: "Do you mean the sergeant was drunk?"— "Oh no, sir, oh no, I wouldn't say he was drunk sir, oh no." The O.C. said, "Damn" under his breath. "Well then would you say he was sober?"— "Well sir, it's like this, I couldn't rightly say. You see, he *acted* sober, but he kept chewing the rag, I mean arguing, with infantrymen, sir."

"You won't say he was drunk and you won't say he was sober. Well I guess you were both drunk. Where did the sergeant leave you?"— "At the pub sir."— "What time was that," asked the O.C. — "Oh about 9:30 P.M." (We had previously told him to say this). The sergeant looked amazed, and the Lieutenant here put in his oar saying, "Sir, these men came and borrowed money from me before 9:30 p.m. I remember first post hadn't sounded."

The O.C. looked dumbfounded, the sergeant was paralyzed with amazement. We looked virtuous. "Well I'll be damned, case dismissed. Will you remain sergeant?"

The sergeant remained, and a few days later he was wearing only two stripes, and for a few days we were at peace with the world.

The hardening process continued and day by day I was becoming what was commonly called a tougher soldier. Booze and insubordination became common among us. We became vulgarized also by the contact with older men, men whose great object in life was the conquest of women. I had yet to have my first experience and I was not concerned with them then. Such incidents as that of the drunk were merely another influence to make me a little more cynical of the world, men and women.

To keep the city of Kingston in a normal state despite the presence of the soldiers, each outfit had to take its turn in supplying pickets, whose business was to look after the soldiers on leave to town at night, and also to keep order. The pickets marched in patrols up and down the streets picking up drunks or breaking up any rowdyism.

One night it came to the turn of our section and I, with the Yank, four others and a corporal, was selected. We marched regularly up and down the main thoroughfare until twelve o'clock, and were just on the way home when a huge crowd in front of the opera house attracted our attention. The corporal immediately marched us to the scene and we felt sure it was some row between soldiers and civilians. Pushing our way through the crowd we came on one of the most curious scenes of my life. A huge soldier of an infantry battalion was standing with one of the signs of the theatre in his hands, and he was swinging it in the air, threatening all and sundry to come and get him. On the ground beside him lay the body of another soldier, held down by his foot. He was wildly drunk, fighting drunk, six foot four inches of huge gorilla shaped body, slobbering at the mouth, his face reminding me of a bulldog. The crowd, composed of both soldiers and civilians, stood gaping as the corporal detailed the Yank and myself to arrest him.

We had no arms or equipment except a belt and bayonet issued especially for the occasion, which we were not allowed to use except at the command of an officer, but we went forward, ignorant as we were of the vagaries of the drunk's nature, and tried to speak to him. He looked at us with stupid gaping bloodshot eyes, a horrible sight, like some great Moloch, and in a flash he picked me up bodily and threw me into the crowd. The people I fell on were more hurt than I, however. The Yank followed me through the air, and the crowds laughed. That kind of jeering laughter raised a fury within me. The slimy dirty beast could manhandle me like that, could he! I was back and at him, half-blind with hate, the bayonet in my hand, held by the blade—and a Ross bayonet is heavy. He stayed before me, waiting, the ignorant beast, his paws up ready. I had the lust to kill him like a snake. But I had cunning, and knew he was watching, and that if I was caught in those prehensile hands that I was done for. So, I waited for him to attack, baiting him, calling him all manner of names. Then I called him the unspeakable thing. He rushed, I jumped aside, the bayonet rose and fell, as I struck and struck. Then I was on his back and he was down, the beast. It took the rest of the picket to pull me off and we took him away, I snarling and hitting at the civilians—anybody in my path—like an angry dog. We didn't like civilians to see army men like this, but even with his head bashed in it took all of us to hold him.

We took him back to camp, and pegged him to the ground spread eagle fashion. It was a rainy night and cold, and with each limb pegged he couldn't move, only moan like a whipped cur. He lay there all night through in the mud and rain, and was sober in the morning, a poor bloody pitiful wreck of a man, and broken. I will never forget it.

We had one more short leave home that fall, then we were off to England. We arrived just before Christmas, in England, the place of our dreams. The story of our home in England had been passed down from generation to generation, and the story of our ancestors' exile during one of the religious wars of the Middle Ages, so that in each one of us had been planted a picture of our ancestral home.

England. Toy houses, toy people, toy towns. Everything in miniature. The people, curiously, reminded me of a maiden aunt of mine who had taken to a Pekinese dog and canaries. Perhaps you understand so sweeping a generalization. If you don't it doesn't matter. I may be biased.

We were duly installed at Bramshott Camp near Liphook and Haslemere, and immediately after our arrival we were given six days leave. Hartley, the Yank and myself naturally selected London for our conquest. Out of Canada and away from home, we felt secure in the fact that we could act like men.

Yet we entertained ourselves childishly. Theatres, food; theatres, food. We kept away from the women at first, not because of lack of interest, but through Hartley's gentle guidance. None of us had had our first adventure, and because of this we had been silent about it at night when the men in tent and hut began to talk of their rather vulgar escapades; we felt we couldn't be men until we too could contribute our share to these circles. So on our last night of leave, when Hartley had gone to see some relatives, the Yank and I gravely debated the subject. We argued pro and con as to ways and means until at last I said in disgusted impatience, "Oh hell, let's pick a couple up. They ought to know where to go." And so, it was decided. We met what we wanted somewhere near Charing Cross and when they spoke to us we halted. I was filled more with the spirit of adventure than anything else. It was a triumph. At last we would be able to contribute our stories. The Yank went on with his woman and soon disappeared in the crowd, while I dropped behind with the smaller and fairer of the two, a sweet quiet pale-faced girl with a slight figure. She was fairly-well educated too, with a beautiful voice, wistful and pathetic.

My astonishment at finding her different from my expectation may appear absurd, but her appealing ways touched me. I was absolutely sober, her voice was soothing, and I forgot my objective and suggested supper, mentioning a restaurant that every Canuck knew. She peered up at me and said, "Did you say the Ritz, Canada?" I said, "Yes, why not?" Again she peered at me. My heavens, I was innocent, I didn't know that their profession showed itself to other women, so again I urged till she gave a rather queer laugh and agreed. In the restaurant, we talked of everything except sex. I gave my impressions of England and of how everybody seemed to make a point of overcharging us. I was a good talker, she a splendid listener, and I made her laugh several times. I noticed she had a nice laugh. We both enjoyed ourselves and after supper we went to the theatre, then for a walk along the Thames where it was beautifully quiet and restful.

After a while we had some more supper in a quiet little tea shop, and my nervousness began. We became rather strained and I felt like someone who, dining with a chap whom he finds rather delightful and human, suddenly discovers that it is his janitor. I became furtive, and she sat watching me with a queer speculative light in her eyes. "Well, Canada," she said at last, "it's my turn now, come on." I followed her, diving my hand into my breeches pocket as I did so. One pound note, three ten shilling notes and several half crowns. I was worried. Did I have enough? How the dickens would I give it to her? These thoughts filled my mind to the exclusion of all others. She talked gently, like an old friend, once in a while giving me a very sharp look. We came to a side street, to a small hotel, and here she signed the register and led me upstairs. The room had cost ten shillings. I was in a perspiration. Did I have enough? I wished Hartley hadn't gone. Darn the Yank for leading *me* into this! I was worried and furtive. So, this was the grand passion! Then her voice came to me: "Sit over there Canada." I meekly obeyed, and sat as I used to sit when getting a lecture from Dad. She sat down too, smiling in a queer way, and suddenly her eyes grew soft, and I thought she was going to laugh.

She turned suddenly face down on the bed. By God, why was she crying,

crying. And suddenly I loathed myself as a vile beast, foul, unutterably vile. I became in my own eyes a gaping stupid debauchee while I stood and watched. At last I moved towards her and clumsily tried to comfort her. She was sobbing quietly, brokenly, with long intervals of silence, every one of which tore my heart. I could have beaten myself with rods of iron. I turned her gently, and took her to me, stroking her head and saying, "What's the matter kid? What have I done? Don't worry, please don't cry, I'll go, I'll go. What *is* the matter, I wouldn't hurt you. My God no I like you too much." The sobs grew slower and finally stopped altogether, and she turned her face up and broke away from me. Her eyes were large, humorous, shining. I loved her then; true, pure, clean was that love. Then she spoke, "Please Canada, go over to that chair and sit there, please, please." I went, like a child.

She sat again on the bed, head cupped in her hands, and looked at me with an expression that reminded me of a picture of the Madonna, soft, quizzical, motherly. I felt like a boy caught stealing jam. Then she said, "Now listen Canada, and don't interrupt or I shall laugh or cry. I don't know which. Listen, you are just out from Canada aren't you, on your first leave?" I nodded dumbly. "I thought so, now listen and don't forget. This is your first experience with people like me, isn't it?" I nodded dazedly again. "Well, let it be your last. You know I almost forgot there were men like you. I am going to quit this business and go home, home to my mother up in Somerset. You never heard of Somerset, did you? Listen, do you know I have a baby four months old, do you know that I am clean, but most people like me aren't and that if you weren't you couldn't have babies or anything, couldn't marry. Look at me, haven't you an idea what I mean? Well you can guess. Now go away and leave people like me alone." She turned to the bed, face down, her arm motioning me to the door. A sob, and that white hand moving slowly.

And even then, I didn't understand. I seemed to feel a dimly sacramental atmosphere. I stood like the gawky bewildered fool I was. There was a dead silence, just the hand moving, I standing there, and the sound of muffled sobs. Then without volition I moved towards the bed, knelt beside her, took her hand and kissed it, a soft white hand, and she fondled my head and then slowly I rose to go. Just as I reached the door, she suddenly leapt up, caught me, took my hand and put it to her cheek very gently, and then pushed me through the door and closed it. I heard her lean against the inner side as I still stood there. Oh, I was a fool, such a fool. I found the stairs, the door, the street, and then I *walked* and walked.

A salute to a real woman, girl, wherever you are, in green Somerset with your laughing child, or yet in the London dark, worn-faced and hard now, or in some still and soon-forgotten grave. You live and are real for me forever, just because I know now what might have been and what could *not* be.

Six

Days and days of incessant drills, until one day comes a startling surprise. In France the Canadian Mounted Rifles had been made into infantry, and automatically we became the same. The various squadrons were joined until they made one complete brigade of infantry in the new Third Division and were known as the 8th Brigade, 3rd Division Canadians. There were four battalions, the first, second, fourth and fifth. One battalion from each part of Canada.

We became a draft depot to replace casualties in the newly formed brigade. When the orders were definitely announced and infantry equipment began to be issued, we held indignation meetings, delegations went to the O.C. and begged for transfers to real cavalry. With tears in his eyes, he explained that he was doing all in his power, and one day we were on parade when he addressed us, speaking feelingly, emotionally of his hopes. How he had grown to love us, harum scarum lot that we were. That he was sure we were going to be great soldiers, and that on that very day when he knew he could not take us as a unit to France he had offered his resignation and volunteered to go as a private. We cheered. We had grown to love him too, the old walrus-moustached, line-faced man. He told us the famous story of the Messines Barricade, when through no fault of their own, they (that is, the new brigade in France) had been put in the line without proper training, without guides, and of how Fritz had taken advantage of it; and now, he said, our nickname among the infantry was not the C.M.R.'s but the C.M. Runs. He begged us then to retrieve our name and make it one of honour and not of disgrace. Let it signify that we were running towards the enemy and not from them. And there and then, like knights of old, we took the vow that in later days made the C.M.R.s the shock troops of a shock corps. The Vow, whose fulfilment cost more casualties than any other brigade in the Allied or German Armies, and that won more battles, that helped to make the Battle of Courcelette in 1916 a byword; that made Vimy Ridge, Passchendaele, and later fights something to remind the world of the Canadians. That was our vow.

That night we held the famous burial parade, when we buried our spurs, and the hopes of the Canadian Mounted Rifles by torchlight and according to the Rites of the Church of England. A burlesque you say? Maybe. Burlesque is sometimes only a transparent garment for tragedy. Gone was our romance, gone was our ambition. We became foot sloggers, poor bloody infantry, became those things we had looked down upon and patronized. Our shame was great, and many were the fights and riots with grinning infantrymen, whose stock goad when they met a C.M.R. was, "I hear you blighters have been promoted, that they are letting you be real soldiers, instead of chocolate ones." There was no other recourse but a scrap. One night in the hut I counted fourteen black eyes including my own, besides bruises, broken noses and sundries.

Even an officer appeared with a shiner one day. They must have been getting it too.

Infantry drill, rifle and bayonet exercises, squad drill, open order. Never did instructors have more unwilling pupils. They lashed us, goaded us, but we were sullen, and the instructors grew afraid of going out at night. Bayonet exercise is one of the most bloodthirsty pursuits you could wish. We were lined up in front of sacks of straw suspended from a gibbet, with various vulnerable parts of the human body marked on the sack, and our job was to lunge, stab and kick at this arrangement, to the continual din of the instructor's voice saying, "Now for God's sake put some ginger into hit. Hin! Hout! Hon guard! Ow! Ow! And they call this houtfit Canadians! You bloodywell couldn't be hannything else. Stick 'im, kick 'im. Ow! Ow! Thank God we got a nivy!" Then if the instructor got too close, somebody accidentally would drop the butt of their rifle on his toes. Such was our prelude.

Rumours had been flying for days that we would soon be going to France. Our training was hardening, toughening us for the slaughter. We were in perfect health and filled with the joy of life. It had to find outlet and it did, in joyous rags, fights in pubs, walking ourselves tired up and down the streets of Haslemere and Liphook looking for girls, and in a thousand other ways.

One wonderful day I remember. It was spring, and in spring England is wonderful. The air was soft and balmy, a caress, the birds were singing, and we had been given the day off. The Yank and I went away off the beaten track and just lazily walked and drifted with the breeze, letting it lead us down the hills, over the railroad tracks, over the next hill, along a lane lined with oaks of wondrous beauty and quaint little thatched cottages, to a tiny little village. It was midafternoon and we lazily sat beside a tree to watch, as the Yank said, "the crowd roll by." Not a soul could be seen. I believe I went to sleep, dreaming of England, the real England which I had found at last. And out of the mist of dreams, I woke to see a fairy godmother, plump, with fluted cap. We sat watching her making her way towards us. And behold she came, nodding and smiling to us. A smile that crinkled every dimple and wrinkle in her dear old face, and made us grin in return and shuffle to our feet, hats in hand. I can't reproduce her dialect but she invited us to tea. Would we? We would, and so up the lane one on each side we went, towering over her, then through a funny little gate into a prim little garden, with flowers already blooming, and into the house, wherein everything was shining, everything spotless. And to complete the picture there was an old, old man, toothless, who kept mumbling away to us or himself, we never knew which, and what did it matter? A cat was purring, clock ticking, the kettle singing merrily, in peace. I had found a little of the real England.

Back to camp in a haze of romance, dreams of cats, clocks, children, wives, sunsets, cradles, all joyfully intermixed. A happy day. It was good to be alive.

Cry Havoc

Next day my name, Hartley's and the Yank's were read out for a draft to France. The farewell from the other members of the depot reminded one of a wedding. Slaps on the back, boisterous talk about our luck, and giving the Germans one for them. Shouts and cheers as boisterous and hypocritical as Rotary Club conventions. But for a different reason.

Seven

It was a dark drizzly day when we arrived at Le Havre. We had a long march up to the Canadian Base Depot, uphill all the way. Our greeting from France was the cries of children for souvenirs and bully beef. They were wise in the ways of the infantry, these children, they knew that after the first few kilometres, when the equipment became heavy, the men would suddenly get generous, as we did. The camp at Le Havre was set on a hill, and it was there that we met a new kind of Canadian. Canadians who had curiously set expressions and who were continually chuckling at some joke apparently on themselves. There was a disregard for petty things. And Ypres! Ypres! Morning, noon and night, the name assumed the spectral proportions of a nightmare. Ypres! Ypres! It grew and grew before us, until it became like the Giant in the story of Jack the Giant Killer, while we in turn felt the willing but somewhat incredible derring-do of Jack.

Then on the second day we were addressed by the Padre: a man seemingly kept there for the express purpose of exhorting troops going up the line. His sermon began by his saying "Kill the–" and ended with "Kill the–." The Christianity of churches is a flexible thing. In peacetime pacifist, in wartime it becomes a composition of stoicism and laissez-faire resulting in a slaughterhouse ethic.

We were issued new equipment of British manufacture, called the Webb equipment, a canvas affair of many intricate pieces but more comfortable than its Canadian counterpart. And gas masks, not the later style, but just a chemical hood to put over our heads. Ammunition field dressing to be sewn in our tunics, identity disks, which latter made us shiver. There were two of them and I asked an old soldier, "Why two?" He laughed and said, "Well if your head goes, they have your wrist, and if both go, they don't give a darn what happens then anyway." And that was that.

I didn't question him further.

We were inoculated again for something or other, and then as we were badly needed we went on our way again to the front, in box cars appropriately labeled, as containing so many horses and men.

We passed through a peaceful country, a beautiful country, that reminded me of Ontario, and as one wag remarked, the French even had cows like ours. The time of the train ride was filled in with poker and crown-and-anchor and a new game we had picked up called "Housie-housie." I nearly got into a scrap once, during a poker game, when I innocently asked at the beginning of the game whether if you held fours and the joker, would that make fives, and would the fives beat fours? It was an old argument, and finally it was decided that fives did beat fours. The game began. I won steadily, then came the hand in which I held four sixes, discarded one card, and when I made a play of looking to see if I had a straight or flush, found I had caught the joker. The betting began, and a big husky McGill University man stayed with me and even raised until all our money was gone. He had a British Warm overcoat, I had a pair of knee-length boots. He said he would bet the coats against the boots for a show-down, we did, and I displayed my fives. He had four kings. There was a dead silence, somebody laughed, and I started to rake in the pot. He put out his hand to stop me, and with one hand on top of the other we sat staring into each other's eyes for a long time, then his hand moved away. We were good friends after that, and as he said later, it did look darn queer to draw a joker with fours. Luckily for me somebody else had dealt.

During a stop in the second day of our train ride (one of many), a funny sound came to our ears. A relentless monotone like the playing of some huge organ with bass notes only. It rose and fell, rose and fell.

We looked at each other questioningly. What was it? Then from the car ahead came a man whom we knew as an old soldier, going back to his unit. We asked him what it was. His chuckle was curiously sardonic. "You'll know soon enough what it is, that's the guns." THE GUNS. My stomach suddenly rose up to throttle me, my body grew dry and brittle. THE GUNS. There was silence for a moment, then talk, talk, boisterous talk. Hectic talk about nothing, sudden enthusiasm to look in the darkest corners of the car. We arrived at Poperinghe that afternoon.

Poperinghe was situated several kilometres behind the lines, yet still within shelling distance. It was the end of steel. Outside of the town were situated the several rest camps, or groups of huts for troops when they were out of the line. They were also billeted in the town itself, as about half of the inhabitants had left. It reminded you of a picture of the gold rush days, except that the pervading scheme of color was khaki.

The troops had established their own canteens, moving pictures, and such like. The town was always crowded with ambulances, motor wagons, limbers, etc. and traffic policemen were a necessity. One of the standing jokes among the infantry was, "Daddy, what did you do in the Great War?" the answer being, "I directed it." This was usually shouted in passing these police, who were looked down upon as bomb-proofers. Possibly it was envy.

We detrained at the station, or rather just outside what had been the station, and stood there like sheep caught in a storm, until a sergeant put in his appearance accompanied by an officer. (In England, we would have said that it was an officer accompanied by a sergeant, but a little experience in France gave us the true perspective, for in our army the officer was only the mouthpiece of the sergeant, he knew nothing and the sergeant knew everything, or at least, sometimes too much.)

Some other E.C.O.s also hove in sight and bore down on us, and the officer stopped and spoke: "Where are you men detailed to?" We didn't know, which brought from the sergeant, "Darn this goddamned army, that's always the way. They tell us they are sending men, but don't tell us who to look for. They ship the men but don't tell them where to, it's a wonder there is any damn cock-eyed army left. The dirty brass hats (staff officers} have got the brains of a dead jackass."

We looked blank, the officer looked blank, and the sergeant still harangued us on the life, the army, the officers, and base camps. Then a transport officer came down. Now transport officers have been dealing with sergeants for a long time, and have learned the axiom, that the best method of defence is attack. This one began, "Here sergeant, why haven't you got these men away? Do you know they haven't had a meal yet? For God's sake get a move on. You blinkin' infantrymen think you have eternity to move in." To which the sergeant replied, "Say, go easy, we don't know whether this is our mob or not, we haven't any papers and neither have they."

We were grinning, the officer was grinning, and somebody behind said, "I bet two bits on the transport officer." The latter knew his business all right, and began to shout. Papers? Papers? Why Godam if he was going in the line and Fritz was coming over he would ask for papers. PAPERS? The sergeant looked sullen while the officer looked away quickly and someone else giggled. The transport officer looked through a fistful of papers and said, "Here you are, sergeant, here are your papers, your nice little printed papers, but don't forget the men." He passed on majestically.

The sergeant looked at us grimly. "Fall in, in two ranks." We shuffled into position. There were four box cars full of us to go to this one unit. "Do you know how to form fours?" Somebody said we did. "My God, a mistake must have happened, they know how to form fours. The last mob we got didn't even know where to put their rifles. Well, form it! Now right turn and follow me." Hartley looked at me and said, "So this is war. Well I'm damned. Why that guy doesn't even know how to give the proper commands." But I remonstrated and said, "Have a heart Hartley, you didn't know anything about infantry drill yourself until we were made footsloggers. Why I'll bet that beggar never let on he saw infantrymen before." For let the truth be known: the C.M.R.s never liked to admit that they were infantry and they wouldn't do infantry drill if they could possibly avoid it. Officer, N.C.O. and private felt the same way. So off we went, following our leader by devious ways until we arrived at a collection of huts outside the town, between Poperinghe and Vlamertinghe. We halted before one and the sergeant and officer disappeared, coming into view again with several more officers and the colonel.

They looked us over, then a short stout sergeant major stepped out, asked for volunteers for the battalion Machine Gun Section and concluded by saying, "Of course you get better grub in the M.G.S." Like one man, Hartley, myself, and the Yank stepped forward with three or four others. The sergeant major smiled and turned to the Commanding Officer, saying, "Depend on the young ones to come when you say "grub." They all laughed. The sergeant major separated the volunteers for better grub away from the others, called a corporal and away we went again, finally coming to rest before another hut. The corporal disappeared within, and out came the funniest, shortest, stoutest officer I had ever seen. (We later found out that he joined the C.M.R.s so he wouldn't have to walk to the war, only to be disappointed.) He wore glasses and had the complexion of a baby just spanked, but had a curiously deep voice. He looked at us, we looked at him, and he had a very companionable smile. He looked at the Yank, short, demure, angelic. At Hartley, tall, sober, funereal. At myself, awkward, gawky, looking my real age. "My God, what is Canada coming to? Are these soldiers?" Then he grinned, with ourselves and the corporal following suit. "Tell 'em to leave their equipment here and assign them to their guns. We will find them beds afterwards."

We gratefully dropped our equipment, and were led by our guide philosopher and friend, the corporal, to an army field kitchen, where a most ruffianly-looking cook was playing poker with a group of others beside the wagon. He had one eye, a face almost black with too much shaving, eyebrows that looked almost like misplaced moustaches, and wore a greasy black shirt. He was absorbed in the game when we came on the scene. The corporal hailed him, "Hey, you gotta give these guys some grub, and for God's sake don't take all their money away from them, I want some myself."

It is a heartbreaking thing to hear a man with huge proportions, and black evil visage, speak, sometimes, for you are disappointed. We were, in this case. We expected curses at the army, corporal, etc. in a deep base voice, and nearly fell over when we heard the cook speak. It sounded like a contralto, a peculiarly sweet, womanish voice accompanied by a smile of welcome that entranced us. We were almost disappointed. "Well, well, well, boys! Just a minute and I will give you the feed of a lifetime." Away he went and in a trice, we had a dish of stew, Spanish onions, bread, butter, jam, and cheese, and tea. It was wonderful. Two days on hard tack and water hadn't killed our appetites, and the cook looked on in pride as we did full justice to his artistry.

After this feast the corporal once more appeared and led us back to our equipment and hence allotted us to our guns. Hartley, the Yank, and myself were left to the last and came to a halt outside a hut that looked even more dilapidated than the rest. There the corporal scouted, "Sam, Sam! Where in hell are you?"

Holding his shirt in one hand and his trousers up with the other, naked to the waist yet somehow still looking personable, there appeared at the door of the hut someone who looked down indolently, insolently at us and eyeing us humorously said, "My God, save Canada, what is she doing? Calling up the class of 1915?" (He wasn't so very far wrong at that.) The corporal laughed and we looked sheepish. The former finally said, "Where's Sam? You ought to consider yourself damn lucky to get these, you should'a seen the rest." The figure spoke again: "Thank God my gun's full anyhow. Sam's gone to town to see a man about a dog" (a wink) "so I'll take 'em in. Come in you guys and make yourself at home." We did. Then came questions; the poor fellow was alone and had to take questions from all of us. Was that a Fritz aeroplane up above? Were we really going to be Machine Gunners? When did we go in the line? Was he killing lice? Were there many of them? And so on *ad infinitum* until at last he cried for a halt and said he wanted some beer, and as we were just out we must have some money. We did, and we were only too glad to have the honor of buying beer for a real fighting soldier, even if he didn't exhibit any extravagant knight-errantry.

Then we had some forbidden cognac and talked far into the night. Sam ultimately came and we found that we were in D. company, machine gun squad, and that Sam was our #1 in charge of the gun. We were merely carriers. In Machine Guns of the Colt and Vickers type there are six men to each crew: #1, who is in charge and actually does the firing; #2, who assists #1 in loading and making repairs; and #3, who takes charge of spare parts. The other three carry ammunition and are spare men, shoving up one when casualties occur, until #6 is #1. And if #6 gets it, the gun is out of action, but not till then, unless certain stoppages occur. In case of attack a machine gun crew *never falls back*. In an offensive war their task is more or less easy. In defence they are a suicide club, actually and in theory. As three casualties had occurred on this gun we were replacements and had yet to be trained. We had had no previous experience whatsoever with Machine Guns, in fact had only fired ten rounds of rifles at the ranges. Our #1 told us that we had better get a lot of sleep, as we were due to go in the line the next night, June 1st. It was to be our last trip into Ypres town, so he said, as we were to go and open a big offensive on the Germans somewhere. But we never opened that offensive, which was later known as the Battle of the Somme.

The next morning, we awoke filled with lice and cheerfulness. My body was one itching, crawling mass, I swarmed with them, and felt loathsome to me; and even Hartley, the acme of cleanliness, had them. We told our #1 about it but he only grinned and said, "If you only knew it, you will find the cooties are your best friends. I was going through for a chemist once and they told us about a thing called a 'counter-irritant' and that is just what you will find them to be." Long afterwards I realized what he meant, for when shells were dropping slowly and regularly near you, with the deathlike certainty of fate, when your mind was ready to break and your nerves were shrieking with the strain, these lice, gnawing and biting, and worrying at you, gave you just the necessary irritant to keep you sane. After trying in vain to rid ourselves of them, we began to compare experiences and found that we were unanimous in our decision that so far, France was better than England or Canada as far as the army went. No drills, no worry about saluting or dirty buttons or anything like that, but peace, relaxation, while everybody, even the adjutant, seemingly had forgotten all about petty things. We had even grown used to that boom, boom, boom, ahead of us. Although we were just a few miles behind the line there was no shelling and our #1 told us that they had a special arrangement with Fritz not to shell each other's rest camps. The funny part of it was that I never heard of troops on rest getting shelled or bombed until 1917, so it was almost credible.

Our #1, or to call him by name, Spence, then inveigled us into a game of poker and took all our money away from us, but charmingly loaned us some of our own money back, as he said he just wanted enough to get some brandy. He gave us a little training in the gun, and then we adjourned for more beer.

There was a restful relaxation about that camp that amazed us. We found ourselves quite happy and at peace with the world. Everybody was so considerate. The presence of death, not too near, is a great tonic to men's higher perceptions.

That night, or rather at dusk, we fell in, to march off to war. The band played, the Colonel reviewed us, we marched shoulder to shoulder, chins out, chests up, with a swing as if being reviewed by the king. Eleven hundred human beings, there were: Dick, Jerry, Tom, Walter, James, John, Terry, and Ronald, all somebody's sons, somebody's sweethearts, somebody's husband or friend. Shoulder to shoulder we marched. Eleven hundred, we marched. My God, the angels in heaven were wishing they were men then.

O Canada, O Canada
True patriot's love, in all thy sons command.

Dear God, eleven hundred of them, Hartley, the Yank, and me. Shoulder to shoulder.

Canada, O Canada.

My spirit soared, I was sitting up there high in heaven, sitting beside God and saying, "See God, there goes Hartley, my chum, and the Yank my friend. Aren't they fine? Don't you wish you were a man?" And God put his arm around me like an old friend and said, "I was a man, these are my sons, every one of them, my sons."

O Canada, O Canada.

Only two hundred and sixty-five answered the roll. The Colonel wasn't there.... Two hundred and sixty-five.

Eight

At dusk, we started on the trek to the lines, in company columns, at long intervals. Each company was to take a different route after reaching Ypres, so that this was the last time we would be seen as a unit, until we came out of the line again. The Machine Gun squad was last, and they were to pick up their guns and ammunition at the village of Zillebecke, where the limbers would leave them. Our turn to move had come at last.

We had been sitting on the ground resting and smoking after the review, when word came. A heave and a grunt and we were off, to the accompaniment of sardonic farewells from odd soldiers who were watching us leave, such as "Good-bye, good luck, a soldier's farewell to you," "Don't let Fritzie bite you," and the unforgivable insult to a C.M.R., "Don't run so fast next time." Then the marching songs. *Pack up your troubles in your old kit bag and smile smile smile*. A mouth organ started to play.

Hats thrust back on our heads, it was getting warm. Then:

Keep your head down Fritzie boy,
Keep your head down Fritzie boy,
Late last night in the pale moonlight
I saw you—I saw you
You were fixing your barb wire
When we opened-up our rapid fire
If you want to see your mother or your brother anymore
Keep your head down Fritzie boy.

Then:

Après la guerre finité
Après la guerre finit. Mademoiselle, etc.

The wistful tones of the unprintable song dealt with how the Canadians left Mademoiselle *après la guerre finit*.

Darkness was falling, and the first flare streaked the horizon, to the accompaniment of

There's a long, long trail a-winding
Into the land of my dreams
Where the ni-ightin-gales are sing-ing,
And the white *mo-on beams.*
There's a long, long trail a-winding.

Darkness had settled, flares threw a greenish ghastly color over the land. The guns boomed slowly at intervals, like a minute gun at a funeral.

I want to go home.
I want to go home
I don't want to go to the front anymore
The whizzbangs they whistle,
The cannon they roar
Take me over the sea,
Where the Allemafte can't get me,
Oh my, I'm too young to die,
I want to go home.

The singing died down, the mouth organ stopped, heads fell forward, plod, plod plod, clump, clump, clump, clump.

My pack and equipment began to weigh heavily upon me. One strap not set right gnawed at my shoulder. Gnaw, gnaw, gnaw, every step was agony. I forgot about the war, life, home, everything, while my mind concentrated on that searing, scorching, cutting gnaw of the strap. Would, it *never* stop? My head went forward and down. Plod, plod. Why the devil doesn't that man in front keep up? I keep stepping on his heels, and when I go back the man behind steps on mine. Damn him, his load isn't as heavy as mine. Why doesn't he keep up? I'll kill the bastards if he doesn't. Wouldn't it be nice to pull out my bayonet and stick it forward, so that every time he fell back he would get jabbed. Now he is dragging his feet. Oh God, I could kill him. Gnaw, gnaw, gnaw; plod, plod, plod. I'll ditch half this darn stuff at the next halt. I should have thrown it away anyway.

At last, thank God, REST. A heave to the side, a hurried search, away goes gun bag, ammunition, water bottles, and other paraphernalia. Ah, now the strap is loosened a little. Now that should be just right. But would it? Too little is better than too much load. A still more hurried search in my pack, and away went socks, knitted doo-dads from home, part of my ammunition. Then a sigh of content, a smoke, peace, relaxation. I looked around. It was the road to Ypres. The flares cast a horrible light over everything, making the country a ghastly green phantasmagoria. Trees were broken and gaunt, and looked almost beseeching, stretching out arms to stop us, as if saying, "Abandon hope, all ye who enter here." Everybody was whispering, no one was laughing, just whispering. The Yank leaned over and said, "Slim, I'm scared stiff for fear I show yellow." I didn't understand what he meant then. I had been so taken up with my shoulder, I had forgotten about war. Shouts came to us, "Fall in, fall in." Heaves, curses, grunts, the creak of equipment. The smell of sweat, and off again.

Plod, plod, darn that man, he was still dragging his feet. The sound of marching feet in front changed tune. Feet rang more sharply. I looked up. Ypres. I never thought houses had souls till I saw Ypres. Row on row of empty shells, that looked and felt dead. Staring out on the world with a sightless, fixed gaze that appalled one. My head dropped again. Plod, plod, plod, not a sound could be heard except the ringing of iron shod feet on the cobbles. I sniffed and sniffed again. My God, what a smell, what a stink, what was it? What in heaven's name had such a vile smell?

It grew worse, the Yank began to vomit, and it didn't take me a second for me to follow suit. I heard Hartley behind curse, the first time I ever heard him swear. Somebody laughed, the corporal came back. "What's the matter with you guys? Oh I see. All right, fall in as soon as you can. Hard luck. I did the same myself the first time. What is it did you say? Well to put it gently it is dead horses—and others. Mostly others. Get back into line. We're behind time now." Oh God, did you make me for that? It was awful, terrible, soul-destroying, that smell, for the first few hours. Plod, plod, plod, through the square, where the city of the dead came to life. For here was traffic, traffic reminding you of Piccadilly circus, only there were no lights. Ambulances, limbers, wagons, troops, traffic policemen, cursing and shouting, it brought us back, to life and reality for minute, the Cloth Hall, the Cavalry barracks, Infantry barracks. Down the road, plod, plod, and then *the Menin Gate*.

When I was a boy I often read the books of Henty and one of his favorite phrases was "Baptism of fire" and I appropriate that same phrase for my own use. There is not a better and more literal description of the Menin Gate than that. It was a baptismal font for thousands of Canadians, because outside that gate was war.

It was early, 11 p.m., when our squad arrived at the gate. The huge towering ramparts loomed above us, and gave shelter from what might be happening outside. Not only that but we could smoke and talk once more. The various N.C.O.s were as busy as clucking hens mustering their charges. We were to go through the gate and over the bridge in small sections running as hard as we could, then to fall into a ditch at the other side. Our section was last, so that we had all the form necessary to make it a ceremony. The long anxious wait, the corporal approaching, chanting, and exhorting us, then the final sudden dart to safety. That long, long, wait, that curious sickening feeling rising again from my stomach. It rose and rose till I was sure it was going to choke me. I was even afraid of it killing me there and then. Fear, fear like some slimy monster rising from primeval muck. I watched it rise, I tell you, like some great prehistoric reptile, to choke me. It wasn't I, I wasn't afraid, yet it was getting me, choking me. But I swear I wasn't afraid, it was something separate from myself, over which I had no control. It rose slowly, inevitably, mercilessly. My God, it wasn't me. I wasn't afraid. Then a new and greater fear came. Was I showing fear? That thought killed the huge beast at one blow. I looked around furtively, tried desperately to laugh and joke with Hartley. My laugh sounded like the gobble of a turkey. "Get ready fellows, and for God's sake don't forget to get in that ditch and stay there. Keep your bloody heads down too. NOW!"

A breathless scurrying dive through a huge invisible foundry of ringing anvils, with shrieks from the shells rising like the wail of lost souls. The corporal or somebody had guessed wrong, we were in it, and not past it as we should have been. Smoke, gasps, curses that were prayers. Free air at last, a dive into a ditch on top of others, with your heavy boots striking them. More curses, curses, curses. "Where the bloody hell are you going?" Keep those damned big ugly feet of yours off me." A gasp of relief. I was safe. Fall in, fall in, single file.

"Put out that cigarette, keep touch with the man in front. Keep moving, keep touch, close up, close up." Plod, plod, plod, heads down. My shoulder hurt again, then the man in front laughed, a queer laugh, that, as if the joke was on him. "By God, I was hit and didn't know it. By God, I'm hit! My guts." Then he drops and I almost fall over him. He is panting like a dog I saw poisoned once. "Stretcher bearers, on the double. Keep-up, don't lose touch. Close up, close up. Never mind him. Stretcher bearers, stretcher bearers, close up! close up!" Plod, plod, plod. "Wire overhead. Wire overhead, shellhole to the right! Watch your step!" Smell, smell; the sickening paralyzing odor of decaying bodies. Past the Zillebecke dugouts, Zillebecke Lake, then the village, and a halt where you drop on the ground dead tired, sick of the world, sick of yourself, praying for death.

The Corporal goads us into life again, we struggle through the darkness over piles of socks and equipment, until we find our gun, left there by the transports. Ammunition boxes, belt boxes, spare parts, tripod, the gun itself, and rations, all accounted for, we are off again in single file, just one small group of six men, tired, stumbling through holes, wire, underbrush, pitch darkness. Until at last the Corporal in front shouts, "Is that the 60th? Where the hell is your #1 gun? Just like you guys to hide the damned things off somewhere." Another voice answers, a voice filled with relief. "Thank God. You blighters did arrive at last. We thought you *had* got lost." Stumble, stumble, dark forms flitting here and there, talk between the corporals about ranges, ammunition and so on. And then quiet again. Off come our packs, our guns thrown down, and sitting in a hole *we* are able to smoke again. We have carried out a relief.

It is the morning of June 2, 1916.

Nine

The Corporal immediately proceeded to break us in to the French etiquette and cooking.

With pieces of sandbag, candles, and an empty tin, one can boil tea very rapidly and without smoke, also fry bacon or do any other cooking that is necessary. The #2 and the Yank were detailed to take the first watch with the gun. The gun was mounted in an exposed position with only a waterproof over it, and thus would be used only in case of attack. Half of the brigade of C.M.R.s were in the front line, on a slight ridge called Mount Sorrell, and the other half acted as a support and were entrenched in Sanctuary and Armagh Woods. There were only two lines of defence, the front line, and supports in the woods, with one 18-pound gun called a "sacrifice gun" also hidden in the woods, directly behind the front line. The nearest supports to us would be or were supposed to be, at the railroad dugouts in Zillebecke. But as the artillery were pulling out of the line that night, it would be doubtful if there would be anything behind us except working parties until one came to the rest camps near Poperinghe. The range in case of attack was 350 yards, which meant that we were within 360 yards of the Germans. Mount Sorrell rose in the darkness ahead of us, silhouetted by flares. All we could see was a pile of new earth here and there. Not a soul could be seen. We slept in the day time, all work being done at night in the salient. And in the daytime, was our period of recreation.

The Corporal explained all this to us, as we sat in a small shelter made of arched corrugated iron, that gave you room neither to sit up straight nor to lie down. It was about five feet square and three high in the centre. And it was in this drain that we had to eat, sleep, and work. We were on watch at night and resting in the daytime. The Corporal had dug a hole for himself close to the gun and in this the day relief sat and smoked.

The Corporal was telling me of his first trip in the line at the famous or infamous Messines barricade, when he suddenly stopped to listen. For the last hour or so he had appeared nervous, and we couldn't quite understand why, as the first line seemed to be quite peaceful and not a solitary gun of any description was being fired. Finally, I asked, "What's the matter, Corp? Do you hear something?" He grinned and said, "That is just the trouble. I can't. This line is too darn quiet to suit me. I have never seen it like this before." He snuffed out the candle. "I am beginning to get a hunch that Fritz is brewing some grief for us." He crawled outside, and the other old member, a man by the name of Hurde joined him. Hartley and I grinned at each other. War wasn't so bad after all. We had visualized a continual rain of bullets and bombs while in the line, and here there wasn't a shell or gun to be heard.

I said, "Say, Hartley, you can never satisfy some guys. If there were shells they would kick, and when there aren't, they're kicking."

Hartley laughed as he answered, "It does seem funny. It is darn quiet though, isn't it?"

Suddenly we heard the voice of the officer outside calling for the corporal, and the corporal answering him, as he came over. They stood just outside our hole.

The officer spoke first. "It seems very quiet, doesn't it, Spence? I wonder what the devil he has got up his sleeve? It must be pretty bad. I hear the brigadiers are coming in the line to look it over. I hope nothing happens this trip, it may be our last in the salient from what I hear. The front is getting the wind up though. Look at the damn flares we are throwing up. The Line's getting nervous."

Then the Corporal's voice: "I'm getting jumpy myself, sir. Gee! I would hate to have anything happen this trip, I got three new babies and they hardly know how to fire the gun, let alone do anything else. But it looks bad, looks bad. They do seem nervous over by the gap. I have never seen our guys more generous with flares."

"Well, don't forget your standing orders. If anything happens you are to head for the ridge if they need help, as soon as seen, or if you see the artillery flare, you move up. The other three guns of D. Company will be in the woods so don't forget to send a runner to them, if they are firing too low. Well good luck Corporal. Well, so long and don't forget to move up if anything happens—and I have a hunch." The earth-deadened voice went away.

"Good-bye Sir, good luck." The Corporal crawled in again, "You guys had better come out of here and stand to. I am afraid we are in for grief." We crawled out again with him. It was a beautiful morning, the sky carpeted with stars, and the wind had changed, so that Fritz was getting the smell. The air felt soft and dampish and it was dark.

I chuckled softly as I crawled out, imitating an Englishman as I remarked, "oo wouldn't be a blinkin' worm." Hartley laughed, and even the corporal gave a chuckle. He then detailed us off to our work, and there we stood and waited, for we knew not what. Dawn came slowly, making us look like wraiths. I shivered with the cold, or what I thought was cold. I had four belt boxes in sand bags to carry. Hartley was about ten feet in front, sitting down hugging the spare parts. I could just dimly discern the machine gun, with the corporal sitting behind it, and what I supposed to be the Yank and the other man lying by it. Hurde was behind me. He had discovered he hadn't got a field dressing, and was softly cursing. I felt for mine.

"Gosh, isn't it funny," I thought to myself, "waiting to be hit and killed?" I prayed I wouldn't get it in the face. I wouldn't like that. There were six of us, like six little pigeons sitting on the fence. Darn funny. How quiet it was, a cough sounded like a burst of a bomb. I kept giggling to myself. Six little pigeons! Was I getting hysterical? I must stop that. Gee! It was quiet.

Then a huge burst of flame, a hundred feet high, that gave enough light for the fraction of a second, to light the whole salient. Then an ear-splitting, deadening, paralyzing boom. Again, it happened. Again, and again. Seven times. By the second time my hearing had gone. I could hear nothing, in a world on fire. Loose dirt came down on our caps like a heavy rain. Then flares of all colors and kinds went up in the air. The artillery broke loose. Fritzies—the whole horizon was lit by stabbing flames of light. For seconds, I watched in fascinated wonder until I saw a man beside the gun leap into the air and fall flat. I was suddenly paralysed. The world was coming to an end. My ear drums were vibrating like a telegraph key. Hurde came from behind pushing me aside to fall beside the gun. I stared around. A cyclone without wind was taking place, trees crashing, smoke rising in sudden bursts of earth, and other things flung suddenly into the air, only to disappear. Although it was not yet daylight, the whole scene was brilliantly lit by exploding shells and flares. I looked toward the hill in front. My God, it was gone! And another hill was there, of new earth with little bits of smoke rising from it here and there. It was nearer to us now. Then smoke came in one huge gasping cloud, and stopped all further vision. I couldn't even see the gun. I heard nothing, my eyes watered, tears in a stream rolled down my face. Burnt powder and cordite filled my mouth with alum.

I stood there like a gawking school boy, choked, blinded, deaf. What had happened? *What had happened?*

The battle of Sanctuary Woods had begun. I staggered blindly forward, the iron belt boxes striking against my body at every step. Out of the smoke loomed a little mound—the gun. I found Hartley. He had a wound in the arm, near the elbow. The corporal was safe, untouched, but the other two were dead. Hurde had received a nose cap in the middle of the face. It was ghastly. The corporal saw me fixing Hartley's arm and came over. I was worried about the latter, he was trying to tell me something, but I couldn't hear him. Oh, artery, that was what he was saying. I tied it up, but couldn't make the darn thing fit properly. Blood bathed my hands, his blood, and my hands grew slippery. The corporal pushed me aside, and fitted the bandage himself, quickly, expertly. He had had experience. He sat down then, fished out a paper and pencil, wrote a short note and gave it to Hartley, shouting in his ear. Hartley staggered to his feet, lurched like one drunk and left. Eenie, meenie, miney, moe, who would be next! Oh God, don't let me get it in the face.

The corporal in taking the gun down, signed to the Yank and me. He took the tripod and two sandbags with belt boxes in, and I took the gun itself. The Yank took the leather case of spare parts and more belt boxes. A staggering, sobbing, cursing half-walk, half-run, trying to keep in sight of the corporal, down holes, up holes, holes, holes, holes. Smoke, flares of flame. An inferno. Over broken trees, with dim figures like wraiths meeting us, staggering past us, going out. Usually the white spots of bandages showed up glaringly. Our fourth man must have been buried! I wondered if the brigadiers had been killed. Sob, sob, sob, with breath whistling, heart hammering, lungs pounding for clean air. A hill now, climb, climb, you poor blasted infantry, climb.

You—I'll make you climb. Climb, you blighter. Oh God, I can't stand anymore. Climb you—climb. Sob, sob, whistle. Damn, oh damn, those belt boxes, climb, scramble, scramble. The air is getting fresher, at last the top. The corporal is sitting head down between legs, wracked with sobs, trying to regain his breath. I fall beside, my breath coming in short stabbing gasps, my head falling forward. Oh God, can't I get my breath back, my lungs are being cut out with a knife! The Yank falls beside me, face downwards and I watch his body jerking spasmodically. At last back to normal. The corporal taps me, and motions toward the gun. We get it mounted, and a belt box in place. He looks worried and gazes at the wood with a puzzled air. The landscape looks so changed he can't get his bearings. The Yank still lay panting, head in the dirt.

I pulled him over, face upwards, and his eyes were almost popping out with the fight to get his breath back. Slowly, slowly it came, more and more even. I pulled the belt boxes off him and put them beside the gun, and there we sat, three lost souls in a world gone crazy, waiting for the next joust with fate. Waiting. We were in a stark dead world, not a soul to be seen and we huddled closer to each other for companionship. Then out of nowhere appeared a lurching, staggering, reeling figure, that stumbled on unseeing within six feet of us. He was wounded and of all things in heaven and earth, a staff officer. He reeled on blindly, and we saw him no more. Where he came from and where he went we knew not. It was weird, uncanny. The corporal motioned to me and started to instruct me in dumb show how to fire the gun. My hearing was slowly coming back, curse the luck, for again I was inflicted with the vibrations. I even caught the dull boom of thousands of guns. He patiently explained the working of the gun.

It was about nine o'clock we judged, by examining the variations in our watches (they were all wrong as I later found; it was about 6 a.m.). We had lived an eternity in those few hours. Our faces were black and streaked with brown dust, and my hands and sleeve were red and caked with Hartley's blood.

Cry Havoc

The Corporal took off his tunic and sat with hands hanging loose, his grey army shirt out at the back, and a heavy Webley revolver at his belt. He looked like a picture of Wild West days. I took off my tunic also, transferring all my belongings to my trousers. As it grew warmer, off came our shirts and we were naked to the waist. The corporal carefully unfastened his field dressing and tucked it all ready to use in the top of his trousers, and as I followed his example fear in one great overwhelming flood came back to me. I had been so busy I had forgotten about it before, but now I had time to think. Sweat oozed out of me. I felt sick again as I looked at my hands caked with blood, deathly sick. By God, I won't have any stomach left soon. The Yank sat beside me, unmoving, staring, staring. The Corporal wrote a note and passed it to me. It is short and to the point. "In case I get it first, you must not leave the gun under any circumstances, until either the hammer is in the position I showed you or you have no ammunition left. Take this letter out with you and post it."

I looked up and he had a letter in his hand, which I took and put in my trousers, where it immediately dropped to my knees. I nodded, the corporal nodded in return, and his eyes were soft and dreamy. He was looking at me but not seeing me. I began to think again. The Corp. doesn't think I am going to get hit, or he would never have given it to me. Praise be, I am not going to get hit yet. My fears left me.

Suddenly the Corp. jumped, and I looked. Here they come, at last! Rat tat, tat, tattetty tat. Shoulder to shoulder, rifles slung and shovels in their hands. By heaven, they don't figure we are here. They think we are dead. Look at them jump, twist, fall, fall like wheat before a scythe. Rat tat tattety tat, they are gone, gone except for odd blundering figures staggering back to their own lines. The Corporal looked at me and grinned. I grinned back, exalted. This is great sport. Look at them kick! I looked around for the Yank and found him lying in a hole, his tunic reddened near the shoulder. He's hit! I went to fix him up but the Corporal pulled me back, wouldn't let me help him. My chum dying and I daren't leave. He lay there in the hole, huddled up, and the stain grew bigger and bigger. Here they come. In little groups this time, running from hole to hole. They were hard to hit. You no sooner got one group down than another appeared from somewhere else. They got closer, several grenades began to drop in front of us, and we couldn't see for the smoke. Damn them, we'll get them yet.

Rat tattety tat, traverse fire now, steady, easy, one belt gone. Another put in its place. I fumbled it. Oh damn, damn, a jerk, a pull, ratetty tattetty tat tat. The grenades stopped, and the smoke drifted away showing odd figures kicking and wriggling not twenty feet away. The gun was hot, damn Colts, they always get hot, just like the Corporal said. Another belt. The gun swung away from me and as I looked I saw them coming up the side. Rattetty tattetty tat tat. That got 'em. Now right around the other way. The Yank is dying. Oh

God, he lies there... The circle bigger now. Suddenly the gun stopped vibrating, and the belt stopped moving. I looked to see what was wrong. The belt was all right, the hammer all right, what the devil's wrong? It's the corporal, —clean, neat, quick, right through the forehead. No blood, just a dark hole. He still gripped the gun, and his face was set in a funny smile, the mouth slightly open. It's my turn now. I threw him aside, sat down, pulled the belt, raised the safety and—rat tattetty tat. Gosh it swings easy, and gives funny little jumps. I had better hold it tighter. I brought it around into a group, and they suddenly disappeared except for a few kicking and wriggling. The belt went and I looked for another. Just one more left, then I can fix the Yank up. I waited for more figures. They came. Then—rattetty tat tattetty tat. An eternity passed. A stoppage. I looked at the hammer. A No. 1 stoppage, I know. I ejected, pulled the belt and reloaded. More figures with hand grenades again. Oh, God I hope they don't hit the Yank. I couldn't leave without him. The gun stopped again, and I found the last belt empty. I hunted for a rifle, but there were none, we had left ours behind. I took the Corporal's revolver, and identity disk. He was Church of England, I saw. I looked for the Yank and knelt beside him. He smiled. What grit! I couldn't have done that. What courage. I tore off his tunic, and found a bad hole, which I covered with my own dressing and pulled him to his feet, motioning him to walk. He nodded, stumbled, then staggered.

Halfway down the hill I looked behind, to see figures closing in after us. Germans! I pushed the Yank on ahead and hunted for the revolver. God! I left it in the hole! I haven't a darn thing. I looked behind again, they were getting closer. What will I do? What will I do? They will start shooting soon. I ran blindly on, thankful to see that the Yank had got further ahead, possible ten feet. I looked back once more and saw a big fellow with a rifle on the ready, bayonet down and aimed at my back, my kidneys. I could feel it going in. What will I do? He doesn't intend to shoot or he would have done it before. He wants to bayonet me, that's it. He wants to stick it in my ribs. What can I do. I have it. I'll stop suddenly and turn on him as he runs at me, grab the bayonet and kick him. Kick him in the right spot, and he's done. Can I do it? I looked behind, he was ten feet away. NOW—TURN—GRAB—KICK. He dropped, screaming, writhing. The other Fritzies were some distance behind. I'll soon make the woods now. Where is the Yank? Where is he? Oh, there he is, sitting waiting for me. I staggered up to him, pulled him to his feet, and began to find how tired I was. But we had to hurry, pant, sob, pant, sob. Oh God. "Come on Yank, you got to." I hit him. He was dazed and weak and I couldn't carry him. It was when my hand went out to pull him up to his feet, that I saw my hand was open from one side to the other, covered with blood, dripping. Oh hell, what does it matter. Must have been the bayonet. Let the damn thing bleed. On again, through the woods, over the ridge, down to the village. Bloody, dirty, dazed, tired, deaf, helping each other, equipment gone, gun gone, everything gone. Patting each other, coaxing each other, forcing each other ahead. Life, death, war, hell itself was forgotten in that one supreme effort to reach the village.

Ten

When you are footsloggers in the infantry you see less of the war than a man ten miles behind the lines. The ones who see the full layout of the puzzle are those who arrange the pieces, the staff officers. For example, we as infantrymen did not find out till after the battle that there were seven German Divisions attacking two brigades of Canadians. We did not know that one of the brigadier-generals had been killed and the other wounded and taken prisoner by the Germans at the beginning of the battle, so that it was practically every man for himself. Our own Colonel had also been killed, our whole staff broken and disorganized. And so by all the laws of war, we should have been in flight; never before in history had so many head officers been lost and the infantrymen left to their own resources, and obliged to organize their defences. It spoke for the discipline of Canadians, not the orthodox army discipline of brass buttons and military police but a voluntary discipline that was stronger than bars of iron. We did not know that our artillery, caught when a relief was in progress, had no chance of fighting, or that the nearest supports were miles away, in fact we had forgotten all about them. We knew that Fritz was attacking as never before and it was up to us to stop him. When army experts think of war, they proceed, usually, on academic lines, lines of cold-blooded logical deduction with the most important factor of all left out, the human factor, and many times they have been proved notably wrong. According to their logic, the Spanish Armada should have defeated Drake. The Germans should have walked through Sanctuary Woods on that day as if no one was there. Seven divisions, one hundred and forty thousand of the fittest troops the Germans could produce, not Prussians but Wurtemburgers, against two brigades of less than half strength after the mines had exploded, probably four thousand fighting men all told. The Germans' total advance was a few hundred yards against this array. What stopped them? The spirit of one brigade, a brigade which had been held in derision by other Canadian units, that brigade called the C.M. Runs. Their determination was to wipe out the blot, which they did with blood. Not weight of men or armaments, not any of the things which war experts take account of, but simply a determination to regain a lost name. The fate of nations hangs on such things.

But let us go on to the village.

At last we arrived, broken, sobbing wrecks of men, hardly able to see, hardly able to wipe the sweat from our eyes with bloodstained hands. I felt like one drunk and was practically carrying the Yank whose legs moved like mechanical limbs at my orders. A stretcher bearer saw us come out and took him, I following to where behind some houses we came on the flotsam of battle. Boots, boots, boots, row on row with toes pointing to the sky, hundreds of them. And there was a continual soft wailing and moaning, with once in a while a shriek from shell shock cases. God, it was awful. By some freak my ears were back to normal again. I had to wait my turn beside the Yank. The doctors were very busy and no wounded could be evacuated yet on account of the barrage. Shells were falling at intervals around, once—well, one dropped close. I hunched against the wall, staring out with dead eyes, and somebody put a cigarette between my lips. I felt a needle go in my arm. It was a shot of anti-tetanus.

After a while somebody took my hand, I heard a grunt and looked up to see that the doctor had at last arrived at me. He looked at my eyes, drew a surgical needle out and stitched the wound of my hand together, after flooding it with iodine which seared and burned so much that the agony of it was delicious. I was alive. I hadn't felt the needle, but there was no doubt about the stitching, which I watched. A tag was tied to my braces and I looked at it stupidly. On it was only one word, "re-open." I wondered dully what it meant, then somebody else came along and a good shot of rum was poured down my throat. It felt warm, delicious, I wanted more, and the angel dressed like a man gave me some. I stood up then, feeling dizzy, weak, with dull aches all over. I looked at the Yank. He looked almost ethereal. Was he dead? No, he had a tag on too, but I couldn't make out the writing. He was breathing quietly, peacefully. Asleep. I was a fool, I bent down and kissed him and said "good-bye old scout." You see I was a walking wounded and therefore could make my own way out to safety.

I was standing up taking my bearings when an officer came, our machine gun officer. He was peering in the face of every man he met, and had his tunic off and his shirt open, ready for wounds and a quick application of bandages. As he came to me he looked at me sharply. "Hey, you're a gunner aren't you." I nodded. "Well, I need you old son, no blighty for you for a while yet. Where are you hit?" I showed him my hand. "Oh, is that all, well, I'm sorry but we need you, need you bad. Come with me." I followed him, still in a daze, and we went behind some more houses, down a cellar, piled high with machine gun ammunition and one or two spare guns. He handed me his water bottle with the invitation to "take a good swig" which I did, letting it gurgle down till I could hold no more. I almost felt normal again. My face began to burn though, and I felt sick. He was speaking: "Say you are one of the new draft, aren't you? What happened to your gun?" I told him. "Oh that was it, was it. I wondered what the hell was holding them up. Good old Spence. He got it, did he?" I nodded again, and leaned against the wall, so tired was I. The officer seemed tired too. Poor beggar, I saw he was having his troubles. "Well," he said at last, "I guess there is no damn good being done here. Say, can you carry the tripod and four belt boxes. If you can I will take the gun, spare barrel and six boxes. We ought to have some fun with them."

"What, you figure on my going back? Into that? You have a hell of an impression of my brains?"

He laughed. "You are coming back to life eh? One more shot of that and you would lick the whole darn army. What are you going to do? RUN?"

"Well, now, not exactly, but good God, I have done my bit. Damn it all, I couldn't walk a hundred yards, let alone carry all that stuff."

He looked serious. "Well, listen, I'll tell you what. You help me out in getting the gun thru and then you can beat it."

I groused, but took the belt boxes, put them in sand bags, and grabbed the tripods. Gosh, but they were heavy. My head was throbbing and burning. I'll bet it was that darn shot the doctor gave me. We staggered out into the blinding sunlight, the officer leading the way, and curiously I felt quite strong for a while. We went over the road, up Observatory Ridge, and on the top we rested, panting. The ground was dotted with khaki clad figures, some whole, some not, and all with the Maple Leaf shining in the sunlight. We weren't supposed to shine them, but we did. Our vanity helped our morale. Evidently Fritz had got his, for grey uniforms were piled in queer heaps here and there. Machine gunnery here. Whose gun was it? The officer shouted. "This is where Speed's gun was, blown up by a shell. He did a hell of a lot of work though before it happened." The scene was a grim one, bits of bodies, parts of machine guns, belt boxes, cartridges, and empty cases all over. We came on lines of dead Germans, almost perfect wind rows where the machine gun had caught them. There were wounded here and there and we picked our way daintily among them. One fellow wanted a drink awfully badly, and his eyes followed me. Poor devil, I signed to him I didn't have a bottle and called the officer, who came back and gave him some of the rum. His eyes were grateful and soft, like a dog's.

The tripod was cutting into my bare flesh and the belt boxes were taking the skin off. I cursed myself for a fool ever to have come back. We arrived in the woods and saw odd infantrymen here and there, resting and doing the queerest things. One chap was wiping off his boots, another was trying to cut a slice in his tunic for a sling. Another was methodically cleaning his rifle, holding it up to see if it was clear. There weren't very many. One man about every fifteen or twenty feet. We came to a halt behind a fallen dugout. There were feet sticking out of the earth. An infantryman crawled over and said, "Got any cigarettes?" The officer disappeared ahead, I mounted the gun, inserted a belt, gave him some cigs from my store, almost having to remove my trousers to get them. They were broken, crushed, but we smoked the pieces, and sat quite companionably, resting.

Odd figures would stagger or scurry past us, wounded and runners going back to report. I asked, "Who are in front of us," as I couldn't imagine this as the front line, it was so quiet just then, and the barrage was falling behind us. My new acquaintance grinned, "Nobody now, there were some machine guns but they have disappeared." I was startled, and said "Well where the hell are the Germans? I came through a while ago and they were right on my tail. And where were you guys? I didn't see anybody when I came through?"

His answer was startling, "I'm not a bloody footslogger, I'm a company cook, and this bunch is a mixed outfit from headquarters. We met the Fritzies in here, hand to hand. See this?" Pointing to a hole in the side of his tunic which I thought was a tear. "Bayonet?" I asked. "Yep. We had one glorious time here for a minute." His eyes locked off in the distance. "My helper got it too. One of the best. The bastards, I'll give them one for him."

Suddenly the officer dropped between us, sighted the gun, and started to fire. Rifles began to crack but I couldn't see what they were firing at. *Then* I saw forms flitting, sneaking up on us. Rifle grenades began to arrive. The officer surely knew his business for the gun cracked steadily and all I had to do was sit and watch for the end of the belt. The grenades got closer and as I sat half reclining with my feet in the bottom of the hole I felt a stinging sensation, then numbness. No pain at all, but I saw a ragged hole in my puttees with blood coming out slowly. Then the end of a belt came and I was back to business and I forgot about it in the next few minutes as the gun was getting hot and stoppages were frequent. The officer was having trouble getting the range too, because of the smoke. My tongue and mouth were again coated with cordite. Another jam. Damn the gun. This time it was hopeless, the shell had broken off and jammed the barrel. We burnt our hands badly changing barrels, as to do this we had to take the gun almost to pieces. We got it fixed—too late, they were on us, and I picked up the jammed barrel as the officer's revolver began to bark. The rest was a daze. Grunts, shouts, curses, a rifle shot blazing right in front of me but facing sideways. Something hit me in the stomach and I went out like a log.

I awoke to find myself in the hole still, but it was evening now, and dusk settling. I felt pains in my stomach, my jaw, and worst of all in my leg. I looked down at my leg, which was very stiff, and the puttee was soaked with blood. If I took it off, the bleeding would start again, and if I left it on I would get gangrene. What the devil should I do? No, hadn't I a shot of that dope! I'd leave it. My jaw was bruised, only a slight cut, and my stomach had a very bad welt shaped like a gun butt. So, that was it. My hand was bleeding again. What a mess! Good heavens, who was coming? Germans! I was behind the lines! Two figures in grey with red crosses on their arms had stopped at the hole. I tried to look brave and snarl, but I'm afraid it was a very weak attempt. They were stepping over the bodies at the bottom of the hole and around the edge. There were two or three other khaki figures lying there beside my own. I heard the moaning and groaning of wounded but couldn't place it exactly. There seemed to be a lot. The Germans gave me a look and then one had compassion and gave me a drink. I wasn't worth worrying over. They went right through the officer's pockets, taking everything, even his boots, nice soft shiny ones. "The bastards." There was a Fritz wounded there in the hole, his jaw nearly off. My gun barrel did that, I said to myself. At last they passed on, taking the Fritz with them. My head began to throb. Well, thank God the Fritzies weren't as bad as they said. They left me alone to die in peace. In war you look after your own side first, naturally.

When there were no German wounded to look after, they would come back for us. I couldn't help it, I thought I was alone among the dead, and I groaned, and groaned again. I would have given anything to cry. Then a miracle happened. I thought I was dreaming, but the officer moved, slowly rolled over, oh so slowly, and said, "Can you see any Fritzies?" I said no. "Thank God. Well, we sure are in one hell of a mess. Where did you get it?" "All over," I replied between gasps. "The devils didn't leave a whole bone in my body." He spoke again:

"I got a beauty, a bayonet in the shoulder. The blighter was aiming at my belly but I knocked his arm up. Are your hands free? Do you think you could bandage it?" He groaned in spite of himself and added, "It is pretty darn painful." "Can you roll over?" I asked, and as he rolled toward me I rolled a little in his direction and stuck his field dressing on the wound. It surely was a mess, a long gash with cords sticking out. I couldn't tie it though with one hand, and said, "I can't make the bloody thing stick." So we both thought it over for a minute, then he suggested changing his Sam Browne belt to the other shoulder to hold it. I had a difficult time rolling him over and fixing his belt as we daren't raise ourselves upward or we would get it. It was finally done, but darn it all, I had broken open my leg wound and unwinding the puttee found it was a bad hole through the calf. I could feel the shrapnel, a jagged piece, under the flesh. Oh Hell, what would I do now? I groaned again, my mouth dry, my head throbbing and throbbing. I slid down and groped among the bodies until I caught a khaki tunic, tore it open with my teeth and wrapped it round but couldn't tie it unless I used my other hand which was very stiff and burned and seared. Sweat poured off me, to the accompaniment of groans and grunts, as I tied the dressing.

The officer was talking quietly to himself and groaning. He was delirious. Oh God, what should I do? I pulled him down to the bottom of the hole among the bodies, and finding a German pack with a great coat, put it over him. I hunted through my friendly Canadian's body for cigarettes and found some. Throb, throb, would that damned engine in my head never stop. Oh God, do something about this. I can't do much more.

I hunted for my cigarette lighter, crouched down in the hole, putting my head between two bodies, cigarette in my mouth, lighter in my hand. Thank God, it lit quickly for once, and my cigarette was going. What a relief. I hunted among the water bottles till I found one that gurgled, pulled the cork and putting it to my mouth, found RUM. I said a prayer of thanks, drank long, and it immediately put fire into me. I had to put out my cigarette or lie down. Which would I do? I placed it carefully on the belt buckle of a Fritz and crawled over to the officer. His mouth was open and I poured some rum into it. He spluttered, sending it all over his face, but he began to lick it with his tongue, mutely asking for more. I gave him a little and reserved the rest to see what would happen later. Throb, throb, would that never stop! I hunted my cigarette, and found it still going, so holding my hand over the spark and blowing the smoke down to the ground, I smoked, smoked, smoked. It was dark now and felt cooler. Not a shell was dropping over us. They would have to be our guns, if there were any, I thought to myself. The German barrage was on ahead. Evidently their wounded went by another route then through the wood, for we saw no one. Flares thrown up by the Germans convinced me they must be up on Observatory Ridge.

RATS! My God, I had forgotten about the rats. I could see their eyes gleaming, hear them rustle. Oh, I can't stand anymore. And now rats! Haven't I stood enough, suffered enough. Oh please, please send the rats away. Oh, please do, please. I am at the end of the rope. Haven't you done enough? Why do you allow it? You aren't a God, you are a joke. Damn you.

I shuffled down beside the officer, hunted for his revolver, found it, and struck at them, and cursed, lying across him to get at him. Scurry, scurry, I could see their eyes. Damn them. Curse them. I forgot about my wounds, troubles, pains, aches, everything, and like a snarling beast, struck and beat at them. I lay there in a world gone mad, and dared God to do his worst, defied Him, preached to Him, and machine gun fire broke out, red and green flares floated in the sky, and the German artillery burst like a flood of bass drums, pounding in my ear. The rats disappeared and figures rushed past and I heard groans, and curses in German, then came men running, stumbling, and someone fell into our shell hole. I struck and struck and struck, and was still pounding him with the butt of the revolver when I heard voices, English, and good old Canadian curses. They passed, following the Germans. I still struck the figure though he had given his last groan long before.

I was in a daze. I believe my mind was going. The officer still mumbled and groaned, another wave of men passed over, not even glancing at us. Then came the third wave, and these were slower, hunting, hunting, listening for groans. I could see them by the flares, and I shouted and shouted. A figure came toward us. "Hey Joe, here are a couple." A welcome voice said, "You can stop hitting that poor blighter now Bud." My hand moved up and down, then somebody felt my body, and my mouth was opened and a pill of some kind thrust in. "God, Joe, these are the C.M.R.s, not our mob at all."—"Well, what the hell do you think of that. C.M.R.s. An officer too, without any boots. Those bastards pinched his boots. How is your guy? Mine's off his bean but o.k. I think." Then another voice broke in, "This beggar hasn't even a shirt. He's as crazy as a loon. Been pounding some poor dead man's face to pulp, and was still doing it till I told him to let up. Can yours walk? I think I can handle this one." Joe's voice again: "By the look of things these C.M.R.s sure put up some fight. Say, we better get out of here before the barrage starts." I felt myself being lifted, my arm put around somebody's shoulder, while my other arm still flopped up and down, up and down. I couldn't seem to stop it. Am I crazy? I must be. That chap said I was.

I felt all right, no pain, nothing, only that arm. I couldn't stop it. My mind seemed perfectly clear. We stumbled on, and I heard my man trying to encourage me. Suddenly his nerve gave, "For God's sake stop flopping that arm. It gives me the creeps." I tried to cut it out, but couldn't. I didn't seem to have an arm. It wasn't there, I couldn't make a connection. Am I dead? Must be. Stumble, stumble. At last a road. We moved along it and I heard the sound of an automobile motor idling. A heave, a push, and I lay on something hard, then rumble, rumble, and we were moving. Somebody else is there now too. The sound of gasps, groans, bump, rumble, rumble, bump. Screams from somewhere, sounding like my own voice. Rumble, rumble, at last a stop, lights, doctors, stretchers, a funny smell, then sleep, blessed sleep, glorious sleep. Thank God for sleep. The battle of Sanctuary Woods was over for me.

Eleven

I awoke peacefully, feeling fine but sort of tired and lazy. I didn't want to do anything but just lie there. I looked up at the ceiling and found even that made me too tired, so I closed my eyes again and went off into another sleep.

I awoke again later. Same ceiling. I moved my head sideways and I saw a window, glass. A big window. That's funny, I don't remember that. I wondered where I was. Oh well, what does it matter? I went to sleep again.

Again, I woke, still in the same place, but this time I heard a rustle, and a woman's face peered at me. Now where did she come from? Funny. I don't remember it at all. The face had a mouth that opened cavernously, saying something. I couldn't quite make it out. She smiled, so I smiled in return, then felt tired with the effort, and went to sleep.

The same thing when I woke again, the rustle, and everything, but now questions were forming in my mind and I tried to ask one, when another face, a different one, peered at me and smiled. Not a nice smile this time, but one of those cold-blooded professional ones nurses give. I didn't answer that smile, I don't like her, I wish she would go away. Then she spoke, after taking my pulse. "Well, how does Canada feel today?" Another smile. Darn that smile. I turned pettish and said, "Oh go away, and try to roll over, that smile gets on my nerves." By Jove, I can't move, can't feel. "Where the hell is the rest of me?" I looked at her again and gaped like a fish. She put her hand on my head and said, "Are you strong enough to tell me your regimental number and to what battalion you belong?" Oh! Still the army. Always a number, never a human being, just a number! Oh well, what does it matter? I went to sleep again.

I awoke at night, at least it was dark, and I was frightened. It did matter. Where the devil was I? "Hey, hey," I intended it to be a shout but it issued forth as a squeak, and sounded so funny. I grinned to myself. Gosh! I seemed easily scared. But it served, for I heard a rustle, lights went on, then off again, and on again, at the top of my bed this time. I blinked dazedly and couldn't keep my eyes open for a minute. A different face peered over me this time, a motherly face, no smile but a look of concern. "Well child, what's the matter? How do you feel now?" She put her hand on my head too, but I liked it and wished she would keep it there, it was nice and cool and soft, not flabby, but soft like silk. I spoke, even managed to grin, she was so nice. "Oh, I guess I'm all right sister, only I woke up scared. Say sister, am I all here? I mean, am I?"—"Now child, don't worry yourself. You are all there, except for the bits of iron we pulled out."

"Well, why the dickens can't I move my body then?" I demanded querulously. She cupped her hand under my head and lifted it up so I could see the rest of my bed. Oh, so that was it, was it? Strapped in. Why should they strap you in? Looney. I must have gone looney. And as if in confirmation she said, "You know, child, I do believe you are going to be worth the trouble, I believe you are going to pull through, but my! Oh my! Haven't you given us a time. You broke open three times to my knowledge just as they were getting healed too." Three times. THREE TIMES! What the dickens was she getting at? "Say sister, how long have I been here?"

She thought for a moment. "Let me see, you arrived here June 4th, and today is July 2nd. You—" Four weeks! Where the dickens had my memory been the last few weeks? "Was I looney sister?"

She smiled. "Looney? If ever a man was looney, as you call it you were. But enough of that, child. Can you remember your name? You know your people probably think you are dead. We knew you were a Canuck because a whole trainload of you arrived. But we never found anything except a crumpled letter ready to post, which somebody else might have given you, and an identity disk *in your pocket*, not on your neck, so we figured it must be somebody else's. You were naked to the waist with not a trace of any disk of your own. So we thought we had better wait till you came to. But we never guessed it would take so long." At the mention of the letter memory came back in a flood. I broke out in a sweat, and my hand began its old motion, rise and fall, rise and fall. The nurse, dear angel of God that she was, soothed me, petted me, coaxed me back to normal again. Finally, I gave her my name and number, and she gave me a glass of hot milk and a pill which sent me off to sleep again immediately.

It was morning when I awoke to find the straps off my bed so that at last I could move. Once of my legs felt stiff, due probably to bandages. I tried to lift my head and found it stiff too. My mouth felt funny and I found that I had lost some teeth somehow, on the side of my mouth though, thank heaven. I felt my chest, and found it strapped with court plaster. Gosh. I must be a wreck. I felt fine though. Then a glaring face came into my line to vision, to interrupt my investigations, and a strange voice said, "H'm, awake, are you. I suppose I will have to wash you." An involuntary "God forbid" came from me, which only made the face glare still more. Then it disappeared, and I heard the sound of a basin placed on a locker beside my bed and I squinted sideways. The face was grinning now, with what I imagined was a fiendish smile; but very gently the washing began, so gently that I looked through soapy eyes, trying to discover whether it was the same face beside me.

It was, but now I recognized the face as being not ugly but friendly, so I ventured a "Good morning sister," very meekly. "Oh, good morning Canada. You must be feeling good this morning to give me a dirty slam like that."

I explained how I had just awoken and was a bit startled. She laughed pleasantly. "Oh, well, all is forgiven. How do you feel?"

"Pretty good, sister." "I thought you must be a Canuck, I am a Yank myself. I thought so. Another of those bally Eastern Canadians who look down on their boastful cousins!" I hastily denied all such ideas. Personally, I loved all Americans, etc. etc. and mentally I kicked myself as a traitor to my U.E.L. ancestors. She only laughed and said, "Cranberries, you can't even lie decently. And now what is your number?"

I gave it, "51394, sister," very meekly.

"Well thank heaven it isn't in the hundreds of thousands like one of your chaps we have here, what do you want for breakfast?"

I suddenly realized I was hungry, so I asked for ham and eggs and tea and toast but she raised her hand. "I said breakfast. You can have tea all right; little toast, and maybe some maple syrup."

MAPLE SYRUP! I squeaked, and such a delightful kindly smile spread over her face. "Yes, maple syrup. When I joined this hospital and saw so many Canadians coming through, I tried to think of something they couldn't get but would dearly love to have. So, I hit up on maple syrup. I wrote to a friend in New York State and got him to send me maple syrup, so every one of you Canucks whenever you come to your senses, get maple syrup just to buck you up." And away she rustled.

It was not a breakfast, but an event. Just when I was beginning to get homesick for some friend, here she came and gave that little touch which made the world look good again. When I gave my thanks in return, all she said was, "Soldiers shouldn't cry," and wiped away something from my eye. She earned her place in heaven, that blessed old Yankee.

After breakfast came the doctor, a woman! Good heavens. I felt like a blushing girl. She poked and probed as ruthlessly as a man, and that Yankee stood grinning at my blushes. "H'm, h'm, temperature normal, how is your head?"—"All right," I replied. Did I hear sounds? Did I dream? Not that I remembered. Did I remember what happened in France? Why yes, I did. I started to sweat. Still questions. Couldn't she leave me alone? Why was it necessary to go back to that? Where was I hit first? I felt sore, and said I wasn't hit, I cut my hand on a bayonet. Oh, that was the first was it? "Yes," grumpily. Was I sent back in the line after that? "Yes." Where was I hit next? "In the leg." And where after that? "Oh hell, nurse, or doctor, can't you leave me alone?"

She grew gentle, put her hand on my head. "Now, now, take it easy, we just want to find out the facts, so we can repair the damage." I was still petulant and said, "I didn't have time to mark the spots, but I got one on the jaw and one on the stomach." Didn't any shells drop close? I interrupted, "If you are trying to make out I was shell-shocked, you are mistaken, I wasn't."

"Well, then what was it?" She spoke still more gently. I kept twitching and sweating, and my head was throbbing again. "Oh hell, give me a chance, I can't answer your questions, leave me alone." I tried to roll over, but again that voice, so gently: "What was it? Come on. Tell us and then you can go to sleep. What was it?" I burst out, "Damn you, it was rats, R-A-T-S RATS." My body was shaking, I felt like crying, screaming, yelling. My hand started to go up and down again, up and down. I heard a voice as in the distance, "Poor child." A hand was stroking my head and I grew gradually quieter, almost peaceful. More hot milk, another pill, then sleep. Why couldn't they leave me alone ... blessed sleep again.

Twelve

The next day I came back to reality. The hospital, I gathered, was in England. I must cable home to let them know I was still alive, and to get some money. So, I blarneyed my Yankee nurse friend to loan me some money to send the cable, and sat back content just to rest and dream.

It would be appropriate here to explain something that the English people often forget. And that was the fact, that England was not the home country of the Canadians. My home was three thousand miles away. I had no friends here to whom I could telegraph, and who would come to welcome me, and bring me those little things that somehow satisfy one inwardly. We had nothing of that sort. Is it any wonder that sometimes we got drunk, just to forget? When an English Tommy arrived in England, he was *home*. But we were in just another country. When they got ten days' leave, it meant something. To us, it was a holiday in London or Paris, it didn't matter which, only in one place they spoke English. And often, often in hospitals I have seen the same scene. An English Tommy on visiting day with a group of admiring relatives or friends around the bed, and in the next bed an Australian or Canuck with no one, nothing for him but to watch, while his heart ached for wife or mother or friend.

Is it any wonder we burst out once in a while to forget? The British Tommies were even worse than we were, in the same circumstances, at Salonica or Palestine, when they were as far from home as we were. Oh yes, we got drunk, I did, often. If I hadn't I would have gone crazy. Oh yes, I went with doubtful women. Weren't they like ourselves, homeless too? At least we met on equal ground. "Let him who is without sin condemn us." And He will be the only one that won't. My friendship with the Yankee grew. I always called her Yank. At first it made her mad, and was almost good looking when she got really sore. We had lots of talks together as I grew stronger, frequent hot debates about the war and nations.

One day I asked her why she had come to England to nurse, and she replied with a counter question, why had I enlisted? "I'll answer yours if you'll answer mine," I bargained. She nearly blushed as she said, "Have you ever read Kipling?" I pleaded ignorance. "Well, there is a bit in one of his poems and it goes like this, 'The Colonel's Lady and Judy O'Grady are sisters under the skin; and that's the answer.'" I told her I didn't get it yet. "Well, I'm a Yank, you are a Canuck, another is as Australian or New Zealander, or South African, but I am afraid we are all children of the same mother, and every real Yankee feels that way. I don't mean the Irish or the immigrants in the States, but the real-old Yankees, and I am one. That's that, now what's yours?" I was very sorry then that I couldn't give such an answer as hers, but I put it as gently as I could, and said, "Public opinion," which seemed to satisfy her.

She argued with me very shrewdly and good-naturedly, but her weak spot was America's efforts in trying to quench the fire with a feather, namely President Wilson's notes. Neither did she like our calling the Americans dollar-chasers. I loved to tease her, but if I caught my English friends jumping into the argument I would immediately support her. It all helped to pass the time and occupy our minds, though of course everything we talked about had some bearing on the war.

One day the matron happened to be present during our argument; the usual hard-boiled English hospital matron. I remember saying to the Yankee, "You must admit that you Americans are getting rich out of the war." That started her; the words came so fast that it was hard to get her meaning. But it went like this:

"Say, listen, you English like to call us dollar-chasers, while you are far above such things. Do you know why? Well, I'll tell you. Back in the States I have a friend, a millionaire, who is just like yourself, looking down on the rest of us. All the common herd thinks of is money, he says, while he, he is interested in the higher things. Sure, he can be interested in the higher things. Why? Because he has all the darn money he needs, anyway. Well, that's just the way with England, now. What about when it was young and poor? Napoleon called your country a nation of shopkeepers, but you didn't care how you got your money. You sold opium, you knighted pirates, you did everything to encourage our people go get money. No questions asked. In fact, a lot of you were made into Lords and Dukes if you were foxy and hoggish enough. Your imperialism has been a blot on history (like that of most colonizing nations) but up to now you are the richest nation in the world. Now you can act virtuous. You don't believe in stealing because you don't need to steal. You don't believe in war because in war you are a defender. So, throw your stones, the worst we do is imitate you. Only we haven't got the nerve to compliment people for stealing yet."

I laughed till the tears ran down my cheeks. By Jove, she had hit them off. That of course was the policy of all governments. The matron grew purple, and pranced from the room. "Well, Yank," I said, "you must admit that you people are imitating us pretty well. You're in a fair way to getting all the money, and I'll bet a dollar that after this war you'll be looking virtuous yourselves, eh?"

She laughed, having recovered her breath and good-nature. "I guess you're right there, Canuck. But we will imitate Asquith and 'wait and see.'"

"You mean you adopt Wilson's policy of 'watchful waiting,' don't you?"

Another way of teasing her was to put the Australians against the Yankees. They seemed to have boastfulness in common, I told her: "You Yanks are worse than the Aussies for "telling the world." Her answer made me laugh. "God forbid!" was what she said.

"I'll bet a dollar you are jealous of the Aussies. Aren't they, according to their own say so, the best fighters the world has ever seen? Haven't they the finest country? Don't they, like you Yanks, call their land 'God's Country?'" She laughed, but then became serious.

"I'm going to turn the other cheek to your insults. I am afraid deep down in my heart that it isn't the Aussies or the Yanks who are the fighters, it is you Canucks."

I nearly jumped out of the bed, and shouted: "What? Treachery! Treachery! What can I do now? I must compliment you in return. Horrible Horrible."

She laughed light-heartedly. "No, 'pon my honor, it's so, Canuck. I was talking with an English artillery captain who was wounded June tenth in the Salient, and he saw you fellows come out of the line, and if what he says is true, you are *some* fighters. He said the Field Marshal offered a British Army Corps to take back the trenches lost, and he was told to go to hell, that you would look after your own affairs. And I read in the papers you took back all that had been lost. Your division was out on rest after getting yours at Sanctuary Woods, so that it left only two divisions which had been in the line all the time, and yet, tired as they were, with heavy casualties, they took it back. So, you are some fighters, even a Yank must admit that. Of course, you come from the States anyway, so it really is a left compliment to us." She referred to the united Empire Loyalists, of whom I had told her I was a descendant. "Yep," she grinned, "you are the cream of both countries. You got kicked out of England for being disloyal, and kicked out of the States for being loyal."

This was the fact in my case, as she had learned. My family, or their ancestors, were exiled to Virginia during a religious persecution in England, then exiled from the States at the time of the American Revolution. I almost blushed at her compliment to Canada, which seemed to have the merit of being sincere and disinterested. I didn't know what to say, but at length I managed: "Now you have played a dirty trick on me, I've nothing to fight you about. I'll have to admit there may be a little good stuff in the Yanks after all." She laughed and departed.

So, passed the weeks, weary tiresome weeks, only lightened by our forensic jousts, and the visits of some brewery duchess now and then. These women did their bit by distributing favors to the soldiers. Sometimes we felt that this was done in the spirit of giving a dog a bone. I had heard from home, so had plenty of money and could be independent of such charity. One day I was a little more tired and nervous than usual. A little homesick too, with no one to visit me, until one of these women came around, accompanied by a nurse. "Oh, so this is a Canadian, is it?" I felt like a new species under the magnifying glass, which did not increase my amiability. "And how are you, my man?" I felt like telling her that I wasn't her man, I never would be her man, and that I wouldn't be found dead beside her, and sat grimly silent.

"Here are some cigarettes," she added, throwing a packet of cheap English cigarettes on my bed. I looked at her, my patience gone, and spoke.

"I have absolutely *no use* for that kind of cigarettes. Nor for you either," I added fiendishly. "For heaven's sake go away. Take her away, nurse, she makes me sick. She thinks she's at the zoo, feeding the monkeys."

I turned my head to the pillow, and had my first real laugh in days. I shook with laughter, until the sister came to quiet me. It was not the Yankee this time, but the quiet little English girl, who made you think of violets and a breeze rustling the leaves. My visitor had reminded me of a mongrel dog that had been trying to imitate a thoroughbred. I told the sister so, and she said, "Hush, hush, you mustn't talk like that." But she smiled.

She was a V.A.D., and scrubbed floors, did all sorts of menial work, and generally acted as an orderly; but my Yankee friend told me afterwards she was Lady Somebody or other. No wonder she smiled. The Yankee was hard to cajole, but I could get anything out of the English girl, even some beer, which I hugely enjoyed because it was forbidden.

She was a good sport. The genuine English, a kind you can't beat. She and the Yankee were good friends. The Yankee learned to say, "Isn't it huge?" and the English girl, "You bet your life," and both practised on me. The Yank had the habit of beginning any sentence to the other girl with, "Now my dear," and the English girl's favorite was, "It *was* jolly," so in self defence I imitated one to the other, until they stopped.

One day the English girl's mother dropped in, a sweet old lady who offered or rather asked apologetically if I would accept some cigarettes and chocolates. I wouldn't mind at all, so she brought some out, some American cigs, horrible things, some of those awful mixed ones, but I accepted them gladly. Then, wonder of wonders, she produced a bottle of homemade pickles. We grew quite friendly after the pickles and she told me she had a son blinded at home and another on the Somme. The Battle of the Somme had been on for some time then. He was in the artillery, eighteen pounders, and she asked, if I thought he would be safe? "Oh sure," I said, lying like a gentleman. "Why the artillery are so far behind the lines that the infantry never see them, I never heard of many even getting wounded all the time I was in France" (which was about five days). I don't know whether I comforted her or not, but she was more cheerful when she got up to go.

She looked furtively around and then dived her hand into the bag again, and oh boy, brought out a bottle of wine, wine. I wanted to hug her. Would I accept it? I certainly would, but I didn't have an opener. Again, her hand dived into that marvelous bag and produced an opener. The sister was nowhere to be seen. She must have one with me I insisted. She fluttered, but agreed at last, so it was opened and baptized with all due ceremony. And then she really had to go. She came and leaning over me, kissed me, and said, "Thank you so much for cheering me up. May I come again?" She was thanking me, for *letting* her call. I nodded and managed a "delighted to have met you," which I hated for its inadequacy, and then turned into the pillow so she could not see my watery eyes. By Jove, when you met a real Englishwoman, she could teach you something.

Thirteen

Then the air raid came. One night just as I was about to drop off to sleep the English girl came into the room and took up her position beside the bed after putting out the light. "What's the idea sister?" I asked, then before she could answer some sort of fire cracker went off somewhere and the street lights went out. It was absolutely pitch dark. Then the sister spoke, briefly, but with a world of significance: "It's an air raid, and this hospital is close to Charing Cross." Charing Cross, as one of the bigger railroad centres of London, was target for the zeps.

"An air raid," I said, "Well, why the dickens do you come in here, isn't there a cellar or something to this place? It would be a lot safer than here?"

She gurgled with laughter. "I'm here to look after you. You know the hospital is all put out of gear with you. This is really a hospital for women. Of course, we have army wards, but you couldn't be put in the general ward, so you have a private room, and now in this air raid you have to have me here to hold your hand and protect you."

I laughed in spite of myself. "What! Do you mean I am the only man around here! And that you are to look after me? What if I get shell-shocked? Do you have to pet me?"

She laughed again. "Oh, no you don't, if that is your idea, I absolutely refuse to make love to anybody while they are off their heads." A hint was sufficient, I protested my sanity, and searched for her hand.

Anti-aircraft gun began to bark, sounding like thunder. A searchlight lighted the room for an instant showing her face, pale, ethereal. I took her hand more firmly and said, "Sit on the side of the bed where I can look at you." I spoke almost harshly. I felt that I wanted to comfort her, pet her. The bark of anti-guns grew louder, the searchlight more brilliant. *It* was coming our way, I felt it in my bones. Her hands grew nerveless, lax. That was dangerous; had she fainted? I waited for another searchlight. I believed she had. I pulled her down, stroked her head, spoke soothingly, then a long mournful shriek sounded right on top of us, followed by a heavy crash, that echoed and re-echoed. The window broke and pieces flew all over. One struck the bed, and I pulled a blanket over her, my bare feet touching glass as I got up. I smelt the peculiar odor of cordite again, and it almost sickened me—but ladies were present. Mustn't get sick. I sat facing the window waiting for the next. She was covered as much as possible.

Another—a heavy boom—farther away. The anti-aircraft grew suddenly furious, then died away. I cursed the Germans for bringing women into it. The sound of guns died away in the distance. I prayed that they had got the airship. The street lights went on, a fire engine passed, another and another. Must be a fire somewhere. Ambulances now, I could tell by the clang of their bells. Then whistles for taxis. It was over. I hurried toward the bed. She still lay there, the street lights showing her dimly. Fear struck me; was she hit? I spoke, rubbed her hands. What the devil did you do when a woman was hit? I heard some women screaming somewhere. Ambulances were stopping in the street now. I rubbed her hands feverishly. "Sister, sister, for God's sake." I rubbed her head, wanted to kiss her, but it wasn't sporting. Finally, she moved a little. "Are you hurt sister? Were you hit?"

"No, no, I'm all right, just a minute," she returned in a dazed voice. "Oh goodness, are you out of bed? Oh, I'm ashamed of myself, so ashamed." She hurriedly jumped up, a quick recovery, I thought. "Now please get back into bed. I'm so sorry, so sorry." She began to cry, and I took her to me, feeling like an old man, and petted her, soothed her, and finally her sobs grew slower and I had a bright idea.

"Say sister, I need some brandy badly, or I will catch cold." She was immediately all apologies again. The light went on and she scurried off for brandy. The centre of the glass in the window had seemingly caved in and broken all over the place. I found two or three pieces on the bed, and threw them on the floor. She ran back in a few moments with the brandy and I made her drink some, also taking some myself. And then, it was a foolish thing to do, but we both grinned, and I said, "Well, you must admit you took an unfair advantage of me. Like yourself, I don't believe in petting somebody who is off their head. But I liked it just the same." We both laughed, but hers sounded hysterical so I made her take a little more brandy. Then she saw the glass and departed to get repairs and a broom. She was very busy fixing up the hole and cleaning up, and then went out to find where the bomb had dropped. After a while she returned full of news. It had dropped about 150 yards down the street, completely wrecking several houses and killing and wounding several people who were now in the hospital.

Then she told me that this was her third raid, and each time a bomb had dropped close by until her nerves were shattered. No wonder, poor girl. Damn the Germans. The light went out again, then a voice in my ear and a sweet breath, as I lay there. "You're a dear, Canada!" And something brushed my lips, then pressed hard. A kiss. "Good night Canada, I shall never forget."

And neither would I.

Next morning I had hardly cleared the sleep from my eyes when the Yankee bustled in, glared at me, washed me viciously and grunted and snorted as if murder was in her heart. I was amazed at the change and finally managed to get enough courage to ask her what the trouble was. She snorted again. "Humph, there isn't any trouble except that the most marked characteristics of you Canucks seems to be that you have the brains of a Tin Lizzie!" I was dumbfounded, indignant, and I pouted. "What the blazes have I done now?"

Another snort and, "That's the trouble, you haven't done anything. Imagine, a pretty girl, an air raid, and the damn fool treats her like a daughter." She actually swore. "You're a beauty. I don't think." With that and a rustle and more snorts, she left. She brought my breakfast in silence, and departed again, when some men came in to put in a new pane of glass.

After they had gone *she* came in on some errand but wouldn't look at me, so I called to her, trying to look stern and fatherly. "Look here, have you been talking to that lantern-jawed friend of yours about last night?" She nodded but still wouldn't look at me. "Do you mean to tell me that you expected me to make love to you?" Again, rather surprisingly, came the same nod. I gasped. I was done, beaten, finished. "What do you want me to do? Marry you or something?" and again that damned nod. She even looked up and smiled. I blew for air. "Well, what the devil do you think of that!"

She spoke at last: "Why, don't you want to marry me?"

"Who, me? Good God, no, I don't want to marry anybody."

Her laughter pealed out, and the Yankee coming in again just then, joined hers with it, and they both laughed and laughed.

I was paralyzed with amazement, then I saw. "Oh, I see, the beggars were pulling my leg," I told the world. I felt sheepish and the imp repeated it over and over again. "Good God, no, I don't want to marry anybody," while the Yank, laughing said, "You are out of luck dear, she simply refuses to have you. Go off and lick your wounds." Finally, I began to laugh, although I still thought the joke was on me. Good heavens, what if I had said 'Yes.'"

"Say," I called out. "What if I had taken you? What then? What if I had been in love with you?" They both laughed again, but the English girl stopped long enough to say, "We knew you weren't by the way you acted last night. So, we thought we would pull your leg."

That put us back to normal. I had wondered how I would meet her after the experience of the evening before. Her mother came in that day and on hearing it all was scandalized at the behaviour of her daughter. I took full opportunity to get my own back, by telling her solemnly that I had to refuse her daughter's offer of marriage that morning.

I was allowed to get up now in the afternoons and could even hobble around a bit. I would be going to convalescence camp soon on the way back to France.

It was then the beginning of August and one morning after the usual visit of the doctor the bandages were taken off for good. I was sent down to the clinic for a more thorough examination and finally pronounced fit, after further treatment in a convalescent home. The nurse, my Yankee friend, broke the news to me. "Well Canuck, you are on the way back now. You are to start on your return trip to France, and, gosh, I hope you get a two-way ticket."

I managed to work up a grin. "You made a darn good job of me, that's the trouble, sister. If you had only treated me a little rough, I might have got home to Canada."

She laughed. "That's you all over, always blame it on the women." There was a silence for a minute, then she added. "Say, child, if I were you I would tell my real age to the doctor. Oh, yes you are! I have been in this world too long not to know a kid when I meet one. Honest, I am sorry to see you go back."

Then the English girl came and the nurse told her the news. "What! Do you go back again to France?" I said it looked like it all right; as I had been pronounced AI, except that I was still weak. She didn't say anything for a minute, and then, in an unusually hushed voice she asked, "When do you leave here, and where do you go?" I told her I hadn't the faintest idea, but guessed it would be soon, as judging by the papers we were getting it pretty heavy and every bed would be needed. The girls went out together then, talking quietly to each other.

A little later I had a visitor from another ward, a Cockney. He was short, thin, used crutches and had a queer bird-like way of looking around. He glanced in first and seeing me reading a so-called humorous paper, he said, "Strike me pink, but some of you blighters get it soft, a room all to yourself, a nurse, ugly but still a nurse, all to yourself almost. Say, tell me 'ow you do it?" I had to grin in spite of myself.

"Come on in, soldier, make yourself at home. Have a fag?" He hobbled in, took my extended cigarette, and sat down on the bed. I was in hospital blues, sitting in a deck chair. We both examined one another with interest. Suddenly he asked, "What are you, a Canuck?" I pleaded guilty. He told me he belonged to some London Regiment, had been wounded on the Somme, and was just getting around. His eyes brightened when he mentioned Canada.

We talked of Canada, my home, Home! My voice grew soft, I loved Canada. Not England, not the States, but Canada, Toronto. Why if I were home today, I would be swimming at Sunnyside or the Humber, or maybe planning to go canoeing in the dusk of the evening to float back in the velvety darkness with the current. Other canoes would be there, some with gramophones which would sound almost beautiful coming over the water. Up by the Old Mill, and over in that old man's orchard where we used to pinch apples. Or just lying beneath the trees dreaming, lazy, content, in High Park. Or maybe hiking to Markham, or doing a thousand and one things I had done—in Canada. Oh God, let me go home. I don't want to go back to France.

I came to myself with a start, to hear him speaking. "Sye Canada, you know I often thought of going to your blinkin' country. What's it like?" So, I told him of Canada, and Toronto. Where you have every sport of the world, in its season. Hockey; by George, there was a real game with life in it. Of autumn in all its glory of maple leaves, with a tang in the air that made you leap and frolic for the very joy of living. Of Spring and maple syrup, of Winter with its thousand and one sports, bob sleighing, tobogganing, skating, sleighriding, snowshoeing, ice-boating and then the theatres and all the things one could do in other countries.

"Sye Canada, were you born in a city?" I had to laugh at this. "Say listen, Tommy, about two thirds of our blinking army, up to the time I left, were born or brought up in the city. The farmers can't be spared from their farms. Our country isn't composed of cowboys and Indians, in fact I never saw either in all my life, except at the Exhibition. I was born right in Toronto, Toronto a city of half a million, that is so up to date and modern that your country makes us think of Quebec. Why, good gosh, it's a real genuine city, about as big as Leeds. You just want to see it, and then you will have seen something. Not a bit like this damn damp miserable hole."

He laughed. "I have never lived anywhere except in this damn damp miserable hole." And so years later, he came to Toronto, managed to get a job as janitor, is doing well, and can even patronize people quite nicely.

I was allowed out now in the afternoons, for a walk or to the theatre, still in those hideous blue clothes, and there was a quiet little tea shop nearby where I liked to sit and watch the crowd roll by. Soldiers of all nations, civilians of all varieties. It was delightful just to sit and watch. Two days passed and on the third day my Yankee nurse came in whistling. "Well Canuck, we have managed it."

"Managed what?" I asked.

"We are going to take you out tonight. Both of us got the night off till twelve and we got you a pass, so we are going to paint the old town red. Tra la la, won't we have fun!"

I managed to look delighted but good heavens, to be walked around London with two nurses! I knew their idea of a good time, to take me to Madame Tussauds, or something like that. I groaned. Her smile became fiendishly impudent. "Oh I know what you are thinking. We will take you to the museum or something." I registered guilt. "Well we will just for that. I can't say you look very cheerful about it." I reiterated my delight but she laughed and disappeared.

Immediately after tea they both came in giggling and laughing at some joke. They put on my horrible blue overcoat and I certainly looked in no shape to go out. Hospital blues are of baggy material with everything too big, and my trousers were turned up at least six inches. But they, the girls, were undaunted, so away we went, in a taxi, a long long ride till we stopped at some hour in a dark street, at last, and I was push and shoved up steps and through a doorway, beside which stood a butler looking as startled as I was myself. But he offered no resistance, and we went on up more stairs into a bed room, and on the bed was a complete suit of khaki, with riding breeches and bandolier, and even a wound stripe on one arm. There were regimental badges in proper place and a British warm overcoat, and even underwear, socks and shoes all complete. The nurses shouted, "Get dressed quickly and properly or we will dress you," and left.

I had a suspicion they were peeking through the keyhole for I heard giggles outside but I dressed and found the things fitted fine, and was delighted to find they had brought a Canadian tunic with a high collar. "God bless 'em": But I had no hat, no hat. I look and looked, but still no hat. I examined myself in the glass and found I wasn't bad looking, for me, only pale and with a funny expression. I didn't quite recognize. I looked old, and there was even grey in my hair. I opened the door and sure enough they had been peaking in the keyhole. I tried to look stern and martial. "Say, don't you know that the book of etiquette forbids ladies peeking through a keyhole at a man while he is dressing?" They just giggled, and the Yank said insultingly, "We couldn't see much anyway, you are so darn skinny." My conceit was pricked like a balloon. I didn't dare them to tell me how I looked.

They stood looking at me critically for a while, then the Yank spoke again, "If had a little more meat on those legs of his, he wouldn't be bad looking at all, would he?" The English girl smiled. "Oh! I don't know, the freckles don't improve him any."

My face got red and I said, "Look here, I am not passing remarks about your legs or shiny noses. You may be both bow-legged for all I know, or even knock-kneed." They both had the grace to blush and grabbed me by the arms and whisked me downstairs, where I had a whisky, then away we went, to some Variety theatre, then a movie, where I held hands with both of them, then supper in a brilliantly lit cafe with an orchestra, where I tasted a meringue for the first time and liked it. Then we took a taxi back, and I changed my clothes again, like Cinderella, and returned to the hospital. And all this to the continual accompaniment of giggles and gurgling laughter that made me forget in spite of myself. It was a joyous evening and I went to bed tired but content, thanking God for my luck.

The next day the news came that I was to go to Uxbridge Convalescent just out of London—a Canadian convalescent camp. They both saw me off, and the Yankee talked and talked while the other was quiet. I had their suit of khaki on. As I kissed them good-bye I promised to see them and write when I could. Then I was off to Uxbridge, and the return trip had begun.

Fourteen

The Canadian Convalescent Home at Uxbridge had been somebody's country residence or estate. It was a big rambling house with many passages, but spoiled by additional huts built temporarily outside of the main residence.

I went through the usual examinations and received a pay book, so that I was once more on strength, and a possible candidate for the line again.

It was here I met Coles. It has been a million years seemingly since we had sat together in the same tent. Yet here he was as large as life, in the same ward as myself in one of the huts. A group of men were playing poker when the nurse showed me my bed. I was tired so I just flopped on it and went to sleep. They woke me for supper and it was then that he came out and peered into my face. "By all the gods of war, it's Slim." (Slim was my nickname.) It took me a second to recognize him, for his face was badly scarred. We had to celebrate our meeting with due ceremony, so we hied away to a pub in town, all the time talking excitedly. "Where did you get it?" "Sanctuary Woods."— "Oh I got her in July at Mount Sorrell, first trip in the line."— "Trench Mortar, say those things put the fear of God in you."

Then at the pub after getting a drink in me I finally summoned up courage to ask, "Did you ever hear about Hartley?" There was silence, while Coles thought hard, and my glass of ale was half way to my mouth where it had stopped, awaiting his answer. "No Slim, I never heard what happened to him. Nobody seems to know." I finished the drink. By God, a fellow felt he needed a drink in times like that.

"Say Slim, did you ever hear about Knight?"—"No, what was it?" "Well, you remember how that big slob had us all scared to death of him? How he kept talking about the South African War, and how we poor bastards didn't know how to fight, didn't have any discipline and all that. Well, that big son of a bitch came with me to the fourth C.M.R.s and on the very first trip in the boob showed yellow, tried to get a transfer, and then on the second night sneaked down to the horse lines and reported sick. Well, anyway (have another drink? I did) we came out of the line to the Zillebeck dugouts and stayed there on a working party, and he was sent back up and reported to the officer there, and the sergeant was wise to him, and put him on the working party with me that night. We had to go up to a place called 'China Wall' (China Wall was a barricade of sand bags built across part of the Salient to stop fire from machine guns) and we just go there when a machine gun opened up and of course we were on the wrong side of that damned wall. Knight was right behind me, and let out a yell you could hear a mile away: 'I'm hit, I'm dying, oh stretcher bearers!'

"Well, the bearers were busy, so another guy and me lugged him out, and all the time he kept yelling and moaning. We bloody well had trouble enough without that, and at last we got him in a ditch and stay to see where the trouble was, as we honestly thought he must be hit bad. Well, sir, we hunted over that idiot from top to bottom and couldn't find nary a hole, though he was blubbering like a kid. We pulled him half a mile, the big over-grown stiff, and we were both little guys ourselves, so you can imagine, Slim, how we sweated. We looked at each other when the next flare came up. We was shell-shocked, so we thought. But anyway, he scared hiself and pulled off his tunic and shirt, even his puttees, and pulled his trousers down look for that damned hole and at last we found it. In the boot!

"Believe it or not, Slim, but that stiff had been clicked with a bullet in the heel, and it had knocked the heel clear off his boot and probably shook his leg a bit. We were so damn disgusted that we told the Lord all about it for the next five minutes, then the other guy says 'He is a casualty, least everybody says he is, except us, so why not make him one?' Well, you can bet your neck that passed me for a minute, but I was willing to learn, so I says, 'How?' —'Well,' says the other guy, 'how about planting a bullet in through his leg? He'll be no damned good anyhow. And he will be happy to get to England for six months!

"Well, Slim, we debated the matter there and then and finally decided to give him a Blighty. We were just going to do it, when I had an idea and says, 'Say, if we give him a Blighty we will have to carry the big stiff to a dressing station!' We tried to make him walk, but he wouldn't so we decided if we had to carry him, we might as well give him the Blighty where nobody could see us, so we propped him over in the bottom of the trench, one leg stuck out nice and easy, and I took a shot, and damned if I didn't miss, so the other guy tried and he missed too. Course, it was pretty dark and we couldn't see properly, but I found out then why so many guys get left in a battle. We fired a whole damn magazine and missed every one. So, we gave it up as hopeless and lugged the son-of-a-gun to the village. There is a field post there in a dugout, and just outside we slammed him on the head with an entrenching tool handle and carted him in. One first class A 1 casualty all nicely fixed up for England. I almost felt like asking the other guy to give me one, it was so bloody easy.

"Then the doctor came, you know Dr. Pike, the old boozer who used to be at Barriefield. Well he looked at the head, bandaged it, gave us a shot of rum, then said, 'Entrenching tool handles leave a mark, next time use the end of a bayonet, then nobody can recognize it." We looked glass I guess, so he added 'Of course never mind, I'm not going to blab, perhaps you had a good reason,' and gave us another shot of rum and away we went.

"Well, I got it myself next trip, and landed at Leeds, and one day, who do you think I met? Knight, Knight in all his glory, with a woundstripe and everything. Can you beat it?" I couldn't, so we had another drink. I missed Hartley. Hartley wouldn't let me get tight, neither would the Yank. I wondered where they were. Oh hell, let's have another drink.

And so, it went on, and I heard of all our old tent companions, all except my two chums, the Yank and Hartley. We were drunk by now, and we had a "crying jag." I remember going back in a haze of maudlin emotion, saying, "Poor old Hartley, dam ol' war," and singing, "In the evening by the moonlight," and ending with a sermon on war. Damn war, poor old Hartley. At last the hut, and a nurse and, "You know, nurse, he was a friend, I loved him, damn war, oh lemme alone. Poor old Hartley." Soothing hands, gentle hands, soothing words, "Poor kid, poor kid." Soothing hands, "Poor kid," then drunken slumber.

I didn't wake with a dark brown taste or with the morning after the night before feeling, but, rather the reverse—quivering with life and energy. I don't know what it was, but that drunk had loosed some pent-up flood of emotion, which I was glad to get rid of. I felt fine, and looked for Coles. Coles, the other whom I had despised.

One day after another, passed, and it was booze and women, booze and women, a different one every time. London was a short distance by underground railway, train, or tram. So, day followed day, a continual orgy. I had the money, Coles the lust, we were well matched, and besides, next time I mightn't come back, so we made hay while the sun shone.

I became sated with debauchery, so that I experienced a growing revolt against it all. We did as we were told at the home, and took our exercise, but as soon as we could find the chance we were off to London. Our train stopped at a huge munitions works, and the train filled with women workers till our compartment was jammed, and as we were the only men in it, we go up and offered our seats. Coles with a smirk, I with bad grace. Giggles, nudges, remarks, passed from one girl to another; gestures, more or less inadvertent or meant for us; more giggle, more jostles, and nudges till I broke out into a sweat. Then for the climax the high shrill voice of some joker wanted to know where we were going tonight while a straight offer came from another to show us a real good time. The compartment was hot, stifling, and odorous. I was packed in a corner. "My God," I thought, "has this anything to do with the grand passion you read about, is this what women are like if left alone long enough?" I grew sick. To the devil with them. No more for me, I was finished. Coles was in his element. How the devil had I ever seen anything in him? We arrived at last and I made a break for the door. He called after me but I disregarded him and ran as if pursued by the devil himself.

I spent the time now on my hands, in a pub. There I met a New Zealander. Fine people, these New Zealanders, quiet, decent, wonderful fighters. We drank our beer together, and began talking about the war generally.

He was like myself, alone in England, and had been badly wounded at the Dardanelles. I was interested. What was the Dardanelles like? The Turks were good fighters and clean. How was France? I told I had taken a Cook's Tour, and only was in France six days in all, so that my impressions were no good. "Were we getting licked?" "We were. Give the Germans a decent chance, with no blockade, and he would have done it. But, of course, he couldn't now. But still he would give us one hell of a run for our money." My new acquaintance had just got word that a chum of his was killed at Polzierres, and I told him about Hartley. He had another beer, drunk in silence. Would the Yanks come in? What was my opinion? "Well—Oh—Um—Ah—We-ell." He grinned. "That is the best speech I ever heard about it, it explains it so clearly, at least more clearly than the Yanks do themselves," he said. We both laughed, and had another beer.

Warming up still more, we undertook to allocate the cause of the war. The New Zealander began to preach. It was a good sermon. "You want to know the cause of the war? Well, listen, I'll tell you a story." (I sat back comfortably) "Once upon a time there was a man, and this man was just like most other men, he was born poor. But he had guts enough to go after riches, and just a little more guts than the other men had so he got them. Just by care, and being smooth, when it was necessary, he got rich. He pinched some, grabbed some, and some just naturally accumulated, until as I said before, he got rich. Up until this time he believed in looking after number one and didn't bother very much about morals, because if he had, he wouldn't have got rich. Then he married, settled down, had kids and became virtuous. And because he knew that if everybody else did the same as he had done to get rich, he wouldn't be wealthy much longer, he very cannily 'got religion' and kept preaching to the other guy about how wrong it was to steal or pillage or hold up anybody, knowing darn well that if they were going to rob or pillage anybody, it would have to be himself, as he had a good deal of the coin and land anyway. He had several sons, whom he started out in life, and of course they were wise to the old man, and imitated him, and got rich and settled down and had kids and preached virtue, *after* they had become rich. So, all was going well, everybody was happy except those who weren't well off like his family. Of course, the other people had kids, too, but couldn't feed them very well, hut finally one or two got nerve enough to tackle the old boy. But he licked them and taught the others a lesson. But still every once in a while, somebody would try it and get licked. Of course, the old gent said he was only defending himself, that he didn't believe in fighting. And there you are, the cause of war, in a nutshell. Just make the old man England, and the sons, colonies, and the U.S. a sort of step-son, and you have it. Of course, England doesn't believe in war, nor the States either. They have everything to lose and damn little to gain. Of course, we are only defending ourselves. Of course, why do we have to defend ourselves so much? Ah, that's the question. Why do the rich people believe in a police force? So, there you are, Canada. A first class, knock 'em down, stand 'em up reason for war. We've got to fight to hold what we've got. The question is whether the step-son will join or let the old man fight his battles for him. I'll bet he comes in, because he knows he is the next richest to the old man."

I laughed and laughed. "You sure get bright ideas," I told him.

"Gimme one more beer and I'll show the old man how to win the war," he said, and willingly enough I did so. "Now tell us how to win."

"Well," he says, "did you ever see one of these old professional fighters who were punch proof?" I admitted my ignorance. "Well, these chaps get so used to punches that you can't knock 'em out. And the old man (England) is just like that, punch proof. And all he has to do is sit back and receive and let the other poor devil pound himself sick, and then you see, when he has punched himself silly, sock him on the jaw. After all, what the hell do a few hundred yards of land mean in a war like this?"

I did not try to point out to him how much a hundred yards of land might mean in this war. It was closing time so we had to walk across the street to another pub that could stay open later. He had enough Bass in him now to try to explain women, even.

"Now Canada, you take women. Did you ever see a widow stay single? Not on your life! That's women, leave 'em alone and they want you, chase 'em and they don't. That's women. If you prefer the chase, feed 'em mush, lots of it. Just like men—they will believe any compliment you tell 'em. Tell 'em they got a will power to withstand you, and they fall like the walls of Jericho. Tell 'em they don't love you, and they *will* love you. Let's have another drink." We did. The "lady" at the bar was a big buxom creature, with a cold eye for mushers. The N.Z. gave her a cold eye in return and impersonally ordered two whiskies, and by all the gods of war, she thawed, melted, softened, right there, and even wanted to talk. He paid no attention. We drank and departed. Outside he said, off-handedly genial, "Well Canada, so long, good-bye, soldiers' farewell! So, long chappie." We parted, and I went home buzzing with admiration.

Fifteen

The Canadians were on the Somme and my brigade had been in the thick of it there and at Courcellette, the sugar refinery and Mouquet Farm, the biggest advance made since the offensive. That was on September 15th. They had heavy casualties, very heavy. Then back again for Regina Trench, after getting drafts to fill in the blank spaces, and again more drafts. They had started to comb England for men. Coles was sent back but I wasn't fit yet, so was left. My hut was nearly cleaned out, with only men like myself left.

Then casualties from the Somme with light wounds began to arrive at Uxbridge and every day I watched for C.M.R.s but none turned up. Everybody told me they had got it heavy. It looked bad.

I went to London and looked about for men on leave, but found none. I gave up hope then and let it drop from my mind as much as possible, but did want news of my friends. I decided to visit the hospital where I had been, just in hope. I asked for my old nurses, and the Yankee came down first, and was delighted to see me, and so on, but really, she was terribly busy, the place was choked with wounded, and she ran off, begging me to see her next week. Then the English girl came, and I saw she looked tired and worn, and I felt like a brute for taking her away from her work. Her face broke into a smile when she saw me, and she took both my hands and surveyed me from head to foot, then kissed me. She was also very busy, but would be off duty at six, and would I meet her then? I said I would, though it meant going A.W.O.L. and already half my pay was gone in fines, but what the hell! I was there at six. She was drooping and tired and begged me to take her to some nice quiet place to eat, and be nice to her. I swore by all the gods that I would do my best. I told her all the jokes I knew, some good, some bad, but what matter as long as they made her laugh? I got some champagne, the best I could find, and fed her chocolate éclairs, which were her weakness. And after a while her eyes sparkled once more.

Then she told me of her brother. He had been killed on September 13th, and her mother was slowly dying on her feet, yet not whining at all, a real good sport. I asked her about herself. Well, she wasn't feeling any too good, but with all these casualties arriving, what could she do? I mentally cursed war, especially modern war, which absorbed women into its horrendous turmoil. We had a private room, so (whatever my readers may think) I nursed and petted her and soothed her, until she broke out into quiet sobs; and I let her cry and cry until at last she began to hunt for her powder puff, and blinked up at me with starry shining eyes, with her nose all red and her face streaked, but somehow looking more lovely than ever before. And so she powdered and sniffed, and dried her eyes, and said, "You know, Canada, you *are* a dear."

I hastily denied all such intentions. "Honest," I said, "I felt like loving you, but I—I—oh, hell, I didn't, anyway." At which she raised her face up to mine, put her arms around me, and said, "Love me now." But I wouldn't. Somehow it didn't seem right. The feeling I had for her was different from that I had felt for other women.

So, she pouted and laughed and said, "That's twice you have given me the cold shoulder, beware of the third!" I grinned, and said: "I don't know what the dickens you want, because I have been losing your reputation for you already, by treating you like a daughter."

She looked very, very wise, a curious expression, and shrugged, saying, "That's the trouble, but as you Canucks say, I'm going to marry you or bust."

I was dumfounded. "Honest, do you really want to marry a dub like me?"
"I don't know what a dub is," she replied, "but I certainly intend to marry you by fair means or foul."

I couldn't say any more, but pulled her out of the room almost by main force, and growled, "Come on, let's go to a show, or I will be making a damn fool of myself." She giggled and said, "Success is at hand, I have you on the run."

I did not know how seriously I took her, but I turned on her, and, "So help me, James," I said, "if you mention marriage to me again tonight I will spank you." She looked at me for a moment. "I do believe you would."

"I never lost a bluff yet," I said, "so just try it."

In the taxi, I had to note that the perfume on her *was* nice. She enquired innocently, "Do you believe in children, Lionel?"

"Yes! And when I marry I want at least a dozen kids, and they will all have to be freckled. Now, for heaven's sake leave me alone, or I will marry you, just to spite you."

Her voice was barely audible as she said, "Would you honestly?" I turned to glare at her, but somehow instead I put my arms around her, feeling never so strong as then, and said savagely: "Damn it, I will marry you now, I love you so much. I didn't want to, but now I will, and be it on your own head. Tomorrow we will do it." Even this was between kisses, and as she snuggled closer at my words I broke out in a perspiration and pushed her away. "Listen," I said, "for God's sake go away. I love you, darn it all, I love you so much, but I'm not fit to marry you, besides you are away up, and, well, I couldn't let you make a fool of yourself."

"I knew it," was all she said. "I knew it, I was sure that was the trouble." Then she began to weep softly, and of course, of course....

Well, anyway, we were married three days afterward. I gave my age as twenty, though in reality I had just passed my nineteenth birthday. I was granted six days leave, and those were the most wonderful days of my life, spent in Scotland, among the moors, far away from war.

I became a man. I came to know the small dear things that focus somehow a man's view of the rest of life.... One afternoon remains etched in my memory. She sat on the ground, looking over the hills, and I lay, head pillowed in her lap. She had a way I loved of bending down and nipping my ear, or of kissing me, gently, sweetly. It was like the peace of God in my soul. She ruffled my hair gently, all the while looking into the land of women, a land that men can never see.

She quoted a poem, her voice sounding like the ripple of a brook.

I may not hold the heights I gain
In those rare hours of ecstasy
When scorning ease, despising pain,
Forgetting self, and winning free
From all that so entangles me
I leave the low miasmic plain
Of sloth, of doubt, of greed, or pain,

To be companion of a higher train.
I may not hold the heights I gain
In those rare hours of ecstasy,
But God be praised, that for an hour
I gained the heights I could not hold.

Her head came down to mine, and such joy as I had never before experienced held me in exquisite torture. It was an hour of the heights, however transient.

Sixteen

On coming back from my leave, I was told I had been transferred to the Casualty Assembly Centre, at Hastings. I had hardly time to phone my wife before I was bustled away. The hospital was getting choked with casualties from the Somme and they were building new huts. We surely must have got it, on the Somme.

At Hastings I went through the usual examinations, and was billeted at Bexhill, and put on medicine and duty, the duty being physical exercise and squad drill. Getting us fit for slaughter again, I told myself bitterly.

The first afternoon that I had off, I went to town to post a letter, and as I was walking along the promenade by the sea, I heard a voice behind me: "By all the gods of war, it's Slim. Hey, Slim!" I turned, to see the Yank, of all people the last I expected to see. Our hands held together, and we grinned at each other like chimpanzees. Neither of us spoke for what seemed a long time. I couldn't; there seemed to be a lump in my throat, stopping me. At last he said, "Well, where the devil did you come from, I thought you were pushing up the daisies!"

"Hear, hear! That's what I thought of you," I replied. There was silence again, while we still grinned foolishly but happily at one another, then he suggested, "Let's celebrate," and so we adjourned and drank damnation to all sergeants, majors, and Red Caps. He was on leave.

"Yes sir, the King says to me, he says, 'I want to show you how much I appreciate your winning the war, so would you come over, so I can give you a little token of our esteem!' And I says, 'You bet your neck, King, you just tell the lance-corporals what you want done, and us bloody lance-jacks will do it!'" It was the same old Yank, the same queer voice with the lilt in it, and the same old devilment. We had another drink while I plied him with questions.

"Honest, are you really going to be presented?" He had the grace to blush, but admitted the accusation. "What for?" I asked suspiciously.

"A V.V.," he replied.

"A V.C? A V.C.?" I almost shouted.

"Yes, a V.C.," he said again, in sort of shamefaced voice.

"Well, my gosh, what for?"

"Damned if I know. Let's have a drink."

"But what the blazes did you ever do to get a V.C.?"

He grinned, such a delightful, wholehearted grin. "I captured a machine gun on the Somme."

"What?" I asked incredulously. "Honest? What did it do, walk over and lay down beside you?" Everyone knows how hard it is to imagine extraordinary things about people whom we have seen in ordinary circumstances.

He laughed. "You would take the conceit out of a sub-lieutenant, Slim. You're the same old Slim. Let's have a beer, and I'll tell you the story.

"You know after Sanctuary Woods, when I came back. Daddy had taken over the battalion. Daddy was a grand old man who had somehow got to France in spite of his age. He had more courage than the whole Expeditionary Force put together. His rheumatism sometimes was so bad he could hardly walk, yet he never left. He would come down the line at night, roaring and cursing, calling us a bloated bunch of tailors' dummies, and so on. How the hell Canada ever expected to win a war with a mob like us, God only knew. Where the hell were the sergeants? Had these men had their shot of rum yet? Well, God help any blasted three stripes caught pinching the ration, and so forth. Yet after a heavy scrap, there would be tears in his eyes when the roll was called. The battalion would have died for him, and he called us 'his boys' and looked on us and treated us as sons. He had a heart big enough for the world to creep in. He was always broke, for the very worst private could borrow money from him any time, if he had it. His roar was like the cooing of a dove to us.... And the very high epitaph should be given him? 'We loved him because he first loved us.'

"Well of course I had to report to him when I first got back, and he said, 'We will make a corporal of you, you aren't any damned good as a private anyway because you don't know anything about machine guns at all.' The men in the M.G. squad were some outfit, with steel helmets, a new kind of gas mask, and all sorts of doo-dads, and oh, yes, they've got the Lee-Enfield rifles now, and the Ross is discarded except for sniping; and they've got hand carts to haul the guns with. We had a couple more trips in the Salient, fairly quiet ones, then we were relieved to go to the Somme. Say, Slim, I forgot to tell you that on the night of our last trip I was detailed off as a guide, and lo and behold, you know the outfit that took over the place where the Aussies and the Guards had been? Well, I spoke to one Aussie and he said, 'We have to come up here and show you blighters how to hold the Salient.' And then I was talking to a Guardsman, and he gave his opinion of the Canucks, as a blank, blank bunch of schoolboys. Well, I don't need to tell you how I felt, but I couldn't say anything as they were big sons-of-guns, and then to cap it all, I meekly asked another Guardsman what he thought of us, and he, well, to say the least, looked at us with high disfavour. Very high. 'Poor bleedin' Canucks, why my God, they couldn't even put puttees on properly. Put 'em on upside down!' Well, you could imagine what was going on in my interior. I was going to get my own back, by hook or crook.

"So, when I arrived at Rest Camp to look up my outfit, and when I reported with my squad, two men for each company, and two for headquarters, my feelings were not improved by the looks of disdain given us by the officers. Maybe we hadn't shaved or cleaned our brass. Maybe our puttees were ragged and our clothes and equipment dirty. But would shaving win the bloody war? Anyway, we started out and by the look on the faces of the guides I had brought, somebody was due for a rough trip into the line. I gave their staff the once-over, and this staff was adorned by one of those officers with a monocle, who kept shouting, 'Are you *theah*?' to the sergeant major, and passing remarks on how he was almost ashamed to be seen with these guides, they were such a dirty lot, *doncherknow*? That got my goat, and I swore an oath that I would make him dirtier than anybody before I got through with him. Well, to make a long story short, I had to take 'em to Canada Street on Mount Sorrell. I would have taken 'em overland through the woods, but when I got to the Zillebecke Road, I had a brilliant idea. Why not take the blighters by the road, and hope for the best? I could go up Davison Street then (that was a communication trench) and it wouldn't be much longer anyway.

"But on the road Fritz had one of those set machine guns, fixed to fire at a certain range always, and this gun was aimed too high for the road, but low enough to throw the most ungodly scare into anybody. And there was a dirty, slimy, watery ditch on each side. So I warned the officer about the gun, and told him that if it started, to pass the word around to dive for the ditch. *The word was passed back*, and Mulvaney, the guide at the rear, nearly gave the game away. We got nearer and nearer, and I prayed that Fritz would open up and at last we got to the spot, and heaven be praised, Fritz let her rip. Boy! You should have seen those guys go for that ditch, and heard the curses when they found what it was like. Oh, boy, I laughed myself sick, and like a fool I stood in the middle of the road, doing it. Well, they all crawled out, and of course found that the gun was set high, but having no experience in this kind of war, they wouldn't have been suspicious then, if I hadn't remarked on how they stunk, and how I was ashamed to take them into the line. Well, that did it, and of course Mulvaney had to come up and say, "What was the idea of that message you sent back?" My friend the officer swore he would report me, and he did. I was duly hauled up, and after I had told the whole story Daddy laughed himself sick too, and reduced me to the ranks, but raised me to sergeant right afterwards, and told me to get the hell out, or he would recommend me for a medal."

"I see how I'm going to retire as Brigadier-General."

"That's nothing. Another guide tried to get the Aussies to walk through the lake, but they got suspicious of that. Oh, yes, we gave 'em a real rough ride in.... Oh, say, Slim, you were wanting to know why I'm getting the medal. We marched down to the Somme carrying and pulling those darn carts, and had a day in the brickfields outside Albert, and I won five hundred francs there at Crown and Anchor. Then we lugged the things right up to the support lines. Royal Engineers' Dump Kit was, along a narrow-gauge railway. And next day we went over the top, carrying the guns. I carried the tripod, another guy the barrel, and since some blighted brass hat got the brilliant idea of putting us in the second wave, of course the gun didn't arrive, the fellow with the barrel got it, so I was the only one to get there, with the tripod. Say, Slim! I spoke for fifteen minutes straight without repeating when I found I had lost the bloody gun, for it meant filling in all those damned incident forms.

"My number 5 got over with me, bringing ammunition, so we had most everything except the gun. Well, when I thought of all those damned forms I had to fill in, I decided it was easier to get another machine gun, so we hunted around and couldn't find one of our own. But there were lots of Fritz's in the sugar refinery, so we went and got one, and Daddy said it was darn lucky I did, or he would have reduced me again for losing the gun. As if it was my fault! Then the next thing I heard was I had got the V.C. So, that's that. Let's have another beer."

We did, without comment, but I heard afterward that to get the gun he killed or took prisoner a whole crew of German machine gunners, and did this lone-handed.

"You wanted to know about Hartley? Hartley, eh? Well—oh, hell, let's have another drink. Hey, give us a couple of double-headers. Canadian Club." We waited for the order in silence. I knew now. We drank in silence.

"Well, let's hear the worst, Yank. Is he pushing up the daisies?"

"I'm sorry, Slim. Yep! Hartley's R.I.P."

I gulped, gulped again, and ordered another drink.

"Damned few of us now, Slim. And you are going back, aren't you?"

I nodded. It was my turn next. I knew, or thought I knew, I was going to certain death. Hadn't I figured it all out? Was it possible for me to escape a second time? Hadn't I done sums and sums in my head trying to figure my chances for survival? I had figured so well and so long that I knew that in the Canadians my chances were exactly zero or less, for staying six months alive, and that in every other I did stand a chance, an even break of coming out. But not so in the Canadians. Wasn't it rumored that our casualties were in the proportion of four to one? Didn't I know that with all the bunk about getting Germans, attacking troops suffer *far* more than defenders? And weren't the Canadians only used in attacks and to hold some desperate point? Didn't I know that even then there was a big scrap coming for the Canucks somewhere near Arras?

Didn't I know that up to that time, from November 1915 to November 1916 that the battalion to which I belonged had been replaced *completely* four times? That for one thousand men or less, our casualties were near five thousand? Oh, yes, I knew. Didn't my life, my hopes and fears depend on knowing? So again, I repeated the Yank's phrase. "Yep, I'm going back, and this time next year they will add me to the fertilizer. Let's have another drink."

He told me about Hartley. "You know, Slim, when he left the gun that time with a message? Well, he got back all right, for an officer told me he asked him for the Machine Gun Officer. Well, I guess he tried to get back to the gun again and got lost. At least I figure he got lost, for he was found about a hundred yards or so to the left. He had picked up a rifle, and when he met the Fritzies he got three, wounded as he was, and I guess he was off his bean. Anyway, he put up one whale of a scrap by the looks of things, and finally got a bayonet in the stomach. Better have a drink, Slim." Poor Hartley. What in the name of God would I tell his people? I guess I'd better tell them something. I heard the voice of Yank away in the distance. "I wrote his people and told them that he died in my arms, and that he asked for his mother, so you don't need to write." I thanked God.

I couldn't finish my drink somehow, and made some excuse, told the Yank I would see him later, and left. I walked and walked and walked. Hadn't I been a fool! I had tried hard to avoid making up my mind irrevocably, but at last I had the courage to measure what was ahead see, two months at Hastings, two months at the Reserve, another month or less getting back to the battalion—five months, with maybe two months more before I would get it, that was seven months, seven months to live. Well, that wasn't bad, if only I could keep that imagination of mine under control. That was it, I wasn't afraid of death, but it was my imagination that kept conjuring before me how I would die. I didn't want to get it in the face like that guy I was passing, or in the legs, but just a nice even hole, like the corporal had got. Now that wasn't bad, it was over so quick. But was it? I remembered once having a tooth pulled, and although the doctor said the nerve didn't stretch, but that he broke it off quickly, I knew better. It had seemed like eternity. Mightn't it be just the same at death? It may seem only a second to the one watching, but what about the poor blighter who is dying?

Damn, oh damn, why in the name of heaven was I ever given such a realistic imagination! Many of the men I knew were considered brave, but it was only because they didn't have the brains to think. Their imagination didn't trouble them as much as a goat's. I had to drug mine. If I could only find something besides booze. Booze was dirty stuff. Something clean and quick, that doped your brain. Then I would be like those damn cowlike men. Hartley was gone, a bayonet in the stomach, and oh, God, I could see him lying there. Hartley was gone, and the Yank would be sent home, and I would go back, back to the blood and the mud and the torture of seeing myself get killed. Oh, God deliver me, am I a damned soul? What have I done to deserve this? Is it my fault that I am as I am? ... There couldn't be a God. No one, not the worst beast of the field, could be as cruel as that! No, we were all a gigantic accident. No use worrying, or trying to depend on somebody that wasn't there, no use. I was caught and gripped like a log at the lumber mills, inevitably pushed into the maw there to be cut, tortured into some other shape. Oh, hell, why worry. I would go crazy this way! So, I went into a pub, and the door closed on God and all his works. Oh, I was cunning enough not to pass out. But I took enough to deaden, to stupefy the brain within me that kept crying out.

Seventeen

I met the Yank that night as arranged, at the clock tower, and we immediately began trying to devise ways and means for me to attend the presentation ceremony, but we couldn't get any practical ideas, except for me to go A.W.O.L., and as I wanted leave to see my wife soon, that wasn't feasible. The Yank was thunderstruck when he heard of my marriage and said he had a damned good mind to tell the O.C. my real age and get me kicked before I did it again. In spite of myself I laughed, for I had a sneaking idea that he wasn't much older than I was. But as to experience, we felt that we were old men. By this time, we were mixing our drinks, that is, taking a whiskey straight with Bass for a chaser. I am one of those curious individuals who can never get really drunk in the ordinary sense of the word. I forget the past, and live vitally, but almost soberly, in the present. When I realize that a friend of mine is getting tight, it brings to the surface an almost motherly solicitude that makes me so anxious to protect the drunk from trouble that it keeps me fairly near a sober state. I knew the Yank was getting tight, because of his harking back to an incident I had forgotten, but which he had evidently nursed in his sub-conscious mind. In this I was a listener, a placater, a mother.

"Say, Slim, do you remember the time you kicked me in the ribs back there at Mount Sorrell? Well, sir, if you weren't a frien' of mine, I'd pound the daylights out of you for that. You're the only guy that ever kicked me, and got away with it, but you're a frien' of mine, see? And blast it, a frien's a frien' and has a perfect right to kick if he wants to. Say, Slim, do you know I was jealous of you then, you looked so damn cool and care-free. Yes sir, jealous, that's what I was, jealous, and I said to myself, sometime I'll make that long drink o' water jealous of me. I'll get a bloody medal, then tell him all about it. You know, Slim, honest, I was no blasted hero, do you know, honest to God, I was scared, but I says to myself (tapping me on the shoulder) 'I says, I'm going to get that gun, or croak. Then I'll get home with a medal, and nobody'll ever know I was scared, see? That's me, and I don't give a damn who hears it.'"

I was getting worried, for he was surely tight. But I was a good listener, and soothing as a mother. After we had another drink, he called a British Tommy: "Say, you blasted Britisher, come here." Luckily the Tommy had a sense of humor, and he came grinning. The Yank went on: "Meet my frien', Slim. Slim kicked me once, but he's a frien' of mine, see? So he got away with it. Have a drink." The Tommy grinned and had a drink. "Well, do you know, I'm going to get a medal from his nibs, the King, the King, God bless 'im. Have a drink. And after he gives me the medal I'm going home, HOME to the States. Yes sir, I'm going to Canada, but I'm an American. You betcher life I am. In the finest bloody army in the world. That's me, and I don't give a damn for Aussies, Tommies, Fritzies, or the whole darn caboodle. You fellows, you Britishers, you can hold the line, the Aussies can attack, but us, we do 'em both.

"An' Slim's going back, but I'm going home.... By God, that's a joke: I will be planting potatoes back in our garden, and poor old Slim here will be pushing 'em up. Tha's a joke, Tommy, yes sir, good joke. Ain't it? What? Me putting 'em in, and Slim pushing 'em up. Why don't you laugh? Ain't you got a sense of humor? *Ha, ha, ha-ha.* Slim's a frien' of mine, see, I'd knock the blooming daylights out of him if he wasn't. Yes sir, there I was lying on the ground, and the big stiff kicked me. But I love old Slim, oh, yes I do. He saved my blasted neck for me once, didn't you, Slim, old boy. Ha, ha, Ha. The joke's on you Slim. The joke's on you, old kid. I'll be putting 'em in, you'll be pushing 'em up. Let's have another."

But I led him home to his hotel, and on the way to my billet his mocking laugh rang in my ears. The joke's on you. *Ha. Ha. Ha*, the joke's on you.

The days passed with daily letters to and from my wife, and I was anxious to see her again. Her letters were wonderful, an inspiration, a joy that never will be forgotten. She was such a beautiful, healthy, sporting creature, and her mind was interesting and fine. I will quote some of her ideas as they came to me in her letters. One day she wrote:

"I have made a great discovery since we were married, and that is, that there is a difference between the minds of man and woman. I was brought up on the teaching that women are equal to men; but they are not—can never be. Between the two, as the Bible says in reference to something else, is a great gulf fixed, and that gulf can never be crossed. If one tries, one only falls into the abyss, and like Mahomet's coffin, stays in midair, neither in earth or heaven.

"I am content to be a woman, to fulfil my task as a woman. This equality business, as you, my dear old wild man say, is the bunk. Men are dreamers, idlers, and want to loll and be idle, being naturally lazy. They would like to dream all the day long. But a woman is anchored to the earth, she must drive and inspire the man to work and slave for her and the family. She is practical, but it goes against a man's grain to be practical, and he may become a beast...."

"My old nurse used to say that marriage was just like making porridge. To make it taste properly you put in two extremes, first salt, to supply the savor, then sugar when you want it sweet. Too much of either is disastrous. You are as different from me as that. I want love, petting, all the manifestations of love; while with you, love is but the thing of the moment, as soon as you have your fill you are tired of it. Oh, don't protest, shouldn't I know? To a woman, love is all; she gives and gives, and only as she keeps on giving does she grow and become a real woman. But as soon as she stops giving, and begins to receive, she dies spiritually. Haven't I seen only too many petted wives, drifting like lost souls, because they didn't know, they thought they were meant to receive.... With a man, on the other hand, it is different. He receives, first the love and sacrifice of his mother, then his wife, his friends. On that he thrives. Stop a man from receiving the love of some woman, and he becomes sour and embittered and a damned soul.

"You wonder, I suppose at all this moralizing. But it is because I love you so much, my mind works and plays all the time about *us*. Oh, sweetheart, how I love you! I would give you my all, my life, joyfully. And I am going to give you a memorial, a son, and he is going to be brown-haired and curly like you, but sometimes I pray that he will be born without quite so much soul and imagination, so that he won't suffer like you. Oh, don't tell me you don't. Haven't I watched you, seen you on the street, stop, almost seen your heart jump, as you saw some child in danger. Oh, yes, I have watched you, Lionel mine.... I used to think when I was a child of how Christ suffered on the cross, but now I know that the physical suffering was as nothing, to the suffering that brought the cry, 'They know not what they do,'—and that greyed your hair.

"Oh, darling, I know that a man suffers far more than any woman—if that man has a soul. That the bearing of a child or any other physical suffering is only a beginning. I can see you fighting God, fighting fate, ready to live, ready to die. I believe in God, oh yes, I am a woman; it is better to nestle content in a harbor, even if it is a false one, than to go out onto the ocean. No woman wants to leave a harbor.

"After all, you men are only children, you still come to us, to harbor, to be petted and strengthened just to go out again. Women love individuals, everyone is a 'one-man woman' as long as she loves; but a man loves the group, his own side. His love for an individual isn't love, but only a kind of affection. But if a man loves a nation, a race or a party, then, and then only does his love resemble a woman's love. It becomes a passion.

"Aren't I silly to talk like this, I feel as if I should be wearing spectacles and a beard. But somehow, I want to get these things off my chest, the time seems short. I don't know why, but I feel like that. Something keeps telling me, 'Hurry, hurry, love him as much as you can, *while you can.*' Oh, darling, darling, I love you!"

Moved by her letter, half-amused, half-impressed by her ideas, I read it again, and the last part struck me. "While you can." I laughed and laughed and laughed. Everybody seems sure, so sure I am going to die. Isn't it a joke? Oh, hell, I can only die once. And they might get fooled at that.

That night the telegram came. "Please come at once." I went to the O.C., obtained four days leave, saw the paymaster, and out of the kindness of his heart he gave me two quid, although my pay was already overdrawn. I left on the train that night, and I had been so busy getting ready that I didn't have time to think; but as I sat in the train, my first conscious thought was, it must be the baby, and if so, wasn't it a bit soon. I had no idea just how short a time it might take, but even to me it appeared a bit premature. I felt more curiosity at first than premonition.... Maybe she was ill. That thought gripped my heart. I spoke to her. Oh, yes, you may say I am a fool, but I spoke to her there in the train. I said, "Oh, Aileen, it is very bad?" She only smiled, in an ineffable way, and said, "Wait and see." But I felt comforted, because I saw she smiled.

I arrived at the house early in the morning. Since our marriage, she had taken a flat in Crouch End. As I walked up the first flight of stairs everything was very silent. I hunted in the gloom for the knocker, and the door opened, and I saw a nurse standing there. Good God, what's the matter? Then I saw the doctor, and in one crushing blow, I knew. Something had happened to her. My head began to buzz. "*Ha, ha, ha!* The joke's on you!" The God I had seen in the shell-hole laughed. With a jerk I pulled myself together. "Don't act the fool, everything's all right, don't go crazy before you have to." Then I spoke: "Are you a doctor? I am her husband, what's the matter?"

I waited, and heard a clock ticking, one I had asked her to buy, as I wanted a real old grandfather's clock in our home, the kind that had a nice fat solemn tick and boomed sonorously. Silence. Then I became conscious that the doctor was speaking. "Now please don't take it hard, go easy."

"Say, what's the matter, I'm all right, what *is* the matter?"

"I'm very sorry, very sorry, but your wife died this morning at four o'clock." He put his arm around me, but I threw it off, and went to the window, and I am afraid I was a coward then; my whole body slumped. As I stood staring out of the window, a messenger boy passed. Funny, what they looked like. He was whistling. "Died, did you say, doctor? How?"

The nurse told me. "She was on her way home after posting a letter, and was struck by a bus, and of course in her condition, it proved serious." The world changed into a grey haze. I was tired, Oh, God I was tired. So, that was what it meant. "While you can" applied to herself, not to me. I groped toward the doctor, whom I couldn't see very well. "In pain, doctor?" I asked.

"Oh, no, oh, no." I knew he lied. "She never recovered consciousness." I knew he lied again. The nurse asked, "Do you wish to see her, she looks lovely." Damn you, you cold-blooded ghouls.

"No, no, I don't want to see her now. I want her alive, alive!"

"I may not hold the heights I gain." "While you can." ... Somebody's laughing at me. God's laughing. "The joke's on you." Then came unconsciousness.

I woke in darkness, but there was a light in another room, and I raised myself and peered in. *She* lay on the bed, and her mother knelt beside it, praying. Poor old soul, she certainly had her troubles, sons dead or blinded, now her daughter gone. No more would we hear that lovely little laugh, so sweet, like bells in the evening should sound. I knelt beside the aged woman, and put my hand on her arm, and she just turned and put her poor, poor, weary head on my shoulder and sobbed quietly, while I eased my grief in feeling hers.

The clock ticked, tick, tock, tick, tock, tick, tock. And she? My love? She lay there, and my hand found itself on her.

Eighteen

I obtained two days extra leave, and then returned to Hastings. My first, appalling feeling at the loss of the only real human being in a world of foggy nightmare was now tinctured with fear and bitterness. Often at night, when men were exchanging stories, I had heard them call things, and even persons, hoodoos; and it came to me that I must be a hoodoo. Didn't everything that I touched or love, die? The fear of that filled me to the extent of certainty. I was a hoodoo, one to he shunned. I must never love anyone, for surely the one I loved would die. My soul grew bitter and morose. To forget, I would get drunk, only to be there. I was different from most men drunk, like a rat cornered, and ready to snarl, fight, or kill. If God was like the police in the military prisons, determined to smash me, break my spirit, make a truck horse to do his will, my hate of Him was greater than fear. I licked my wounds, but was ready to fight again. He wouldn't break me. I'd show Him. I swore an oath, that I would die cursing Him. He could get me down, beat me, kill me, but I would show my hate to the last. I carefully schooled myself for further blows, and tried to put on a veneer of hardness, a poker face that would not show agony. But my hair grew greyer.

I attended every drill for physical exercise, dieted myself, cut out whiskey and drank stout, took eggs in brandy, and doped myself with patent medicines. I worked hard to put myself in condition to be accepted and passed by the various boards. My leg looked pretty bad and I was afraid now that it might stop me from going to France. So, whenever I was asked about wounds or scars, I mentioned only my hand, which was perfectly normal except when it was struck in a certain spot, then it tingled in most exquisite agony. I prepared to endure pain by striking this hand, every day, but it took all the courage I had at first, and some I didn't have and I broke out in cold sweats when waiting to muster sufficient nerve to do it. But I did it, daily, and it was then that I made a discovery. That you can be hardened to pain as to anything else. That pain, like the strings of a violin, can only go to a certain pitch, and then it dies. Or if it continues, after the first few minutes you become used to it. That the most deadly pain is that which comes at specified intervals, and it is that only because your mind is imagining it beforehand. I would have killed my imagination too, but nothing could be done for it, that was where I was beaten. The only thing I could do was to dull it with beer or stout, or wine, perchance.

The peculiar thing was that I grew popular among certain of my fellows. I attracted men who were quiet-looking, who had the expression of coming death in their eyes. Oh yes, you can laugh, but I knew, and often later on, in France, I amused myself by picking out the men who would get it that trip, and I was never once wrong. It was something in their eyes. I knew. And these men came to me, seeming to get support; and we would drink together. They usually were the type that makes bookkeepers or parsons in civil life. Quiet chaps who wanted nothing more than peace, and now were in war, like a bunch of sheep without a shepherd, hunting blindly for truth. My hardness and coolness attracted them, I could do anything with them. I think that at that stage, I would have made a good officer.

One night we were in a pub, three of us, just drinking quietly, not bothering anybody, when in came some Australians. Now we were deadly enemies with the Aussies behind the lines, and one of these had a fighting jag on. Just drunk enough to want trouble, he swaggered in and the door swung after him. We had just ordered another beer each, and it stood there untouched.

"Blasted Canadians, eh? Blasted, bloody, blinkin' cockeyed Canadians! Think you are the whole bloody world, don't you?" And with these words, he seized and drank one of the beers, then threw the mug on the floor. Three Aussies and three Canucks. It only lasted a few minutes, but in these few minutes I rid myself of all my troubles and resentments. I became a raging, cursing demon. One of them lay on the floor after I had struck him in the stomach, and I strangled, beat him, whipped him, until I was pulled off. For one brief minute I went mad. Strange as it may sound, it brought me back to normal. I felt as if I had rid myself of a heavy burden. I was almost lighthearted, and then the Red Caps came in (military police.) The bar-maid supported our story, and two of the Aussies were taken to the hospital, while the other had disappeared. We finished our beer. I was almost happy that night. I felt as if I were getting a little of my own back.

A few days later I was boarded, and sent to the reserve battalion at Shoreham. I was there three months. The Methodist was there, the same old patronizing, ingratiating polite but insulting Methodist. It gave me a great deal of joy to beat him up, one night at Brighton. Of course, I was hauled up and given fourteen days in clink, but when the O.C. asked me why I did it, I just said "on general principles." As he was a Sergeant, I should have been sent to the Glass House (jail) but I almost believe the O.C. sympathized with me, for he said, "taking into consideration that you were drunk (I had not said I was drunk) and the fact that a draft will be leaving soon, I give you fourteen days in the guard house." And that was that.

To be placed in the battalion guard house was not as bad as it sounds, the guards were usually your friends, and, also, they were better fed and had more to eat than the soldiers on ordinary duty, besides having a supper at midnight. One was very lightly let down, and it was almost a holiday. One played poker with one's guards, ate their meals, even to the late supper, and they usually supplied one with everything one wanted, down to a couple of pints of beer a day, if one had the money. I enjoyed it, as the first real relaxation I had had in some time.

Christmas Eve came, and I went to Brighton and spent it in a pub. It was there that I met Allen, one of the greatest influences of my wayward life. Allen, who if he had lived was going to found a new and greater religion. Allen, who gave me belief in God and faith in man. Allen, who made me see wondrous things in this world of ours, and who even to this day keeps me looking for a rose in a cabbage patch. Who developed all unconsciously the soul in me, who made me wake in heaven, and see into hell with untroubled eyes. I often wonder how many geniuses such as he were lost in the maelstrom, how many inventions were lost, how many men who might have given birth to—oh well....

Considering what he was to become to me, our first meeting was curious. I sat in the pub, half occupied with my drinking, and half watching the crowd drink, a motley of Canadians, Australians, French Canadians, British Tommies, harlots, and girls who were trying to be. Several accosted me, as I sat there, but I put them off with the old story of wounds to stop their swearing at me for refusing. Just watching the world roll by, lazily, unseeingly, yet dreaming romances of everyone. "That Cockney has the wind up, I'll bet he's on leave and it is up soon. He's afraid to go back, and I don't blame him, and he's trying to make up his mind about overstaying.... The Canuck must be going back after being wounded, and he's married, with a wife and kids somewhere, because he's drinking alone. Looks bad, he is as badly off as I am, poor devil."

Then Allen came in, though I didn't know who he was then. He was tight, riotously, gloriously tight; and I thought, "What a fighter, what a handsome, daredevil rascal."

"What ho! Here we are again, cough up the plunder, shovel up the booze, this is my night to howl, everybody drink! What, you won't let me? Be damned to you, set 'em up or I'll walk all over you, ruin you. Set 'em up!" The crowd, composed nearly all of colonials, laughed, the bar-maid laughed, everybody was enjoying it. "It's Christmas Eve! Santa Claus. I'm Santa Claus tonight, and rolling in it. Hey there, Lonesome Luke (to me) come and drink."

I smiled in spite of myself, and walked over, and when he saw my badges, he shouted, "Well, by—Here's another C.M.R. Best bloody outfit in the best bloody army! Hey, drink up!" I drank. "Are you an original?" I modestly stated that I was not, but an 8th C.M.R. "Well sir, put her there, I'm no blooming cavalry man, I'm infantry, yes sir, infantry, 74th Battalion. When did you leave?"— "June second."—"I heard about it. Some scrap, worst scrap Canada's ever in. Put her there! You sure made your name for us that day. I joined after Sanctuary Woods. Did you know — —?" (Here he strung off a list of names, but again I was forced to deny knowing any of them, but explained I had only joined the outfit two days before getting hit.

"Well, by God, a Cook's tourist, eh, in again, out again, on guard!" I grinned. He certainly was tight, "Well, brother, let's go. Where shall we go, C.M.R.?" —I didn't care. "Well, let's go anyway." And go we did.

We ended up next day in a hotel (Christmas Day) with splitting headaches, a link of sausages, an alarm clock, and a collection of knives, forks and spoons, evidently collected from different restaurants. We had a cold bath, H.P. Sauce and soda water, and felt like new men. Then breakfast, after which we both felt stronger again, and hack to normal. And Allen expressed it nicely when he asked, "Where the devil did I pick you up?" I explained, and we both laughed over it. "Well, it was a glorious battle," he said. "Have you got a pass?" I said I had one until midnight, but it was evidently after midnight now. He was in the same position, so by mutual consent we decided that we might as well be hung for a sheep as a lamb, and stay away over Christmas. I said, "Well, I just got out of clink, anyway, and I owe the army enough money to make me work for nothing for the next year, so they can't fine me, and as for clink, well, I'm due on the first draft, so it doesn't make any difference."

"What? Are you due out on the next draft? So am I, and I'm in debt too, so let's go, Sobersides, and have one whale of a time. How much money have you got?" We both counted our resources, and I had two Canadian ten dollar bills sent in the last letter from home, two ten shilling notes, and about a quid in silver. He had five twenty dollar bills, evidently from a similar source, and about five shillings in silver. "Now," he said, "You got to take charge of the exchequer, and when you say we are broke, we will go home."

Cry Havoc

I agreed, and we found a place to change our money, keeping back one twenty-dollar bill in case of emergencies, and away we went. We chartered a taxi and looked at the town, coming to the conclusion that it wasn't up to Toronto (he was from Toronto too) then we had a gorgeous dinner on the promenade, and after that a theatre, then picked up two girls, and dropped them again as quickly when we found they were hungry, had supper ourselves, went to the theatre again, found a place to dance, and danced with drinks interspersed, until we felt like going back to our hotel to bed, well content.

Next morning, we walked the parade, looking for God knows what, and found a charming old couple who invited us to tea, and with whom we spent a glorious hour. And so passed five days, and we were broke. We went home, reported, were scolded by the sergeant major, hauled up the next morning and given fourteen days more in the guardhouse, which was cut short on the tenth day of the draft for France.

We left for France on the thirteenth of January. I wanted to live again, and had forgotten about God and His world in my new friendship.

While getting ready, I heard from a chap who said the Yank was on his way back home.

Nineteen

It was a pitch-dark night and we sat on the deck hunched up against some stanchions. The ship was crowded to the decks with humanity, and several were ghastly sick. To go inside in the nauseating air meant getting sick yourself, so we endured the cold and wet in preference. Allen was holding forth on war, and telling me of the changes I would find when I got back.

"You know, Sobersides, the war has changed a hell of a lot since you were there. We are all experts now, we've got new gas-masks, with new kinds of gas, and the Stokes gun. Say, that is some gun, you just drop a shell in and away she goes, you can have eight shells in the air at once. The Fritzies are as scared of it as we are of their sausages (trench mortars). The bloody Australians had to let them capture one on the Somme, so he has 'em now too, and believe me, they get your goat. And besides this we got Lewis guns, and colors on our backs and shoulders, and efficiency. Why, they even have the C.M.R.s able to form fours now without falling over each other. We had a Welsh guardsman drill us for six weeks before we went into the line after Sanctuary. But they haven't killed the old outfit yet, it still can steal and forage as of old. We got a bunch of prisoners on the Somme, and I got me a nice wrist watch," he suddenly laughed.

"Gosh, I got to tell you about Frank and his wrist-watch. It's a beauty. We were both in B. Company, and when we went over at Courcellette, we were in the second wave. Well anyway, when we got over, near the sugar refinery, I was detailed off to take a squad of prisoners out, along with a little Jew by the name of Gurevitch, he taking the front and I the rear. Well! We had one hell of a time getting them out of K.R.E., but we got them there, which wasn't bad, considering Sanctuary Woods. And when we lined the beggars up I saw one that had a lovely wrist-watch, so I traded a package of cigarettes that were all wet for it. He didn't want to trade, but he did. And then I took the officer's buttons (there was one) and I saw the moppers up searching them for more souvenirs when I left.

"When I got back, I showed Frank my nice new wrist-watch and the Jew showed some more watches he had picked up. Well sir, Frank got real sore, at being left out of it, and he made up his mind he was going to get some real souvenirs. So he made the round of some Fritz dugouts which we had bombed and left, nobody going into them because we figured they were all stiffs in there anyway, and the sight wouldn't be nice. Well, as I said, Frank started out, and we sat in the hole waiting for what was going to happen next. It didn't take long. There I was sitting nice and peaceable, when who should fall into the hole, right on top of us, but Frank? I pushed the blighter off, and gosh, I never saw a man so scared in all my life, and on top of that he had the most beautiful black eye I ever saw. Gee, it was a beauty. He was stuttering with fright, but finally we got him calmed down, but all he could say was that a stiff had socked him in the eye. Well! Even the Jew laughed at that, but we asked him to show us where, so we crawled out, and over about twenty yards, and sure enough, just as he said, there was a Fritzie stiff with a nice gold wrist-watch, a sergeant or officer or something, because he looked nice and neat.

"We sat down there trying to figure it out, and the Jew said, 'My Goodness, he can't be dead, or else how could he hit Frankie?' and I was sort of coming to that conclusion myself, but still, he *looked* dead. Stiff as a poker, eyes open, hands sprawled, as if he had got it from shock. I went over and stood with my rifle and bayonet poised over his belly as if to stick him, and his eyes didn't even blink; but I took his gun away just in case, and then got down after the wrist-watch. Well sir, I got the finest smack in the eye I ever got in my life! I was dumfounded. The blighter was alive, and yet he still lay staring as if he hadn't moved. It happened so darn quick I wasn't even sure whether he had done it or not. Well, I didn't like to stick him lying there, and yet I wanted him to move. How the blazes would I do it? He was a brave son-of-a-gun, anyway. Finally, I called Frankie out of his hole, and told the Jew to come too. Of course, they kept their heads down, for though one isn't noticed, three would be. We moved him over into our hole, propped him up and spoke the only German we knew: '*Raus mit uns. Mercy Kamarad*,' and then in English, 'Wake up, you blighter, we aren't going to hurt you." And by Jove, he came to life all of a sudden, his hands shot right up into the air, his eyes took on signs of life, and he spoke. Two of us blinked at him with one eye apiece, and in spite of himself he grinned, and we naturally grinned too, and gave him a cigarette. He spoke in English.

"'I'm awfully sorry to have to hit you, but I did not want to lose my watch, it is a keepsake.' I said he could keep the blasted watch, but how the devil did he act dead so naturally? He laughed and said, 'Your first wave came over, and I can't go back, and I can't fight because there is too many, and I am afraid of being taken prisoner by first wave, because maybe they don't take them.' He was right, they didn't. 'And as in Germany I am an actor and practice doing what you call fits, I decided to act dead. Then that man come, and I thought he going to kill me, but when I see he only want watch, I decide I'll hit him, and he being scared will run, and maybe be ashamed to tell his friends.' The Jew and I laughed loudly at this, and Frank looked sore. 'And when I see you, I decide to try it again; and then behold, you brave men, so it does have no good effect.'

"Well, we gave him a shot of rum, then he told us there was an officers' dugout just a short distance away, where we would find wine and beer. So, we started, and sure enough, we found it. There wasn't a soul in sight, but on a table was bread and sausages and beer that was flat. But we found some wine and a little more beer, and as we had some bread, cheese, and onions, we had a feast. The Fritz was a real good sport, and sure was an actor. He sang *Burlington Bertie* just like an Englishman. And the Jew gave us a Russian dance, and as Frank was over being sore by this time, he gave us a step dance. Then we all sang, and oh, boy, it sounded glorious, and then we got Fritz, to sing us the *Hymn of Hate* that we had heard so much about. For an encore, he gave *Deutschland Uber Alles*. Say, that's some tune, Sobersides! We all caught it, and tried to sing, but made a mess of it. Then we noticed that by the sound of the barrage, Fritz must have been counter-attacking. So we went up, and the sergeant, who had been looking for us, gave us hell. Fritz never got far, for we had lots of machine-guns. In fact, we took a few more prisoners and sent them down to join their friends. We went down ourselves later to get same breakfast, and gosh, that Fritz put up a real good meal from our rations and his and the officers'. There was one Fritz that acted sullen, so just to show there was no hard feelings, one of his mates clouted him and brought him to order.

"Pretty soon we heard footsteps, and who should walk in but the O.C. and some other officers. Well he roared and bellowed as usual, then asked us how we got our black eyes, and after we had told him, we all had some beer, and the O.C. said, as he lifted the canteen, 'Here's to the C.M.R.!' And those Germans drank with us.

"We were relieved that afternoon, and tried to take the whole bloody outfit back to our horse lines to give them a real feed, but the battle police stopped us. The Fritz offered me his wrist-watch, but I wouldn't take it, although I should have, as some of those damn bomb proofers would get it anyway."

I laughed till the tears ran down my cheeks, and said, "I believe the part about the black eyes and the watch, but you ask too much when you bring in that dugout story."

"I'm a liar, am I? I'll show you!" We wrestled, or at least he did, but I couldn't for chuckling.

He was a cheerful beggar. He told me next about Regina Trench, where they couldn't spare men to take the prisoners out, and hit on the brilliant idea of cutting all the buttons off their trousers, so their hands would be kept so darn busy holding their trousers up, that they were harmless. Gosh! I would have given a thousand dollars to see those Fritzies running among the shell-holes, with their trousers dropping down and tripping them.

We sat silent for a while and Allen tried to sleep, putting his head on my shoulder, and cuddling up like a child. There is no more beautiful thing in this world than friendship between man and man. No passion here, no seductive line or limb to disturb one, but just understanding. Not agreement, just understanding, and that friendship which allows you to remain silent, that does not call you into action and force you to try always to appear something which you are not. Suddenly I started. In this friendship, I was already forgetting the Yank, and Hartley, and, what else in my life? But Allen slept, apparently, and I drowsed half awake, and half asleep.

He spoke, after a while, without seeming to wake up. "Say, Sobersides, do you believe in God?" I was startled into wakefulness.

"God, did you say? Well, if he exists, He and I are bad friends."

Allen was silent for a minute, then he said, "I suppose you, like everybody else, are passing the buck to Him for allowing the War, aren't you?"

I was nettled. "Are you going to tell me that story—that He isn't to blame?"

Allen sat up. "Look here, Sobersides, I have done a hell of a lot of thinking since I enlisted, and after serious and prolonged debate I have decided whose fault it really is."

"Well, whose?"

He spoke quizzically, so that I did not know whether he was in jest or earnest. "Well, when I am pushing up daisies, and they hold a court of enquiry to place the blame, if I were able to speak I would say 'My old man. My dad!'"

"Your dad!" I ejaculated.

"Yep, the same old man who is responsible for my being in this world. Yep. I have decided it is the old man's fault."

"But why?" I asked. "Surely you can't load the whole damn business on to him? Why that would almost make him a murderer."

"That is so, Sobersides. Almost. You have hit the old nail right on its blinking head. My old man, your old man, the other guy's old man, are all responsible, all murderers...." Suddenly his tone changed, it grew low and passionate. "Listen. When we have licked the Germans, the whole nation will turn around and say, 'Our Kaiser did it,' and the rest of the world will believe it. But listen, Sobersides, can you imagine sixty million average intelligent, fairly well-educated people letting one man run them into trouble, *unless they want to go*? I either got to believe the whole German nation is in it, or that there are sixty million damn fools in Germany. And I think the former is right."

"It's right both ways, "I proposed. "Everybody's in it, but they're in it because they're damn fools. They're fools because they believe whatever is told to them. Like a bunch of school-boys. One tells the other one, 'Jack called you so-and-so.' 'Did he? Well I'll fix him.' So, they start at it. That's what the politicians and press told the people in every country. You can't blame the poor people when they're hypnotized like a lot of sheep. But you can blame the Power that created them."

We were both so intent on our separate ideas that we scarcely listened to each other.

"You are startled at my calling your old man and mine murderers, and saying it was all their fault. Well! If you live to see life after this war you will see what I mean. When peace is declared, everybody will howl, 'No more war, no more war!' Then in a few years they will forget all about it, and will be so busy loving and living, dancing and picnicking, that they won't have time to see about it, and will let the same old grafting politicians into government. Won't attend a peace meeting if they are paid for it, will begin to take pride in their armies and navies again. Pretty soon—war again. It's what always happens. Democracy is the bunk. I would rather be governed by one intelligent man than by a thousand fools. Take a look at any picture of the members of parliament. Why were they elected? They were good mixers, and had made successes of their own businesses. Their opponents weren't quite such good mixers, or they were even pessimistic about the direction the country was going, and wanted to change something."

"Yeah, one side's as had as the other. It's no use blaming anybody, it's what's behind it all—"

"My old man hasn't voted in an election in twelve years, and he wouldn't have voted then, if they hadn't come to fetch him. What do you think of that? Whom do I indict for the war? My own father and grandfather. The trouble is the average man is a damn fool, and as long as the Government promises to reduce his taxes, he will vote. I'll bet you a dollar right now you don't know who your local M.P. is."

I confessed I didn't, and that neither did Dad, as far as I knew.

"Well, that's it. The people in a democracy are supposed to have the voice in directing affairs; therefore, for success they are to be commended and for failure condemned. They will say they don't, that the politicians run the country, or if they are Yanks, Wall Street. Bunk! Absolute, unequivocal bunk. Who allows the grafting politician? Who supports him and upholds him? The people, the good, glorious, bull-headed, sentimental people, like you and me. And as for God above, about the most merciful thing He could do would be to take over this old world and run it properly; but He can't do even that without our consent, or that would be taking free will away from us. I say, Damn the people, not God. Look what they got me into!"

I almost collapsed. This was indeed a new Allen. There was silence. I couldn't think of an answer, while through my head kept drumming his words: "The best thing He could do would be to *take over this old world*." I had been brought up a Presbyterian, and a firm believer in God's government of the world. I spoke at last. "But listen, Allen, do you mean to tell me that God doesn't run the world?"

He laughed, and replied, "How the hell could God be running it, if we are? Don't we make up our minds as to what we shall or shall not do? So, if we do it, I ask you, how could He? It isn't reasonable."

Was it reasonable? My ideas had become confused, but I put a concrete case. "Well, now, listen to this. Suppose, suppose now, just suppose that you had a little girl of your own, and one day she was run over by a bus and killed. Couldn't God have stopped that?"

"That I am going to answer by asking you a question in return. Was God running the bus, or the driver? Was God walking in the road, or the girl? And again, who allowed the buses to run on that street? I'll bet a dollar, if it was an actual case (he little knew how nearly it was) that the ratepayers allowed the buses to run on that street, and that when one man got up in the meeting and said, 'This will endanger the lives of our children,' that the others all shouted, 'Keep your children at home where they should be.' Was God consulted? He was not. But still murder is a terrible word, so instead of blaming an actual council which can kick back they prefer to blame it on God, whom they know won't. A sub may blow us up tonight. Well, who was in the sub, God, or Germans? Let's go in and have a smoke."

I felt that I had learned a lot, but that I wanted to argue further. I followed meekly, revolving my friend's philosophy in my mind.

Twenty

The slow, rickety, dirty, lousy French train creaked on. We were packed in like sardines. Nearly a month had passed since the talk Allen and I had had on the channel boat; a month filled with incessant tests, from the gum to teeth, and after the customary blood-curdler from the parson (which sounded standardised by this time) we were on our way to the rendezvous with death. The whole trainload was made up of old soldiers who had been wounded and were returning for their second, third, fourth and fifth doses of the line. By this time, we knew the ropes, how to beg hot water off the engineer for tea, how to milk stray cows, and to flog (trade) our blankets, spare boots, or anything else, for brandy. And not only that, but we had acquired the divine art of patience, and we didn't give a tinker's damn whether we ever arrived at the front or not. So all was well. In the car were a few trying to read between jolts, and others enjoying a card game that some Yankee had introduced, two or three groups of poker, and one of Black Jack going full strength. If money played out, we bet our rations. At another game, they were playing for cigarettes, once in a while a little money would be in evidence, but mostly it was mind bets, or oath bets. Of course, these latter were the most reckless games of all. One chap was sitting in a corner, enjoying the stomachache, or religion, because he had his Bible out. Allen and I were sitting in the doorway, feet out, swinging idly as the country rolled by. We were watching for stray hens near roadways, and gazed after them with longing eyes as we were carried on.

Allen could kill and skin a hen in five minutes, and we could cut it up, make a fire in the car out of sandbags and candles and stew it. The French of course objected strenuously to this practice, but as our authorities always paid them double, they won both ways. For they got the pleasure of being virtuously angry at those thieving Canadians, and also of getting paid for their losses. My imagination had always conjured up Frenchmen as emotional, excitable, kind-hearted gentlemen. But reality, startling you, shows them as selfish and cold. Their excitement is carefully planned and executes to gain a desired end, the same as a woman's tears. They hoard each copper like gold, but are most delightful people to meet when you are doing them a good turn. In Belgium, which is close enough to have similar characteristics, there have been times when the people charged money to individual soldiers who wanted a drink of water. The troops, however, grew accustomed to this attitude, even grimly relished it.

And as for the French women! Well, the least said, soonest mended! Allen said to me once, "You know, Sobersides, you can tell a nation by the women. For it is in them that the next generation lies; and today the only nation whose women are worth loving is the Jews. The English, American, and Canadian women are nothing compared with them, they are mere bags of bone. My God, when I make love to a woman I like to feel they are women.... Well, let it go at that."

I grinned. "I gather, Brother Allen, that you are an expert on women. I have met a lot of experts in my time, so come on, let's hear your views." Allen laughed in spite of himself, but was only too glad to hold forth.

"No sir, I absolutely repudiate the idea of being an expert, I am only an observer. And believe me, I have observed a lot." I could readily believe it, for he was the kind that women fall for, but who prefer to flit from flower to flower. Maybe that's why they love them. There was a silence while we watched the countryside for hens, as it was near a town. None showed near enough for us to swoop off, grab one, and jump back onto the train, however. The sport reminds you of fishing you have long intervals for meditation. Suddenly Allen spoke.

"You take these frog women, they have made love into a business in life. I don't mind that in the right way, but blast it all they show it, just in the same way you can tell a vaudeville actor. They try to please, and their feelings are carefully hidden in the background. They are in competition, and they know it, with the bad ones, or vice versa. Now in Toronto, the city of virtue, the women are so tame that they have to be taught about love, poor beggars. Now as for me, I like the Russian women, they are good, virtuous, aren't afraid of marriage, or children, and always look as if living with a man didn't hurt them, but rather as if they enjoyed it. Did you ever see one of our women who was honest enough to admit she loved to live? No, everything's for the sake of their one child—who happened accidently—or their husband, my dear." He finished mincingly.

"Oh, for God's sake, Allen, give the poor dears more credit." But I had to laugh, he had such amusing ideas, and expressed them so delightfully.

"Well, Sobersides, maybe I will some time, but I have my doubts. But it is our own fault. One of the curious things about life is that the best women are those who are attracted to absolutely rotten husbands, like myself, or who have a large batch of kids. A woman's soul thrives on suffering, physical and mental. Now take my wife. She knows that I am no good, that marriage with me is a joke, that I only appreciate her when I come home and have my tears wiped away, and yet she grows more spiritual, more kind, every day. She knows what I do, and just because she knows, she would never go wrong. Once I left her and went to Buffalo with another one, a chit of a girl." His eyes grew cloudy. "I came back again, and she was waiting for me, and she didn't say a word, but had supper ready, put on my slippers, had everything comfortable, and of course I cried, and she *comforted* me. Of course, I swore 'never again' and of course she knew I would. But still she keeps on loving me, loving me all along. Why, she would no more think of leaving me than of flying to heaven. I heard her mother ask her once why she didn't and she said, 'Why Mother, what *would* Allen do then?' Right across the road from us at the Beach is a good husband who gives his wife everything, doesn't make her have children, and treats her like a queen. And what does she do? She goes out tangoing, joy riding, even drinking, and he stands it, or maybe doesn't know. While mine has got two kids. I like kids myself, at a distance. I wouldn't like having them.... And there she is. And you'll find that's true, a woman must give to live, a man must receive. Ain't it darn funny?"

I didn't know whether to laugh or cry at hearing these ideas once more, and said, mock-seriously, "Have you really given many kids to the world, Allen?" He laughed as he replied. "If you hear of any great man in France, Russia, England, the United States or Canada, he will be my son!"

I only recovered from my laughter when we saw a hen, and made a dash, the train being stopped.

After our feast of stewed chicken that wasn't quite cooked, but tasted satisfactory all the same, we were again back in our doorway. I was anxious to start him off again, so I asked, "What do you intend to be if you ever get home again, Allen?" He considered it gravely, and then gave his decision. "Well, if I ever get home, which I don't think I will, I believe I will be a parson."

"A parson!" I ejaculated. "A parson!" He nodded grimly.

"Yes, I will get the old man to put me through the Church of England and, believe me, when I get to preaching, they will hear a few home truths they never heard before!"

The phantastic idea interested me. "What would be the text of your first sermon?" He looked at me to see if I was joking, and went on: "I have had my first sermon picked out ever since I joined the army and it would be, 'Thou shalt have any other gods but me,' and I surely would give those psalm singers some sermon." He moodily watched the passing landscape, and went on, "You know these people today think of how darn civilized they are, and how high above the poor ignorant heathen. But are they? After all, what did the poor benighted heathen do about God in their day? They couldn't write like we could, yet they believed there was some kind of a God somewhere, maybe more than one. So, they built idols. But what were those idols? People today say they worshipped them. That's the bunk! They knew as well as we do, that they were only stone, but what they did do was to express their ideas of what God was like and worshipped the conception, not the stone or brass. Don't forget that, Sobersides. They worshipped the conception, and they weren't bad conceptions at that. Well, then Christ came and he told them God was Love, and let it go at that. He wasn't such a fool as to try and *define* it. Today we have fifty-seven varieties of Christianity—and the knowledge of writing. So, what do we do, imitate the poor ignorant heathen and build wonderful sculptures of God? Not on your linotype. We *write*, write down our ideas of what a god of love is, and what Christ meant by love, such as throwing poor devils—into purgatory—"

"You mean poor humans, don't you?"

"Both. Or they write that this God of love made us to be born in sin. And after we have carefully drafted out what we think God is, or should be, we worship that conception. If I go into a Presbyterian Church, I want to hear about God. But all I hear is the Presbyterian *idea* of God. And the same with them all. The only difference between us and the poor benighted heathen is that they were able to express themselves better. We are the heathen, we still need to be converted to Christ."

"But Allen," I said, "why join the Anglicans, if they are all the same?"

He grinned that delightful grin of his. "Because they didn't have the nerve to write down what they thought, and if they did, they are doing their best to live it down. I never met an Anglican who agreed with another Anglican yet, so they must be nearly right."

I chuckled at the idea of Allen preaching this sermon, but I do believe it was more than reckless fooling.

We arrived at St. Pal at last, and had a long march to reach our battalion, which was reported to be out on rest, somewhere. Finally, we located it at what the soldiers called "Gooey Serving" which was probably as near as they could get to it in English. For Allen, it was like an old boys' reunion. As for me, I looked hard and long to find someone I knew, but the old battalion machine gun section was broken, now Lewis guns were in vogue, so that I was really unattached. Allen, having had nearly four months in France before getting wounded, was an old soldier, and you know there is a saying in the army that old soldiers never die, they only fade away. In other words, they know the ropes. And so, putting a fatherly hand on me (he was about four years older than my army age, which would make him about twenty-five) he said, "Now listen, Sobersides, I am going to try to get a bloody bomb-proof for us, so stick by me. Nearly all the N.C.O.s and officers are from my old outfit, the 74th, so just watch my smoke, and swear to everything I say."

I meekly agreed, and after all the others had been detailed to their old companies, we stood alone like children of the storm. Allen had told me that you get on if you looked meek, so we tried to find an expression of resignation and martyred virtue. The Regimental Sergeant Major came over to us grinning, "Hello there, Allen, got back from Blighty at last, eh? You must have swung the lead pretty darn bad to stay that long."

"Hello, Major. Oh, no, I really am back sooner than I should be, my wounds were so bad. But they said the old battalion was short of men, so I came back."

The R.S.M. retorted, "Oh, yes, MEN!" Allen looked properly crushed, and I burst out laughing. (I forgot to mention that Allen had collected a Military Medal for bravery.)

The Major was put in good humor because his joke was appreciated. He was a big-framed, blonde, fat, merry-faced man of thirty-five, and had probably been a bartender or barber in civil life, I thought. I found out later that he had been a designer of women's dresses. He scratched his head and said, "Damned if I know what to do with you two. This feller Thor (looking at me) is an old Machine Gun man too, isn't he?" I admitted I was, and he went on. "Well, I'll be a good sport and make you battalion runners. How does that suit you?" That is the way of Regimental Sergeant Majors the world over. We found out later that the O.C, had already detailed us for that and the R.S.M. merely tried to make appear that *he* had done it, for his own glory and our praise.

We were both more than satisfied, as it meant lots of grub and darn little drill, with the privilege of appearing in the know to the rest of the battalion. We speedily made ourselves at home, and then hunted for the nearest canteens, wet and dry. We found the dry and then adjourned to the wet, where we drank each other's future in beer. Allen was in one of his many moods, this one of boisterous good humor.

"Well, Sobersides, that's a slice of the best luck we have had yet, it means a chance of prolonging our days on this mortal sphere. We might, by dint of hard work, sheer perseverance, and losing enough at poker, even become Lance Corporals. And believe me, Sobersides, it is the Lance Corporals who will win this blinking war. Just think of the day when with your grandchildren sitting around you, the whole damn platoon of them saying, 'Daddy, what did you do in the Great War?' you won't need to speak, but just go off upstairs, find your tunic, and silently display that one stripe to the admiring and gaping throng. That will be enough, for history will already have written that it was the Lance Corporals who won the War."

It was hectic in that canteen. Allen was determined to make a speech, so hoisted himself on an empty beer keg, and his hand shot up in the best dramatic manner, commanding silence, and silence was given.

"Gentlemen! I am here this evening to put forward for your approval very important and vital points for your consideration. The first that I deal with in this group, one that will make you weep tears of gratitude, is the fact that I have been promoted, promoted from a rear rank buck private to the position of runner. I know that you will feel gratitude at the fact that your Dominion has at last recognized the services of her best lead-swinger (cheers) and I want to say, gentlemen, I worked hard for this position. Like a Yankee billionaire I sold newspapers, chopped kindling, shined boots, and licked them too. Who is there that will say that this army is not a democracy, where every man carries an entrenching tool in his pack?" (Loud cheers). "Byng, your revered and well-known general, when he heard I was wounded, came over with tears in his eyes, say tears in his eyes, gentlemen, and said, 'We cannot do without you, the war must adjourn till you get back.' And so, gentlemen, I am here, I arrived by my own private car this afternoon, so I telephoned the Lord (laughter) I mean Byng, and said, 'General, you can let the battle proceed. I am here.' (Loud and prolonged cheers.) He sipped his beer. The canteen was jammed, others held out their beer to him and he drank his fill, and they shouted and cheered for him to proceed. He did, waving his hand for silence, which was rather surprisingly given.

"And now, gentlemen, the next point I want to deal with is, shall we or shall we not allow the Yankees in this war? It is a vital point. The Yankees have licked us in everything, and put their noses into everything. Boxing, wrestling, golfing, tennis, and they tried to claim that Tommy Longboat must be a Yankee because he didn't look like a white man." (Laughter) "And so here we are, gentlemen, we have a nice little war here, made up of a select group of people. And now, gentlemen, the Yanks are not going to leave us even that, they want to sit in. But into this nice peaceable circle and disrupt it." (Cries of "No, no.") "Will we allow it? Here we are fighting, and if the Yanks come in, we will be talking. We Canadians have enough grief now trying to train the Australians the way they should go, you know the way I mean." (They did, and laughed hilariously.) "Just before I left Canada, I dropped over one day to see President Wilson, he had been asking me to come for some time, and he says, 'How are chances to get into this war?' And I told him plump and plain that it was a family affair, that you had to get an invitation, and he gave me a look as if to say, 'An invitation, eh? Well then I will have to get one.' And now he thinks he's got it. We must decide, gentlemen, it is a very important matter. Are they old enough to come in? I maintain, and I think rightly, that the pool room law should apply here and all minors be barred."

(Cheers and more cheers. We stopped for more beer.)

"We older people know how to conduct ourselves. Why, I'll bet these Yankees will play to win, for the sake of winning, just as they do in everything else, when, as you know, all Englishmen play only for the sake of the game." (Laughs.) "And we Canucks just play to keep the other people in their places. I would like to hear this right from some representative of that great nation. Is there any member of that nation here? Any Levinsky, Morosher, O'Hagan or Didtyoshen, if so, let him speak." He bowed gracefully and finished his beer.

As the newspapers say, the speech was most effective and well-received. There was prolonged cheering and cries from members of another battalion for a Yankee. "Hey, Yank, go up, do your bit, don't let him get away with that." And to the front was pushed the fattest man I have ever seen in the army, with perspiration simply rolling off him. He wore the Military Medal, also, and after being well primed with beer, he was hoisted on the barrel by willing hands. He was evidently well-educated, and had the brightest, happiest grin it ever has been my pleasure to see. He struck a pose, and began to speak. The crowd was really amused, yet interested. It made them forget.

"Canadians, and if there are any English, Australians, or Yankees here, I will say also, gentlemen!" (Laughs.) "It has given me a great deal of pleasure to listen to the remarks of my brother from the land of the snow and the tightwad people who do not know how to play a gentlemen's game like stud poker." (Laughs from members of his own battalion. I later found that his greatest ambition was to clean out the battalion at stud poker after pay day.) "In answer to the remarks of my learned and drunken brother in arms, in regard to the possibility that our nation is desirous of entering into this circle, I would propose to answer that with one question: is it necessary? I ask that in all solemnity. Is it necessary? And why, you say, do I propound that question? I do so because, as you all know, I joined the battalion to which I belong on September 13, 1916. On September 15th, we went into the line, and advanced farther than ever before. Up to that time, the Canadian Army had been merely holding its own. But you, you can read history for yourselves. Look what happened when I joined. It is on that, gentlemen (and Canadians) that I base my question. It is not necessary for us as a nation to enter the war, it is not necessary for us to send divisions, but just imagine for a minute, one lone American enters one battalion, and the result, an immediate advance. I say, gentlemen, that all we have to do is get one good American in every Canadian battalion, and you would then multiply that advance a hundredfold." (Prolonged laughter). "The result, the war would be over. If one Yankee can do all I did, what would a hundred do?" The cheers shook the ceiling. The Yank and Allen were both given all the beer they could drink, and then were led, still solemnly debating the question, to their bunks.

The next morning I was the first to waken, and the sight that met my eyes would have made a cat laugh, as the saying is. Our billets were in an old shell-torn building of some kind, with bunks made of chicken-wire that sagged in the center. As I had been the most sober, I had taken the upper, while Allen and the American had crawled into the lower one with all their clothes and boots on. Somehow Allen had managed to stay on top, and they were clasped in each other's arms, each with the beatific expression that angels are supposed to wear, and both snoring blissfully. Their combined weights had been too much for the chicken wire, it was giving, and every little while there would be a twang! and they would protrude a little farther, below. I got out of bed, and taking a bayonet, I cut what was evidently the key wire, for there were three extra loud twangs, then a crash, followed by snorts, groans, and faint, almost mild curses, then a voice, protesting, "Get off me, you big, overgrown product of Chicago."

After sundry squirms and rolls they got dazedly to their feet, and the American was the first to come up for air. He looked around, and in a voice that sounded almost frightened, said, "What the hell time is it?" I told him that, so far as I could judge, it was somewhere near eight o'clock. He groaned and whispered, "Oh, my God, my outfit will walk all over me." "Why is that?" I asked. "Why, dammit, man, I am the cook, and my helper is in hospital, so there won't be any breakfast ready, and I was late last week too! Oh, let me out of here quick." With which he departed with as much haste as his hulk would allow. I could easily imagine a howling mob of hungry men, ready for murder, waiting him, and I pitied him.

Allen got to his feet, scratching and rubbing his eyes. "Drunk again, Sobersides. What did I do last night?" I told him of his speech, and he laughed. "Let's eat, gosh, I'm hungry." So we hunted up the cook and his hearse full of dead horses, and had breakfast. We had hardly finished when the R.S.M. appeared.

"Well of all the bloody wrecks I ever saw, you two take the biscuit. Not back one night before you get tight. You look worse than Mary's little lamb. Go and clean up and report at headquarters at ten. The O.C. wants to look you over."

We did our best, and in our eyes, looked quite presentable, but a sergeant in the imperial army would have had his heart broken if he had seen us. We were duly presented to the O.C. (the famous Daddy) but before we went in we heard him roaring at somebody and quaked in our shoes.

"Right turn, quick march, left turn, halt!" and we stood facing him. He gave us one look and grunted (his rheumatism was bad). "Ho! So, these are the men who know how to run the war properly, eh?" Another grunt. "Well, I don't think either of you are any good as privates, so I am going to make you corporals. *Lance* corporals. In fact, you there, Thor, are already one, though you probably didn't know it."

"What, sir?" I managed to gasp.

"Here it is, you were mentioned in dispatches, and given a King's Corporalship, reading from June 28, 1916. I don't know what the hell I ever recommended you for that for, but there you are!" Then his tone changed, and became a bit softer. "Now for God's sake, men, have a good time, but keep sober as much as you can. I'm glad to see you back." He stood up, shook hands with us, with what was, for him, a smile of welcome, and said, "Dismiss." We dismissed, and stood outside staring at each other goggle-eyed. The R.S.M. had a fiendish grin on his face. "You will knock the poor bloody lance corporals, will you? Now try it out on yourselves and see how you like it. Say, Thor, I want to congratulate you on your stripes. If you only knew it you are the luckiest beggar in the whole blooming army. Nobody can reduce you except by court martial, and it has to be a field general at that. Why my God, you can get away with murder and they can't touch you."

"Is that right, that they can't really reduce me except by a field general?"

"Absolutely, old bean, there has been only about a dozen given in the whole war. You are a lucky beggar."

Allen didn't miss the chance, and said, "Say, Sobersides, if they can't reduce you, just give him a poke in that fat belly of his, and see what happens."

The R.S.M. only laughed louder. "I could beat the stripe out of both of you. Lance corporals! Oh, my God!" and he went off, still laughing.

We departed also, in the other direction, and sat staring at each other, until at last a grin spread itself over Allen's face. "Oh, gosh, every buck private and N. C. O. on this blasted army will be giving me the Hee! Haw! over this." And they did, for wherever he went, somebody would shout, "Who won the war? Why, the blinkin' Lance Corporals." He had the grace to blush more than once.

Twenty-One

Two days afterward we went into the line on a working party. We were billeted in deep dugouts during the day, and worked all night digging communication trenches. A tribute must here he paid to somebody, evidently a Canadian higher up on the staff, who at last managed to make us really work. If there was one thing under Heaven that a Canadian soldier loathed, it was working parties, and even when sent out on them, he did as little as possible, and growled about it all the time. "I didn't join the blasted army to use a pick and shovel." And so it was a notorious fact that whereas on the Fritz side of the line, work would go on continuously, deep dugouts being built, trenches drained and made habitable, and so forth, on the Canadian side it was all the officers could do even to get necessary repairs made and the barb wire strung up. The result was that many lives were lost through this laziness, but perhaps it was attributable to the fact that to work in this fashion impressed on us the permanence of it all, which we didn't like to credit. As we would say, "We aren't going to spend the rest of our blasted lives here, are we?"

That was the difference. The German was content to dig in, but the English and Canadians loathed it because it made it look as if no advance would *ever* be made. But this officer decided that we must work and he made us work, by hitting on the brilliant idea of starting the working parties early and making them stay there until they were finished. You were given so much to do and the sooner you did it, the quicker you got home. But if you dawdled, well, Fritzie loved to catch working parties that were getting home in the daylight. So it meant work or die; and faced with this alternative, we worked. There were many stories of Fritzie catching working parties, and many actual casualties, so he made the men almost like work. He deserved a medal from the king, and kicks from the privates.

We went out on our first working party. Oh, yes, the O.C. took jolly good care that everybody participated except the cooks. He took the battalion roll, not the company, so that we were included. We figured it was getting near our turn, so we both reported sick. Allen already had had one trip, as his name was among the first, alphabetically. But I was lucky, mine beginning with a T. But as there weren't enough after T, the A's and B's had to go out again with us. Allen managed to scare up a bad cold, while I affected rheumatism, but sad to say, it didn't work, for the Doctor, a hard-hearted and brainy man, gave us several 9's which we had to take then and there, and dismissed us with medicine and duty; in fact he shouted as we left: "Those pills will make you work harder tonight than you ever did in your sweet lives before." They did.

Behind the lines an area had been taped out, as nearly similar as possible to the actual ridge itself, and daily we went over the ropes, familiarizing ourselves with the ground to be taken. Not only that, but maps were issued, and another startling departure made. The soldiers themselves were asked for advice, and many valuable suggestions were made. Many people considered the Canadians were just more lucky than other troops in their attacks, for already they had a name to be envied. Hadn't the French lost thousands of killed trying to capture Vimy? Hadn't the British tried and failed, the same as the French? And wasn't it immeasurably stronger now than ever before?

Our luck, if you call it luck, was an intelligent recognition on Byng's part, that here he had no ordinary army. It was not composed of all classes, like the English, French, and German, but one class preponderated, and that a class of intelligent, independent human beings. His greatest stroke of genius was the recognition of this fact. He treated us, as did Currie after him, as if we had brains, and used them. We could work independently, and when shown what had to be done, and the way they thought it should be done, we could be left to do the rest ourselves. Now we were even told to expect heavy casualties, which was showing trust in the intelligence of our men. We took the Ridge.

For days now the air had been vibrating with the sound of the guns. Our guns were nearly wheel to wheel, and one would have thought that the sound of them would hearten us, but we knew that Fritz had concentrated more guns than ever before at Sanctuary, and yet men had lived to hold them back. Hadn't it been the same at the Somme? Wouldn't it be the same here? Didn't we know of the dugout forty feet below the level that would hold five hundred soldiers? Didn't we even hear rumours from a raiding party, of trenches built in cement? Oh, yes, we knew that there would be a welcoming committee waiting for us. Our men were busy making preparations, private preparations for the encounter, everyone trying to get rid of the lice and get clean clothes, so that there would be smaller danger of infecting wounds. The spirit of men in adversity is a miracle to behold. Imagine the men cheerfully doing all this in preparation for their own death or wounds? Yet it was so. Morale had never been higher. Cheerfulness and high spirits were abroad in the land. Some were getting letters ready to post, just in case. In billets at night, you could hear queer conversations.

There was the company pessimist, usually a man who was only cheerful when it was pouring rain, or the battalion was having a tough time of it in the line. Couldn't he then get great joy out of saying, "Didn't I tell you we would get it this trip, didn't I tell you, well, what are you crabbing about then?" So, one night he was getting primed for the occasion: "That's right, get a letter ready to send home, but there won't be anybody left to post it, except the parson. You wanna give it to the first Fritzie you meet, then it might get there. I'm telling you, nobody will be left out of this bloody outfit, except the adjutant, and those — — never die. Imagine it, he wants us to shine our brass. *Shine it, shine it!* He must think we are in the bloody army or something. I'll bet the next thing they will be for us to shine our boots up the line. Just red tape, more red tape. If those bastards were given a little real work to do, it would do 'em good. Shine your brass! Gosh, I would like to give him a shine, the broken down, knock-kneed, half-baked spawn of a jack-ass. Shine your brass. Humph!"

Somebody shouted, "Oh, for God's sake give us a rest. You know bloody well we ain't gonna shine it anyway. I only hope that if you get it, you will be peppered in a place where you can't sit down while you chew the fat for a month." The Pessimist subsided, growling, among the laughs.

Another voice chimed in, "Say, Bert, will that Froggie take any more blankets? I would like to get a bottle myself."

More laughs. "There will be enough army blankets left in France after this war to keep the Froggies warm for the next hundred years. I'll bet a dollar there aren't ten blankets in the whole company!"

Then another voice. "Well, what did you do with yours? I notice you stick pretty close to your water bottle." More laughs, then the Sergeant comes in.

"Say, haven't I told you guys about those damn candles before?"

This is a chance for the Pessimist, and he makes the most of it. "Oh, Sergeant, I *am* surprised. How do you expect us to polish our brass in the dark? You knew very well what the adjutant said. 'It is a disgrace to any army, even the Canadian. I want to see that brass all clean to-morrow.'" This in a good imitation of the adjutant's voice.

The sergeant gave a growl. "Damn the adjutant, I want those lights out, or else some blankets put over the holes," at which somebody chortled.

"If you will loan us some blankets, Serg., we will be very glad to cover the holes."

"I thought so, I thought so." The sergeant's voice was half-delighted at the chance to rub it in. "Flogged all your blankets for cognac, eh? Someday, some day, I am going to see Daddy and tell him to hold a kit inspection, and then you blighters can show your cognac, and see what you get!"

Another voice: "I'll bet a dollar you haven't a blanket yourself. In fact, I'll bet ten dollars, for I saw you down at that Froggie's place not long ago."

The sergeant grinned. "Well, anyway, I'll get lots of blankets after this trip. I'll have the whole damn lot of blankets to myself, and all the grub I wanna eat, too. I heard we go in tomorrow. Toodloo, you guys."

The men all began to talk at once. "What, in all this snow and rain?

"Yep, I guess somebody else needs a little courage, or maybe the people at home are yelling for action, so in we go to-morrow. Toodloo. I'll bring a deck of cards with me, and we will have a game of poker at Foley Farm—maybe." He disappeared again, and a burst of conversation broke out.

Twenty-Two

Curious as it may sound, we had got used to the thunder of the guns. So well, that in spite of the uproar, the first thing that sprang to my mind, as we filed slowly, so slowly, into the line, was thoughts of the silence. Not a sound could be heard of human voices, but just the steady splash of slipping feet along a creaking and groaning duckboard walk. Once in a while would come the low voice of the man in front: "Wire overhead," and I would mechanically pick it up and give it to the man behind. "Wire overhead, shell hole to the right," or "Shell hole to the left." All hilarity had left us and we were, or at least the others looked to me, dogged and grim. There was a dirty job to be done, and we were going to do it. The ghastly green of the flares thrown up at intervals showed me the waterproof cape of the man in front, streaming with rain, then in quick succession three red flares went up from Fritz's line. He was worried, or had seen something. Then came the long, dreadful "Whizzzz," and shriek of shells aimed directly at us. We could hear them going into the ground with a thud, and apparently die without exploding, slither, slip, splash. We heard the thud of shells dropping just outside the trench, a sickening, deadening thud, that made your heart stand still, while you cowered momentarily against the wall of the trench. Then the shriek came, for if a shell is landing near you, you hear the shriek afterward, and if at a distance, the shriek comes first to your ears. Thud, thud, thud, thud, the whining heartbreaking shriek of a thousand lost souls.

"God, it was lucky they were duds," was our thought. Then came shouts from in front, "Gas! Helmets! Gas! Helmets! Put on your helmets, you bloody fools, they were gas shells." I hunted blindly for the mask. Like many another silly ass, I carried an extra pair of dry sox in the holder and of course I tried to put the sox on as a mask, before I discovered my mistake. Thud, thud, thud. Thank God, I had it on at last, but I had caught then the odor, an odor to make me cough and water at the eyes. I prayed that it would work properly. What a fool I had been to miss that last inspection! Gurgle, splutter, it *was* working. Dim, ghastly figures with faces from some infernal region showed in the light of the next flare. With eyes like a bullfrog's, a figure approached us, pushing and gesticulating, to tell us to keep moving. We plodded on.

I tripped on something and fell. It was a body. Then another, and another, and still more figures writhing and groaning in a most horrible fashion, were before us, with stretcher bearers trying to get them out of the way. We *had to walk over them* and keep moving, keep moving, keep touch, don't bother about those fellows. Keep moving! Groans and shrieks, and worse still those silent figures we stumbled over. The shells hadn't been duds, but gas. Depend on Fritz to catch you napping. I staggered blindly on, wondering vaguely who they were. One I turned over was an officer, as I could tell by the cloth of the trench coat. Then came a halt, and there we stood in the thick of it, waiting for some traffic jam in front to be cleared up. Then, plod, plod, stumble, stumble, slipping from one side to the other, like drunken men. The command of, "Gas masks off again." God, that air felt good. My face was dripping with sweat, my eyebrows were on fire, my mouth felt dry and huge, and tasted like alum; my heart was pounding.

We came to a blank wall where a figure stood like fate with hand outstretched. Turn to the right, on again, with the rain still pouring down upon us, then another figure appears, who asks in a whisper who we are, then Allen's voice in reply, sounding hollow and sepulchral, with the single word, "Runners," at which the figure points back. "We must turn back." If you want to see how easy that is, imagine a line of hundreds, even thousands, of men stretched out behind you in a long narrow hole, about ten feet wide and you try and turn back to pass these, try and squeeze past, when they are loaded with machine guns, bombs, ammunition boxes and all sorts and varieties of extra equipment! We turned blindly, only to bump into the men following us, who tried to keep on going, while our little squad of runners began to cuss and squeeze past. All at once a voice, low but concentrated with passion, said, "If you bloody runners don't shut that gab of yours, I'll come back there and tear you limb from limb," at which we subsided, pushed ourselves as close to the side as possible, and waited, to the accompaniment of a continual mutter of curses from those who were trying to pass us. At last the voice spoke again, "Get out of that bloody trench, you guys should know better than to follow us, you are delaying the whole damn show."

We meekly hoisted ourselves over the parapet, breathing curses on the lieutenant who was supposed to be taking us in, and crawled and stopped. (You have to stop every time a flare goes up, which is very frequently.) Feeling that the whole German army had their eyes on us. At last the intersection was reached, where we had turned to the right, and we jumped gladly back into the trench, and finding it clearer in this direction, we hurried on as quickly as circumstances would permit, about two miles an hour, till a faint light gleamed at our feet. I being first, pushed aside the blanket, crept down several steps, and asked if this was H.Q. It was, and our friend the adjutant was there. He immediately asked, "Where is Lieutenant Holwortt?"

"Hasn't he arrived?" I asked in turn. Allen and I looked at each other; and another runner spoke. "He must have been the one I fell over, and if it was, he's a stiff, sir, from the gas." Out of six runners and one officer we had had the bad luck of losing the officer and two men. It was a bad beginning.

We boiled tea in silence. A question was pounding into my brain. It was bad enough to have the worry of your own soul, but a stabbing thought in my brain suggesting that I was a jinx that brought death to those about me, was worse than any hell. Was I to go through it all as a damned soul giving death to those I loved? The more unreasonable I told myself the fear was, the more it grew within me.

There were thuds and steps on the stairs of the dugout, and the O.C. with the balance of the H.Q. and the company commander came in. The dugout was dimly lit by many candles, and there was a roughly made table covered with maps, a telephone, piles of blankets, equipment and boxes, thrown haphazard over the floor. There was a signaller standing at the phone making sure the wire was not broken by shell fire. A cook was busy in another corner getting the officers a meal, and another signaller with the blue and white on his arm stood looking at the maps. The company commanders gathered around the table with the O.C. while he pointed with his fingers at certain points on the maps. I heard the word "machine guns" and I knew the main thing on his mind at that moment was the German machine guns, machine guns that hid in the deep dugouts during the barrage, then as soon as it was over, came up to the surface and opened fire. I looked at my watch and saw that it was twenty past five. Zero hour was set at 6:40. Then came more steps on the stairs, and a brass hat appeared. More quiet talk followed around the table, and machine guns were mentioned again and again. Allen slipped over to me, nodded his head toward the group and whispered, "They have the wind up about those guns all right. It looks as if Canada is going to increase her Roll of Honour tonight." I whispered back, "Do you think they will get across?"—"I don't think we will get more than the Ridge itself, if we get that," he answered. "But we haven't as much grief to handle as the 4th Division at the Pimple. Gosh, those guys are going to get it. If I was the O.C. I'd take it easy. He can't do any more anyway than wait. I suppose that bloody brass hat came up to see why we were late getting in." I hadn't realised that, but the gas shells and resulting casualties had put us nearly two hours behind time, which meant corresponding lateness for all behind us.

Indeed, we heard Daddy's voice delivering an impassioned harangue, cursing the artillery for not silencing that particular battery. His voice rose. "You yourself told me yesterday that every bloody gun would be out of action. And look at it, when a battery gives us three salvos! What the hell is the matter with the observation that that happens? How am I to know now how many of his damned batteries are still in action? If that damned sissified air force only had the nerve to go out and take a look, they might have been silenced. And why pick out today of all days to go over? I'll bet it was because some of you brass hats thought nine was lucky. And if I come out with thirty per cent, you will send me enough damn forms about it to keep me busy till the next war. Here it is snowing (the runners looked at each other. Snowing?) outside, it has been raining for weeks, but what does that matter? You men don't have to tramp through it. But my men do, and by God I will give that staff an earful when I get out."

The staff officer left hurriedly, and I could imagine his report to the Brigadier, and how *he* would go after the division commander, and so on back to the corps.

There was silence for a moment, then a company commander spoke admiringly, "By George, sir, I feel like giving you a medal for that, it is just what I thought, but didn't have the nerve to say." They laughed. Allen and I were smoking in a corner, and presently the telephone rang and after many bellows and damns the adjutant caught the message. Another battalion was being sent in from supports to follow immediately after the first wave. We cursed to ourselves, for if the two battalions got mixed up it would be an awful job trying to sort out the officers in command.

The O.C. stood up, looked at his watch, and said, "Listen, with that other outfit right behind us, we are going to get all mixed up, so why not begin to move at 6:30, get through the wire, and stay there till 6:40. You will be better off, and it will give you a good start." They agreed, and departed to their companies. There was nothing to do now but wait. It was 5:45 a.m. Fifty minutes yet. Daddy's fingers kept drumming on the table, and the adjutant walked up and down biting his lips. The signaller at the phone was chewing gum like a regular "hello girl." The other signaller had to wait and do nothing unless the line broke, then it was his business to find it and repair the damage. One of the nerviest jobs in the whole war. The four of us squatted on the floor smoking and talking of everything except what actually was on our minds.

Suddenly the barrage was laid down, and the earth shook, while trickles of dirt kept falling between beams of the dugout. It grew into a huge roar of steady pulsating rhythm. The O.C. looked a little more relieved. "Ah, that's better," I could imagine his saying to himself. "There won't be many Fritzies left after that." It kept growing louder until our ear drums were vibrating, then Fritzies guns joined in and we heard the voice of arriving shells, some right on top of the dugout. The beams creaked and groaned with the strain, and I heard Allen's voice near me, "God, Sobersides, wouldn't it be awful to be caught in this hole like a rat? Gimme the open air and the blasted flares." I agreed with him, as my mind took hold of the idea, and at the vision of the one entrance to the dugout blown in, I broke into a cold sweat. A rat caught in a trap! I looked furtively around and everybody had thoughts of their own along similar lines, to judge by their expressions, all except the C.O. We could see he was worrying more about the men, but at last he turned to the adjutant, and said, "Let's go up and take a look. Those damn German guns seem to be still alive." I stood up to follow, only too glad of a chance to get out of the trap, but he motioned me back, and I slumped again on the ground. "6:20 a.m. Is that all it is? My watch must have stopped." I looked at Allen's. 6:20. God, time was rolling slowly. The O.C. came back looking troubled, and going over to the map he studied it again, and gingered his watch nervously.

Rolling banging thuds, accompanied by moans, were heard on the stairs, and Allen and I dashed for the door, to pull the gas blanket aside, as a body rolled to our feet. We lifted him up and carried him nearer the candles and found he was badly hit. The O.C. came over and said, "That's a B. Company runner. Try and get the message." While we busied ourselves putting his field dressing over a hole in his stomach, the adjutant tried to get the message, but the man was moaning, evidently unconscious. The adjutant spoke sharply: "You, Thor, hurry along to B. Company and tell them, try and get the message. You have only ten minutes."

I threw off my equipment and ran up the stairs, only too glad to get away from those moans and that hole. The trench was jammed to suffocation with men and one told me that it was blown in farther down. That must have been where the runner caught it, I thought. What will I do? Eight minutes! I heaved myself up on the parapet of the trench, and ran along the top, I say ran, but it was really a staggering blinded, tripping, falling walk. Fritz had this trench pretty well lined up, and black gusts of smoke kept blowing against me and choking me. I ran and ran and dived down into the trench asking the first figure I saw, "B. Company." I was lucky, their dugout was only a few feet ahead. I turned into a bay, but it had disappeared, the whole trench was blown in, and probably the dugout too, and in the dugout, the men. I crawled over but couldn't find the entrance, and asked another figure for an officer, and was told that a lieutenant was just down a little way, but the O.C. was buried with two other other officers and the sergeant major and a private. I daren't look at my watch in the flicker of the next flare but hurried on, and at last found the lieutenant, very nervous, a new man in his first engagement, poor beggar, left to take charge of a company. He told me he couldn't do it, his nerve was gone, and he kept twitching. "Where's the other officer?" I asked. "Wounded? Oh, hell, is there a sergeant?" He told me there was, an old original man, in the next bay, so I hurried on, to find him. He had heard about the O.C. but not about the lieutenant, and I said, "Listen, Sergeant, you will have to take charge, the officer's lost his nerve." He nodded grimly in reply and we both looked at our watches. "Can you get them over?" I asked.

"Leave it to me, I'll get this mob over, or bust," he answered. It was now 6:39, and he left to hunt for runners, and the officer and I went back to H.Q. The trench was empty, or rather emptying, and the barrage was growing more intensive. We were off!

Cry Havoc

Then I noticed one of those things that can't be avoided in circumstances like these. The second and third waves began to file in from communication trenches, in preparation for their turn to go over. German machine guns had begun to rattle, and wounded began to fall back into the trench, and the dead came slithering down also, to lie in the bottom, so that the trench became a hell, filled with dead, and wounded, gasping and groaning and calling for help while all the time the second wave came on, having to take its place, or hold up thousands of men and probably cost the first wave hundreds of lives. And on top of all this the runners and stretcher bearers and all the necessary adjuncts of war were trying to work in opposite directions in an area two feet wide and six feet deep. The snow and rain were falling still, it was no time for sentiment, and iron shod feet clumped, pulled, and kicked their way clear over wounded and dying, one group determined to take their places and go over the top, the other group just as determined in their way to get to dressing stations. It was no time for sentiment, as I say, but the wounded were naturally the weaker.... Oh God, oh, God! I heaved myself up out of that ghastly mess of living flesh and hurried on if pursued by the devils of hell.

Twenty-three

I found the dugout at last, almost falling down the stairs, where Allen was waiting at the bottom for me, and I could see by the grin on his face when I appeared how relieved he was. Gosh, he did like me.

The O.C. was there too, his face grey and haggard, and his hand still tapping the table. I reported, "The Q.C. and officers of B Company were buried, sir. Lieutenant Struthers badly wounded besides, and that new officer's not very fit to take charge."

Then seeing his shoulders droop, I lied, that is, partly.

"I saw Sergeant Hillier sir, and he said he would take charge. He had already organized new runners and platoon commanders and went over with the company only five minutes late."

Such a look of relief overspread his face that I was glad I had lied, and anyway Hillier would get them over by hook or crook, maybe a little late, but he would get them over. The O.C spoke, "That's all, Thor. Is any attempt being made to get the officers and men out?" I told him I didn't think there was, as B. Company hadn't the men to spare. "Oh, I see, all right, Thor." Then he turned to the adjutant. "Take a runner with you and try and find B. Company, and if Hillier is doing all right, leave him alone, but if he needs help you take charge, but for God's sake, take his advice. He has more experience than you."

I prayed that he wouldn't take Allen, but if I had known what was to happen later, I would have prayed that he did. He chose, instead a tall, solemn-faced Scotchman as his guide, and departed after looking carefully at his automatic. The adjutant was always very picturesque, and he managed a dramatic exit even now, standing with the blanket half drawn aside, and his hand on his gun as he said, "Good-bye, Colonel." The Scotchman winked at us and disappeared. Disappeared is the right word for they were never seen again. I looked around, after squatting down as comfortably as I could, and saw that the signaler who looked after the wire had disappeared, which meant the line was broken. The other one was standing at the phone, jingling the bell at regular intervals and listening intently, and judging by the look on his face, the other chap was a friend of his. The cook was sitting in the corner, placidly reading a Sexton Blake story by the light of one candle. The regimental Sergeant Major had appeared in my absence with the transport officer, and they stood talking to the colonel in low tones. The wounded runner had died, evidently, for he was laid off at one side with a rubber sheet thrown over his face and his feet stuck up in the horrible fashion typical of the dead. Another runner had been posted, so Allen said, up at the entrance, to stop wounded from coming down and jamming the dugout. I felt tired, and pillowed my head-on Allen's lap, and went to sleep almost instantly. My last impression was of him slowly and gently stroking my hair.

I awoke later to find my head pillowed on a pack. Allen was gone, and I started into wakefulness and looked around. The dugout was like a tomb. The O.C., myself, and the dead were the only occupants. His head was in his hands, his eyes being closed, and I almost thought he must be dead too, but when I moved he started and said, "Oh, you are awake, are you, Thor. Had a good sleep?" I nodded, and looked at my watch. Nine o'clock. There was silence again; even the guns were sounding quieter. I was trying to summon up courage to ask how things were going, but he spoke first. "Well, Thor, as usual we have made a name for ourselves, all objectives taken except the Pimple by the Fourth Division, but they will get that. We have captured the Ridge, but can't find B. Company, and your friend Allen is looking for them. I haven't heard a word of them yet. Our losses"—silence; and a sort of half-moan. "Our losses are heavy. My boys...." (How I loved to hear him say that) "My boys deserve a V.C., every one of them. No one else on God's green earth could do, except my boys." His eyes stared broodingly into space. "Those bloody brass hats say we haven't discipline. Well, who could discipline boys like mine? I can't. Let them have a good time, let them play. My God, they haven't much time to live. What if they get drunk, what if they can't form fours like a blasted machine? They can fight. By God, they can fight." He woke to his surroundings with a start, and growled, "That's none of your business, Thor, you didn't hear that." I never mentioned but cherished it in my heart until now. My thoughts were broken into by the O.C.'s voice. "I'm waiting to hear from Brigade, that damned phone is broken." We waited, each filled with our own thoughts. I moved over and laid my overcoat over the dead man's feet. The Colonel thanked me with his eyes. We waited. At last, steps on the stair, and I jumped up, holding the blanket, and as I waited to see who would come, my heart seemed to stop beating. Thank God, it was Allen. He gave the O.C. his message, and came back to me. We stood looking at each other, holding one another's hand, grinning like the silly asses we were. "Gosh, you can sleep, Sobersides." The commonplace remark was enough. Allen was alive, what mattered anything else?

All at once the dugout seemed to fill with officers, runners and N.C.O.s, and an excited jumble of talk began. The supports had come up, our H.Q. was to move, runners appeared from the other companies, and to the general activity was added the ringing of the phone again. Everything seemed to be happening at once. The regimental sergeant major reappeared with the transport officer and some man who worked in the orderly room. The second in command, it should be mentioned, had been killed in a previous trip, and no new officer was appointed. We got the command to gather up our equipment. We were on the move. Headquarters was to be moved to the old German Front Line in a dugout near Foley Fern, which was carefully pointed out to us on the map. The bustle of departure began with shouts from the officers of the supporting battalion.

It was approaching ten o'clock when we came in, and the German guns were comparatively silent. There were no light shells to be seen, only coal boxes, the heavy ones that emit a dense black smoke. Even these were falling haphazardly, which made the situation worse as we didn't know where the next one would come. I surmised from this that Fritzes' light artillery was either captured or was retiring to a new position, and as it turned out, both suppositions were correct.

The scene was, to say the least, interesting, though scarcely aesthetically satisfying for here and there we could see bodies in our trench, or just over-the-top, sprawled in queer ways and with the inevitable boots showing that they were dead. I didn't know that feet had such expression until the war. Allen and I sat on the parados waiting for the O.C. We saw a long single line of men, digging a C.T. trench, and another line laying a duckboard walk. We could see several hundred yards, as the ground rose slowly upward before our eyes, and lone figures appeared here and there staggering, walking; and scattered couples supporting one another denoted walking wounded coming out. A gang of men was employed in desperately trying to pull an eighteen-pounder field gun into a new position. Figures which we took to be runners were going hither and yon, and a staff officer, resplendent in his bright red tabs, made his appearance. We watched, with a detached interest, a couple of wounded come in, one man badly hit, evidently in the leg as he was supported by the other, and we could see the white splotch of a bandage. The other had got it in the head, and probably couldn't see very well. They were making slowly and desperately for the duckboard walk, then the smoke of a shell hid them from sight for a time. Had they been knocked out? We watched with renewed interest for their reappearance. There they were, out of the smoke, still coming bravely on, then another shell hid them from sight. There they are again! By Jove, that guy had guts. You could almost hear the gasps. I waited anxiously to see if the working up ahead would seethe, and if so, would they send anybody to pick up? The officer in charge saw them at last, and watched them too with detached interest.

But our speculation changed into pure admiration. That man did have guts. The officer looked back at his gang, then back to the two strugglers. A decision had to be made. Could he spare two men? For that is what it meant, you would have to go back with them to some dressing station. He looked around to see if anybody else was available, saw us, and waved to us. But we daren't leave, as the O.C. might appear at any moment, and strange as it may seem to you, it would have appeared like cowardice to go and get them, for it would seem that we were seizing the excuse to get out of the line. Just then an infantryman appeared in the trench, and we shouted to him, pointing to the two men. He looked at them, our opinion again with averse remark, "By God, that guy has guts!" then hurried along the trench on his appointed way. They fell down, and slowly, slowly, slowly raised themselves, and that was too much for the officer, who disobeyed orders and sent out two men to pick them up. Allen laughed. "I was wondering whether that blighted officer would have the courage to do that." Then the O.C. appeared, and we were off.

The whole incident took perhaps five minutes. In a big battle, every man has his particular job to do, and if he neglects that to do something else, well then, many lives may be lost. In the case of that officer, his business was to dig a trench for the hundreds of wounded to pass down in comparative safety. Every shovelful of dirt thrown up by his gang meant safety to a life and every shovelful not dug by lack of those two men sent to aid the two wounded, perhaps meant a life lost, in preventing other wounded from getting out of the danger zone. The officer could not spare two men for such a vital work, for he knew or we did, that a German barrage might fall at any minute, and if this trench was not finished the wounded could not be evacuated. Not only that, but we ourselves were vitally important, as there were only two battalion runners left. So, it took a supreme appeal to the officer's will, and caused him to disobey orders.

We started on at last, on the duckboard walk, which a continual stream of men was laying as quickly as possible. We found a place in this line, and slowly plodded forward. That walk saved hundreds of lives, for it meant one was able to more than double one's progress. In the mud, you were lucky if you made a half-mile an hour, but on the walk you could make an easy mile and a half. That sounds slow, but not one half as slow as it was to us, even then. Time is a relative thing, and thirty miles an hour is slow, if one could go sixty. A mile an hour is fast after you have been used to one half-mile per hour.

The walk came to an end eventually and then we had to take to the mud. Old as he was, the O.C. would allow no one to help him, but waded and grunted and heaved on in his own way. We were separated by spaces often or twenty feet for safety. The rain had stopped and through the little rifts in the clouds the sun glimmered once in a while. The scene after a battle is not a goodly sight, with arms, heads, etc., sticking out of the ground here and there. Such was the intensity of the German barrage, that if a man fell, he was buried or drowned in the mud and water. There was not six inches of the old surface left uncovered, one hell hole joining another as far as the eye could see. A group of trees, or what had been a group of trees, far in the distance, was our objective. It grew slowly nearer. We even saw the black and red trousers and whole bodies of the French soldiers who had tried so gallantly to take the Ridge, and which were now brought to the surface again by the shell fire. It was said that they lost sixty thousand in the attempt. We recognized dead English by their cloth caps, for they were uprooted too. The Canadians wore steel helmets. I shuddered. There must have been over a hundred thousand dead of all nationalities lying in this area.

We saw at a distance the 4th Division working to take the Pimple, that is, we saw a huge cloud of smoke, which denoted that they were still at it. We came upon a group from our own battalion, dead. The O.C. stopped and looked at some of the men, the transport officer with him. The men had been caught by a machine gun, and there were at least twenty bodies in a group, then a trial of corpses at intervals, in front of the others. We could read the story, the guns had opened up and caught several, the others ducked into shell holes, while one man went forward with bombs. The first was killed, another went up, he was killed, and in all nine had tried one after the other, and failed. Then a concerted rush took place and we followed the trail, as it was along our route. One hundred yards away from the group we came upon the gun. It had been hand to hand, as I read the tragic story, for I counted six Canucks and eleven Germans, dead. Two men were locked in a death grapple, both bayonets having their place at the same time.

We passed on, shuddering. Fritz's artillery fire had almost stopped as had ours, but we could hear the rattle of machine guns ahead. Airplanes buzzed low, taking a look at our colors, and then zoomed on. The dugout was reached at last, and a detail from B. Company were, well, we shall say, making it habitable. We waited. The men looked tired but cheerful.

Vimy was a ridge that when captured showed the result of your work. Looking back, you could see Neuville St. Vaast and many other towns down the long gentle slope. It was easily realized how well every move was under observation, as there was a clean sweep for several miles. We were hardly installed in the dugout before business began. Allen and I were detailed to find the location of the new front line, if any, and report back. This was usually a company runner's work, our job being to keep in touch with the brigade, but O.C. had decided that he would take some of the men from the working party and give them an easier job, and make us do a little work, as he put it. We had had an easy time, and were comparatively fresh, so after boiling more tea, we started out.

It was eleven o'clock, and we had scarcely gone twenty or thirty feet away from the dugout, when with shrieks and roars that drowned out all other sounds, and left us blind, gasping, choking, vomiting wrecks. The barrage opened, a German creeping barrage that followed us as we made for the line, till we lost all sense of direction and time. We clung hand to hand and staggered on, on, and on. A thousand demons pursued us, mud flew up and covered us, and water splashed as shells plunged into holes near us. Bathed in sweat, mud and water, gasping, choking, praying, swearing, on at any cost. The Yank's words rang in my ear like those of some fiend of hell saying, "*Ha, ha,* the joke's on you." Oh, damn the Yank. On, at any cost, and find the blasted line.

Then Allen fell, a dead weight on my arm. Killed? Oh, God, is he dead? Don't let him die, don't let him die. I groped for him, seeing him dimly through the smoke, and knelt beside him, still afraid to let go of his hand for fear of losing him in the smoke. Like one demented, I felt feverishly over his body. Head all right, chest, stomach, okay, then his legs. I breathed a sigh of relief. I could feel his heart pounding, pounding. Oh, Allen, Allen, my friend. At last I found it, a huge hole, clean out of his leg above the knee, but the bone untouched. When my hands touched that ghastly hot flesh blown clean out of his leg became slippery with blood. Arteries, arteries, what is it you do in case of arteries bleeding? Some long-forgotten lesson of tying above the wound came to me. Damn that smoke, I can't see what I'm doing. I haven't any cord, oh, what a fool! Everybody should carry a cord. Oh, I have it! The tape of my puttees! I pulled it off, soaking wet and covered with mud, but I found the tape. Again, the search, for a knife this time. Again lacking. Oh fool, God what a fool I was! Had Allen one? I reached into his trousers pocket, already wet and sticky with blood, and found one, then ripped the trousers far above the hole and tied the tape tightly, desperately above the wound. His heartbeats seemed to grow weaker. Oh, God damn that smoke! My field dressing next, too small, but put it on anyway. Then a tremendous heave, and I have him on my shoulders but I'm sinking in the mud! I can't lift my feet. Damn that smoke, what will I do? What will I do? Pull him? No, his leg would drag in the mud.

I have it, tie his puttees to his feet and pull him feet up. Again, that agonizing work, and a shell drops so close that the shock knocks me over, and a shower of dirt and stones strikes me. Up again, while I pulled off my tunic and tied it around his head, then attached the puttees. Then, pull. Damn, you, Thor, pull! Slowly, agonizingly, and prayerfully we moved. Don't stop, you fool! You will drop. Keep moving, keep moving. Just a hundred yards and maybe you will get out of it and save Allen. Move, move, keep moving! My breath was corning in short sobbing gasps, uphill and down again, be careful of the water. Don't drown him. My feet seemed to fairly sink into the ground, and each step required a tremendous tug upward to release them. Oh God, I am done, I'm done. See, I can't lift my feet. I can't budge. God help me, don't let that damned Yank laugh. I dropped sobbing, beaten, unable to move, and felt myself sinking slowly, inevitably, to bloody hell. I will do it. I will, I will. A lurching, gasping, striving upward for balance, and on again, on, on. Like the finger of a lighthouse, I saw a tree, or rather, a stump ahead, just a few feet. Damn you, haven't you got the guts enough to get just a last few feet? On, on, on, then a figure looms up, takes me by the shoulder while I try to find my hands.

"My God, I hear him," I hear, then blackness, darkness, and the shadows of death. I awoke into a hell of pain, my body stiff and racked, shot and seared through and through. My head was aching and as I turned over I found myself lying in several inches of water. Allen was beside me, his face as pale as a sheet, lying motionless and stiff, and his boots were up. I raised myself cautiously, every move adding another twinge. I saw a whole line of us, seemingly endless with boots, boots, boots, all toes up to the heavens. I was directly beneath a stump of a tree, and on this was drooping, like a drowned cat, a Red Cross flag. But no one moving. Then my ears began to take notice of sounds. Over there somewhere a fight was going on, a hand to hand affair, to judge by the continuous explosion of hand grenades. I got onto my feet and leaned against a tree, then the bombs suddenly stop. Who has won? Immediately comes the staccato burst of a machine gun. We have. I knew that because it meant that the gun was trying to pick off those who had fallen: back, and it sounded too close to be German. Shells were falling in the same way. My dazed and stupid brain was coming back to life and I saw a figure coming along a path, a real path. Leaning forward, he was carrying someone; and other figures followed in rapid succession. Our wounded coming back. Then a long line of men trying to run. Germans, prisoners. I could tell that by the lone figure in the rear, with the rifles and bayonet, who is keeping them on the run, trying to get them away before Fritz attacks again....

Curse those pains. Stretcher bearers appear now, poor devils, and the badly wounded. I looked at my watch. Half past twelve. Is that all it is? I wonder if Daddy knows where the line is? Everybody is busy looking after the wounded and have no time to notice me, so I start hobbling along the path, and every little while I have to get off to allow somebody to pass. As I began to walk, the blood began to pump through me again, making an agony that was most delicious. That may sound queer, but it is true.

At last I came to the edge of the Ridge itself. Good Heavens, what a hill! On this side the Ridge goes sharply down for at least one hundred and fifty feet and a magnificent view is before one. I could even see the German artillery pulling out at a gallop, and halfway down, khaki figures scurrying here and there among the trees, and I caught the glint of bayonets. I could see the three waves distinctly, the first almost down to that little village, in fact in it now, for the smoke and pop of hand grenades could be seen and heard. The second wave was at the bottom, advancing slowly, looking into holes, dugouts, anywhere, for possible machine guns over looked. The third was halfway down, but broken, and looking for the wounded, a continual stream of which was passing up a road over to the right. British and Germans all mixed together. Directly off to the right I saw a machine gun, and headed over that way, for that was where I might get information.

I came up close to the gun, which was mounted on the lip of a shell hole, and saw three men, all machine gunners. Their numbers told me that half their crew was either killed or wounded. They were taking it easy, one lying on some belt boxes, another snoring, while a third, a corporal, was carefully cleaning the barrel of the gun with a ramrod. It looked almost ludicrous, with battle, murder and sudden death below, to see these men going about their business as though on a hunting expedition. They were covered and caked with mud, but the gun itself was spotless, and steam was coming out of the water jacket, showing that it must have been firing a short time ago. I spoke to the corporal, "Say, Corp, do you know where the C.M.R.s are?" He looked up sharply, saw my runner's armlet which I had slipped over my shirt and said, "Trying to save yourself a trip down below?" I managed a grin. "Don't jump on the judgment so darn quick," I answered. "I just came to life a few minutes ago, and I don't feel like going down, because I am darn sure I couldn't get up that hill again."

He eyed me up and down and I must have looked a wreck, no puttees, no tunic, and just an armlet to denote my business. Then a most delightful warmhearted grin spread over his face and he said, "If an English officer ever saw you like that, he would be sure to say 'There you are, those bloody Canadians can't even keep clean in a battle.'" I had to laugh, and sat down painfully.

"Well," I said, "this doesn't get me anywhere. Daddy will be tearing his hair out because we haven't reported, so where the devil are they?" He pointed down. "There they are, cleaning out the village. Say, a guy told me that there is an old French couple down there, so they decided to take it by hand, instead of turning the guns on it. That's our bloody army all over, throwing away twenty or thirty lives to be sentimental! Say, you aren't any good to go back." He looked at me sharply. "What you need to go back to that dressing station and stay there. Listen, that guy over there needs a rest bad, so I'll send him in your place. Then he can get his rest."

I thought it over, and asked, "Are you sure he will get out?" He laughed. "That chap could get through hell and back again. You watch." He crossed over and woke the sleeping man, who growled and groused prodigiously, and finally got to his feet. "That's it, wake me up, what the hell do you care if I never get my sleep!"

The corporal grinned. "Wake up, you lazy beggar. Here's a chance to get a real sleep. I'm sending you back." The man became suddenly wide awake, and as he turned I noticed that he had two wound stripes. I listened as the corporal told him what was wanted.

"Gosh, thanks, Corp. Believe me, when I get back with that, I'll hook right down to the horse lines, and have a beer and a sleep. See you tonight, maybe." As he spoke he was shifting his equipment and preparing to leave, explaining that he didn't want to be bothered with anything to hold him back when he went through the barrage. To get out, he had to cross a part heavily swept with shell fire. After listening carefully again as to where H.Q. was, he started off. He had to go half a mile, that would take him about two hours, and he had about ten chances in a hundred of getting through. Yet you would have thought we were doing him a favour in selecting him to go. After he had gone, the corporal turned to me and said "I'm sorry I can't help you back to first aid, but I guess you will get there if you take it easy." So, I started back to find Allen, and after traversing the same area I had come over, I reached the spot where I had left him, and found a scene of great activity in progress. Some infantry had been detailed off and were hustling all the stretcher cases into a dugout near at hand, while the walking wounded were being sent out to the duckboard walk. This I learned from an infantry sergeant of another battalion who was superintending operations. There had been so many casualties that it was impossible to move them all through the mud until some sort of walk was made. I looked around for Allen, but could not see him, so I asked where the dugout was, and followed the line. It was an old German dugout, of huge proportions inside, and strongly built. They would be comparatively safe here for the night anyway. A doctor and staff of stretcher bearers were also there, so I went up for examination and found that many small slivers of steel had peppered me from top to bottom. The doctor said he could do nothing, and that I would have to go to the hospital, but not to try to walk out, as that would work the slivers in farther. So, I joined the badly disabled in the dugout, and hunted for Allen. I found him at last in a side passage, a very quiet place, for every case on the stretchers had been doped into silence.

Allen was sleeping and breathing easily. He had been given the usual shot against gangrene, and as far as I could judge, although weak he might have a chance. An idiotic prayer came to my mind, and I went down on my knees. "I know, God, you and I aren't very good friends, and possibly never will be, for I still hate you, but listen, God, Allen isn't in on it, he thinks a lot of you, even stands up for You, so why let him die? It will hurt me, but it will hurt his wife and kiddies worse. For God's sake, be a sport and let him live."

I felt relieved at least, and went back again to the lighted room where the doctor was, borrowed a knife and tried to pick out as many slivers as possible, though my legs especially were very painful. The doctor saw me again and gave me a couple of pills he said would ease it a little. The dugout was filled now, packed as closely as possible and there was that peculiar smell of blood, fresh blood, and chloroform, in the air. I shuddered as I saw parts of arms and legs and hands cluttered in a corner that one of the men was cleaning out. It had been necessary to make some quick operations. I lay down and slept.

Twenty-four

What wakened me was the shaking of the dugout, caused by the arrival of heavy shells. I crawled painfully out of the little side passage where I had been sleeping, as I was worried about Allen. It was very difficult making my way in the semi-darkness, among the many forms. But I found Allen and he was awake and lying with an intent look on his face, not of fright but of acute interest. When he saw me, he smiled and said weakly, "Hello Sobersides." I said, "What's the matter, Allen old boy? How are you feeling?"

"Oh, not so bad. Where the devil did you come from, and where are your clothes? How did I get here?"

I had to grin in spite of the dizziness in my head. "Well, you poor old sucker, I came with you, or rather you came with me, and I had to loan you my clothes to keep you from drowning. But why all this sudden interest?"

"I've been listening to that damn row going on upstairs for the last half hour, and am wondering how long this bloody dugout will stand it. Being wounded isn't so bad, but to be buried? Well, I don't like it."

The thought paralyzed me. Buried! I too listened, then said, "I'll be back in a minute," and crawled away to the entrance, one of my legs being now practically numb and not much good. At the entrance room, there was a scene of activity that made my heart pump with gladness. We were being evacuated, several men removing the groaning figures from their stretchers and from where they lay on the ground, and lifting them as gently as possible onto the narrow stairway. The sound of hard-suppressed groans cut me to the heart, but it had to be done. They had to crawl up the stairs themselves, as these were too narrow for the men to be carried up. The doctor was giving each man a look as they were carried by him, and some he motioned to be put back, others he gave a pill and bade them Godspeed. "Good luck old chap, I'm sorry, but you are better off outside than in."

My heart quaked. Was it as bad as that? Several minutes later little streams of dirt were running from the roof in places here and there. The men were getting farther and farther away now, and nearer to Allen. Would he, could he make the stairs? Thirty steps. The men hurried, carrying their burdens swiftly, and giving furtive glances toward the roof as went. We should have known better, for if there is one place Fritz would have the range on, it would be his own dugouts, and he knew we would probably use them. Weren't we fools? I watched for Allen, unnoticed myself, and at last he came. My heart stopped as the doctor looked, held his place, motioned him back!

Oh, God, he wasn't worth taking out! Then the thuds grew heavier and at last the right one came; an ear-splitting roar, a smell of cordite, the rumble of dirt down the stairs, a crash of timbers, followed by the extinguishing of the candle, and I was knocked to the ground by a burst of air, and lay there. I thought I was dead, for a second or more there was silence, then a heart rending, ear splitting scream sounded, then again it came! Oh, God, I am done, done, a sobbing gasp, then silence. Then something scraping along the floor. I wasn't dead! I mastered all the forces of my will and courage. For God's sake now, be cool, don't get excited, it doesn't make any difference. Cool, cool, cool. Damn you, hands, stop trembling. Now feel around, and see what you touch. Ugh! I vomited, tried again, then heard a voice. "Is anybody alive there?" Thank God, somebody else. My eyes were weak and wavering. "Well then, come on over here. Can you crawl?" "Yes," I replied, then the voice said again, "Wait, I'll light my torch." A groan, the flare of a torch, and I crawled toward the light, each movement agony, as I heaved myself over several bodies lying between. Ugh, at last I reached him. It was the doctor. He threw the torch downward, and I saw that his legs up to his thighs were in a mound of loose dirt that was growing bigger. His voice came again between sobs. "Can you—you—pull me out? I—I'm afraid I can't help. The scissors, they're buried in my shoulder."

A sudden burst of energy on my part, drawn from God knows where, and I dug feverishly away at the dirt with my hands, and yet had time to say, "Put out the torch, may need it." I worked on. Was the dirt going? I didn't know, but just scraped and scraped, while sweat poured out, and I forgot all my own pains. "Flash the torch, Doc." The light came on and I reached for his shoulders, grabbed him by the hair, and pulled with all my might. He moved. Then another heave, and another, then a pull sideways on his legs, and he was clear. My head was throbbing, and I was gasping with the effort for breath, but I heard his low-breathed "Thank you."

I took the torch and crawled over to the boxes where he had been operating, and finding candles lit them. He was moving slowly toward me, hunching along on one elbow, between gasps, and I helped him, hurried him over. The scissors had gone in open, and still stuck in the muscles; and because they had gone in open they couldn't go much farther, though one point had slipped beneath some bones. "Better take a pill, Doc." He pointed to his pocket, and finding one, inserted it and waited for a few minutes. "All right," he said, "pull—quick." I wrenched them out, and he moaned, then whispered, "Iodine." I found the bottle on the table and poured the whole thing over the cuts. "Plaster," he said again. I hunted and found one half buried, and tried my best to draw the flesh together before binding it. He was moaning quietly, but at last I got it, then the bandage, which I wrapped securely at his request. I gave him another pill. "Rum." I looked blank. "Bottle." Oh, there it was. I took a darned good swig first, as I didn't want him to see my trembling hands—hands over which I seemed to have lost control. I trickled some down his throat then he said painfully, "Leave me ... Rum, pills ... others."

I understood. It was a big water bottle, so I took another swig, and started out, the fiery stuff making me feel better, giving me more nerve. I looked around. The entrance half-way up had caved in, evidently with a direct hit, and there was a jumble of boards, beams and mud, with here and there a trickle of water. A hand jutted out from under the dirt and I felt the pulse, but it was dead, quite dead. Then I took a thorough survey of the bodies, about fourteen in number. Five were alive, and I went down the passage and found several more, but the shock of the explosion had clearly finished them, as they were all dangerously wounded cases. Allen my God, where was Allen? I had forgotten. I hurried back as fast as my legs, including the numb one, would carry me, and rolled over the bodies in haste.

I found him at last, close to the door, but to the right, and against the wall, motionless, stiff, dead. No. Thank God! He was smiling, smiling, but he was dead....

That flickering flame also had been quenched by the terrific blast. I knelt beside him, while the torch in my hand slowly died. I looked at it stupidly. Such a fool I was, such a fool. I fell on my Allen, the Allen I had loved and who had loved me. "If I ever get home, Sobersides, I am going to be a parson, and believe me I will tell them something."... I wept. Oh, Allen, why should you die, while a worthless life like mine lives, to suffer! You brought me joy, happiness and now you are dead. I wept.

How long I lay there I did not know, nor care, but slowly my surroundings came back to me. The doctor. So I raised myself at last, took the identity disks and papers from Allen, and as my own tunic was gone and I was shivering with cold, I took his, found a blanket and covered him.

He was R.C., I noticed, and some dim memory of candles coming into my mind, I found a bit of one, lit it, and placed it at his feet. It flickered and went out, and though I tried again four or five times, it did the same thing each time. So, at last I turned and groped my way to where the doctor lay, guided by his candle, which had stayed alight. He was standing with his arm in a sling, watching me, when I faced him, and he spoke, evidently having seen everything. "He was a very great friend?" He made it a question, yet a statement of fact. I nodded, and he came to me and put his free arm around, while I, like a fool, slumped to the floor. I was so tired, and my body ached with wounds. When he knelt down beside me, he put his arm around me again, said, "Poor kid, poor kid," I burst out, "Oh, Doc! Everyone I have loved, every friend I had, has been killed. My wife, Hartley, and now Allen, my brothers. Why, oh, why am I always left?"

He didn't answer, but just stroked me and said "Poor kid." After a while he forced some of the rum and a pill down my throat. I didn't want to live then, but he made me, and suddenly became boisterous, cheerful. I started, amazed, and got to my feet. "Can you beat that? Can you beat it?"

I looked as he held a candle to the floor, and saw that it was wet, wet, water! Where the hell was it coming from? We hobbled over to the entrance, and the story was told. The shell had broken a hole, and naturally water from roundabout would dribble in and drown us. Drowned! We looked at each other, and the doctor laughed, laughed loudly and boisterously again. "Can you beat it, can you beat it? We get through one damn thing safely, and then comes the water, and we are going to be drowned. Do you hear, drowned. *Ha, ha!*" Oh, my God, he was off his head. It had been too much. I stared in stupefaction, first at the water dribbling in, and then at the doctor. I shook myself—then laughed. Wasn't it a joke, a hell of a joke, so bloody sure we were safe, and I pitying Allen, when I was as sure to die as he was. Ha, ha, ha, was I going crazy too?

No, no, no! Keep cool, for God's sake keep your head, you mustn't go off your bean. Cool, cool. One of the stretcher cases groaned. The doctor, damn him, was still waking the echoes with his laughter. He would drive me crazy too. I hurried over to the table, nothing there. But one of those infantrymen would have one. I looked among the bodies, found what I wanted, and with the doctor still laughing, I crept up, hit him square, and he dropped. I hit him again to make sure, then put three of his own pills in his mouth. That will keep him quiet I thought, and now for the wounded. I looked at them, and found some had died since I examined them. The one who had groaned still had a chance, so I hunted for a dry spot and pulled him and the doctor over, laying them down side by side. It would take a long time for the water to drown us out. In fact, when I began to think, I realized we couldn't drown, as the average shell hole had only a foot and a half of water in it. Could we get out, that was the question. I shuffled over to the entrance, but saw no chance there. I took some more rum, and it warmed me, and as I was beginning to dry out, the mud was drying off my breeches. I took a second drink and sat down to ponder. The Fritzies wouldn't be such damn fools as only to have one entrance. Well, but where was the other? The candle seemed to flicker, and remembering the one I had tried to light for Allen gave me an idea. There must be a draft of air somewhere, and that must mean there was an opening. I watched the flicker, and noticed the way the flame was pulled, and going in that direction came to the blank wall. Fresh air must be coming from somewhere. I felt elated. I had an immediate purpose in life at last. To find an entrance. I looked the passage over carefully, but there was nothing there, so I came back to the room, and began to search the walls. Hurray, a blanket in a corner, a gas blanket. How did I come to miss it? I pulled it aside and went along another passage, till the candle burned my fingers, then I had to feel my way, and suddenly I stumbled and fell. More bodies! I felt them over.

Germans. I could tell by the brass buckles. I went on more carefully, but the whole passage was cluttered with them. I stopped to think and rest. How would they get here? Then I remembered the moppers-up. Their business was to throw a stoke shell in each passage. They had all been killed by the shock. But wouldn't that block the passage? I dared not think of it, for as soon as I did, my body wanted to die. I must keep on. Then I saw a light, but no, it was just my imagination after all. I bumped against timbers, broken. Oh, God, blocked! I was beaten, and slumped to the floor, but was instantly aware of a cold draft that started me into sudden life again. I felt about with my hands. There was an opening. The beams of one side had fallen against the other, making a passageway through. I had to crawl now, and fall again and again. My body's all in, but I must keep going. At last the air, and I crawled over a pile of loose earth and found darkness, with stars overhead, and flares rising and falling. I fell senseless from my efforts.

It was daylight when I came back, but what time of the day I could not tell, for a fog hung over the earth. I could not move myself at all this time, and must just lie there and die. Poor Allen, he had wanted to die outside, and I am glad that I am able to. I tried to shout, but it ended in a pathetic squeal. But I must have made some noise, for a figure bent over me, a khaki one. Am I delirious? I saw he was wounded, his arm in a sling, and he said, "Are you alive?" I managed to form a "yes." Can't the fool see I am? "Listen," he said, "I can't help you, but I'll get somebody to come back for you. Don't worry. I'll make sure." I blinked my eyes, trying to make him understand that I comprehended, and he pushed on.

An eternity passed, then two figures appeared, but I could not speak to them, my jaws were stiff and locked, and they began to pick me up. How, oh how am I going to make them understand? They put me down, not comprehending, and I wondered if I could move my feet, which pointed toward the hole, or sign somehow that there are others in there. I gathered myself for one supreme effort, to force it into their thick heads. Now! Oh, God, what agony!

Up, up, up, they are almost pointing toward the hole. Then I knew no more.

Sway, sway, sway, up and down, stars overhead, night again. I tried to move my mouth, it opened just a little. Sway, sway, sway, I was deathly frightened that I would slip off the end of the stretcher when it dipped. Down another hole, all the weight of my body going to my feet, and piercing, searing pains racked me, then I groaned, and again knew no more.

Pain again awakened me, and I found myself in an ambulance, still on the stretcher, and with something warm dripping, dripping unto my face. Even in the midst of the pain it fastened itself on my mind, that drip, drip, at regular intervals. I began to wait for the next, imagining it again and again before it fell. It was warm, what could it be? Blood! I shrieked. Rattle, rattle, rattle. Doesn't the driver hear? I shrieked again, and the rattle stopped and a figure loomed over me in the quietness, and there was a flash of light "All right, old boy, take it easy, we will stop that. Take it easy." He wiped it off, and went back to his seat and I heard him say, "That guy in the 42nd, his bandage got loose and dripped down on the guy below. I guess the 42nd chap croaked. Giddap you, you damn mules." For some curious reason the sound of his voice calmed me, it was so natural.

I woke again still on the stretcher, in a tent this time, and the pain so bad again that I groaned, and at once a nurse bent over me, gave me a pill and some water and said smilingly, "it won't be long now, you will soon be moved." Then she left me, and I lay again staring at the ceiling and thinking, "I don't care if they do move me, kill me, or leave me." A car stopped outside and a doctor came in saying, "Take this one first, Jim," pointing to me, "and then take that one there, and then we will give you three walkers besides." I was lifted again, carried out to the car, pushed in; and feeling no pain now, feeling nothing, I started on the long silent ride out. "I guess I'm going to die after all," I thought. "Well, that won't do any harm." The car stopped after a while, and I knew we were in a town because of the ring of wagons on the cobblestones. I was taken out of the car and up a big stairway, and I felt the pain returning as another doctor looked me over carefully. I was put on a sort of wagon, stretcher and all, and was wheeled along several corridors into a room glaring with light, where I felt something put over my mouth. Then came a dizziness, and wild dreams. My wife was alive again and bending over me in the same old way. I felt her kisses, and her hand on my head. Peace.

I awoke quietly and presently a nurse bent over me offering me water in a teaspoon. I could see it was daylight now. Time passed, men came and lifted me again, and this time I felt no pain in fact I couldn't feel my body at all. I was too tired to think. I only partly sensed the long, long ride on the stretcher, and being put on a train. My head lay against a window, and I fell asleep with the sound in my ears of the wheels clicking over the rails.

W. Redvers Dent

Twenty-five

It was a beautiful day, and the sun shone full upon me as I awoke from a glorious sleep, feeling tired, and yet not tired just lazy perhaps. I had no desire to move, but I felt glad to be alive once more, and absolutely content, like a cat on a rug before a fire.

I looked around and found myself in a large room. With the re-awakening of memory I felt myself for bandages, and was relieved to find my face free, and my jaws all right again. Nothing wrong there, thank Heaven. I became conscious of a slight throbbing in my legs and a hint of pain in the region of my stomach, but neither was anything to worry myself over, so I began to interest myself in my surroundings. I saw rows of beds on either side of mine. I moved my head, and instantly became full of delight that I could do so. I could smell some kind of oil, but felt delightfully clean and fresh. When I turned my head, I saw a man in the next bed playing solitaire, and when he noticed me watching him he came over and said, "Hello, Canada, how do you feel now?" I grinned and said "Fine!" Then we both grinned, rather to say next. He was in hospital blues, a nice-looking chap, and fair, plump and blue-eyed, with those china-blue placid Saxon eyes. He had a complexion any girl would have envied, and I noticed his arm was bandaged tightly at the wrist or just above it.

"By Jove," he said, "The nurse told me to tell her as soon as you came to life again," and he hustled off. I was hungry, very hungry. When was it I had eaten last? Oh yes, in the dugout, before Allen and I had left. Allen—oh, well, maybe he is better off. The nurse appeared just then and luckily diverted my mind. She was one of the bustling jolly kind, and she said, "I suppose you want breakfast now, or dinner, or probably supper, or maybe all three." I assured her I wanted all three, but added, "I have an idea that all I will get is a glass of milk and a bun."

She smiled. "So, you have been in hospital before?" I admitted the fact and told her laughingly that I had been to France twice, and had total of two trips in the line and one working party. She looked amazed, and I, delighted to have an audience, went on: "That's a fact, sister, my total time in the line isn't five days yet. What day is this?" she told me it was April 17th. I could account for the 9th and 10th, but the rest was lost somewhere. April 17th!

"How about it, do I get anything stronger than milk?"

She looked at my chart, and said, "You are special. So I will see what 'special' means for you."

My new acquaintance came over again while she was gone, and began to talk. "I didn't know there were so many Canadians in the war," he said smilingly. "By Jove, every ambulance brings some. You chaps certainly gave Fritz a biff in the eye, didn't you?" Had we really? I was anxious for news. "You certainly did. The papers are still full of it. Thousands of prisoners, hundreds of guns, and a big advance at that, and not only that, but even an Australian had to admit it was possible!" We both laughed. "Well, if an Aussie praises us, we all deserve a V.C."

"By Jove, I can't understand you colonials!" Then, seeing my look, "Eh, oh, I mean you chaps from the Dominions. You are like two bally old cats, you spit at each other on sight. By Jove, I had to laugh, an Aussie in the next ward, when he heard that there were Canadians arriving, called the nurse and said to her, 'Nurse, you go get me my clothes. This place ain't going to be fit to live in for one Aussie now.'"

He was a jolly chap, and kept my mind occupied till the nurse came and put a rest behind my back, then brought me a real breakfast too, boiled eggs, toast, tea, and strawberry jam. It was a feast. I lay back after it was over, content.

I had lots of time to think, in the ensuing days, but I was in a quandary, because I actually didn't know how or what to think. I charted my life and experiences, but in a half-hearted way. There seemed to be no other conclusion but that God or Fate—some malignant being or influence—was chasing me, trying to break my will, make me his to do with as he willed. But I wanted to remain as myself. I had had enough of that being one in a mob. If I gave into this being, it would be just like the army again, with myself as the order taker.

I couldn't see any light except Allen's ideas about war. He had promised to give me the rest of his philosophy some time, but his death had ended that. One day he had said something about free will, but I dismissed it from my mind. Free will! I laughed at the absurdity of it. If I was supposed to have free will, where had I ever exercised it? Why, the fact that I had the mother I had would naturally give me a bias against life.

With these thoughts in my mind, I was ready to give them away to the first Padre I saw, and one day one came to visit me. The usual padre in France was as stereotyped as a Ford car, with the exception of such men as Canon Scott and "Woodbine Willie." The very nature of things made them of not much account, and they knew it. They weren't even useful in burying parties if you could get one. But in England they once more assumed their attitude of venerable wisdom. So, with this one when he visited me. He did his best to be bluff and hearty. I disgustedly thought he was like an insurance salesman, looking on you as a sucker, but not daring to say so. When he asked me what denomination I was, I assured him that I wasn't a customer of his, and drew him on into an argument.

I told him that the theological conception of God was rather contradictory. They said that God was infinite, eternal, and unending. But on top of that they said that He was complete, perfect, almighty. But nothing could be complete or perfect without having an end. When anything is made perfect, it means that nothing can be added to make it more beautiful, and that any touch added could only do one thing, make it imperfect. If it had reached perfection, there is an end to its progress. Therefore, God has clearly defined limits, and these limits are perfection. You also say that God can't be bad, that He is perfectly good. Well, if I can only do but one thing, and that one thing is good, then I haven't freedom, and I am not almighty or all-powerful. Because there are something's I cannot do. Freedom means choice.

The Englishman in the next bed was listening with enjoyment.

But when I told the padre that I was the orthodox, and he and his denominations with their dogmas were heretics, because they worshipped incomplete conceptions of God, while I came to Him as a little child, as Jesus had said, he caught me up. He showed me a few things about my conception. However, his voice when he finished had a new note.

"I can very well understand how you felt, Canada, when you saw me come into the ward, and you knew that I would ask questions and possibly make you appear in an awkward light. You decided to turn the tables. But I should not be so ready to hold other people's beliefs or lack of them up to ridicule. You have come through a very hard school, and done a good deal of logical thinking. Perhaps the beliefs of most of us would not stand up before logic, which is man-made after all, but the intimations of higher things are the best thing we have; we feel; therefore, we know. We wouldn't know that two and two made four unless we had had four apples or four pebbles to show us in the first place. You mustn't depend on logic so much. We shall meet again sometime and then we shall know all, and then guesswork will be over. I am sorry you feel that way."

Why, there were tears in his eyes, and he left hurriedly. I looked at the Englishman in stupefaction. "Good night, is he as easily hurt as that?"

"Well, you gave it to him pretty strong, Canada, pretty strong."

There was silence, while I stared moodily. I was thinking of how I might have sown seeds which would end by making him an outcast, an Ishmael like myself. I came to myself with a start. For the first time in my memory I was aware of pitying somebody else.

For days afterward, my sick fancies and my brighter ones when I was on the mend, roved about these problems. But particularly I was interested in the question, how had I got that way? But nobody had given me my ideas. I must have been inspired! Seriously as I took the problem and my own fate, that notion made me grin. I remembered that, left to myself, my facts and discoveries wouldn't marshal themselves, but when I got into an argument, things straightened themselves out into neat patterns. I came to the conclusion that my mind was like a dynamo, which must travel at a high rate of speed before it could work.

My harangue to the Padre had aroused the interest of my English friend, and one afternoon when the ward was quiet and the nurse away, he gave me something of his opinions regarding God.

"You know," he said, "I was wondering where I could place God myself, after this war. But what you said the other day seems to have given me a solution."

"Have you found a solution?" I inquired eagerly. "What is it?"

He reddened. "It sounds idiotic to think that we can pigeon-hole God. My wife always laughs at me because I am so fussy and neat at home. But just the same the war has made feel that everything was out of kilter, and things were in their wrong places, and I have been trying to arrange them again.... You know, I feel almost although I had been converted."

"Well, what conclusions have you arrived at?"

"It's like this. You said something to the effect that if God was perfect he had an end. I couldn't swallow that, so I figured that if God was anything He was, or had been, almighty, or at least that He had what we would like to have—free will in its perfection. So, I began to argue from that that God grew just like we did, only that of course he was millions of years ahead of us. What makes man a man is the fact that he can do something that other animals cannot, that is, see possibilities. I mean that we can not only see what thing is, but we can also see what it might be. But if God knew everything before it happened, he wouldn't be free, because his own knowledge would stop him from doing what he wants to do. So that's how I figure God doesn't know everything, but that His power lies in the fact that His possibilities are endless."

My dynamo began to work. "That means to me that God is progressive which makes a big difference."

"That's it, that's it."

"But why doesn't he progress a little faster, instead of feeling the same as he was three thousand years ago?"

"Well, what I mean is that God keeps growing and growing all the time. That his perfect freedom doesn't lie in his judgment, but in his wishes that freedom is the right to try to attain any desire or wish that you may want. That if he knew what he was going to wish before he had the desire, it couldn't be freedom."

"That is," I chimed in, "His wish must come without any previous knowledge on his part, or going to the other extreme, must come with perfect knowledge."

"Good God, we're getting in deep. Let's stop, my head's aching." So we sat silent for a time. "I know that sounds a queer jumble, Canada," he said at last, "but anyway it has helped me. Shall I get you the sister?" I held up my hands in horror. "No, no, for heaven's sake don't get her, or she'll see that I'm kept in bed several more days!" I rolled over to try and sleep it off. I didn't dream this time.

Twenty-six

The days passed slowly, their monotony relieved somewhat by the arrival of mail which was catching up again with me. The army had evolved a wonderful system of tracing a man, and mail that had followed me to England, back to France, and then back to England, finally reached its destination. I noticed that it was marked "killed," "missing," "believed killed," all of which had been scratched out, and "wounded, England" written upon it, which meant that they had to find me in one of the hundreds of hospitals in England. It was wonderful. There were several letters from Dad; he said Mother was very worried about me, but had recovered the shock of the deaths of my two brothers, and seemed much easier in mind. Dad himself was fine, he said but had retired from the army, as his rheumatism was very bad.

There was a letter from my old friend Mrs. Braithewaite, who had heard that I was killed, and then that I was alive after all, and she told me how happy she was that I was alive, and asked if I would have my picture taken and sent to her, which I made up my mind to do as soon as I was able. The children were all in splendid health, she said. Then there was a letter from my wife's mother, saying that she had just heard that I was on my way to France again, wishing me Godspeed, and asking if I would accept a little gift (ten pounds) and a parcel she was sending. There was hope for her son's eyesight after all she said, in an operation that the king's private surgeon was going to undertake. I prayed that it might be successful.

Another letter was from Hartley's mother, who had also heard that I was on my way back to France, and if this was true, she said, would I do an old lady and a mother a good turn and try to locate the grave of her son so that she could visit it after the war, and she did hope I would come back safely. She said she and my mother prayed daily for my return, and would I mind very much if she kept sending parcels to me, as she had got into the habit of it, and it seemed to give her something to do and established a link with Hartley.

Then there was my mother's letter, telling me how she had heard of my death but couldn't believe it, and how, sure enough they had received my telegram next. Another letter was filled with anxiety about what kind of nursing I was getting, and still another, dated much later, when she had heard I was going back to France, saying that nearly every house on the street was in mourning. The church seemed to be made up of women now, all the young men gone. She thought it queer that the Canadians appeared to be in so many battles, and had so many casualties, and now they were talking of conscription. Was I getting my parcels? Did the salted peanuts keep fresh? (I was fond of salted peanuts) and so on.

One day a letter arrived from Allen's wife, and I give it in full from memory, as the contents are still written on my mind. She had traced me, after

Cry Havoc

hearing of Allen's death, and this was what she wrote.

> Toronto, Ontario, April 24th /17
> Corp. Lionel Thor, 519S4
> C.M.R.s, 8th Brigade,
> 3rd Division C.S.T.
> Believed Wounded.
>
> Dear Mr. Thor:
> I have just received the news about my husband. I received a telegram last night stating that he was "missing believed killed" and another this morning stating definitely that he was killed.
> I suppose that you will be surprised to hear from me, but my excuse is the fact that Allen, in his letters, was always speaking of you.
> I believed he called you Sobersides, did he not? He called me Spud. He had the habit of calling anyone he liked by some nickname, always did, so when I heard him calling you that, I understood that you must be very good friends and that (a blot here, possibly tear) if he was killed you wouldn't be far away. I knew he loved you very dearly, in fact, I believe he loved you more than anyone else in the world, and at times I am ashamed to say that I was jealous of you. But now I want to meet you, to see what you are like, for there must be some great handiwork of God in you, to rouse such love in my scalawag. Oh, yes, you know he was. A dear, dear scalawag, who went through life doing whatever he wanted to do, without fear. But I? I thank God that he always came back to me.
> You see, Sobersides (I must call you that) his was the character that provoked love in others. Everybody loved him, but seldom did he return any deep affection, except when the mood seized him, and then, ah, then one took it gratefully, like a dog night take crumbs from his master's table. But with you it was different. He loved you permanently, steadily, enduringly. I do want to see you. I want to hear from you how he died. But please, please don't make up a story about how he died. Tell me the truth. I have always seen him in truth, and I want to see his death the same way. He told me once that he always opened his heart to you, so that I know you understand more about us than I do. I can only say that I am one of those practical women whom you hear about, and of course you know he was just the reverse. I suppose I should have married a practical man, a virtuous man, a godly man, who went to church every Sunday and took an interest in the house and children. But I didn't. I married a will-o'-the-wisp whose only idea was to love and live and even die, as he pleased. He used to say it was the only thing to do, but if I had done it, I would have lost him. I knew that, and instead of hating him for it, I loved him all the more. He was a scalawag, a dear lovable scalawag, a vagabond in life. But he made me a woman, and made me see

the heights that I never could have reached but for him. I loved him, and sometimes I think that in his way he loved me too. Did he ever speak of loving me? I know I shouldn't ask you, I know you will think I have lowered myself to do so. But, dear God, I love him so much, so much. Could you—would you? Write and let me know?...

I tore the letter into thin fragments, stared at the wall, stared, stared, stared. I answered her letter next day, told her how he had died, and lied of course, but still it was justified. I gave her a picture she would never forget. I told her he had been taking a message and had been wounded but had kept on until the message had been given into the hands of the O.C., and how he then fell exhausted. That he had been sane and free from pain at the end, had called for me, as I had been in the dugout when he had come in, and given me a message for her. "Tell her, Sobersides, I was always hers, always, just as she is mine. We can't part. I want her, love her." That was my message to his wife, scarcely coherent, perhaps, but still the best I could manage.

The next day I was allowed up. It was May, and two weeks afterward I received my board from the doctors, and was marked fit. I had twenty-eight scars on my body. The doctor told me afterward that they had received notice to examine all Canadians, and discharge from hospital any of those considered nearly fit, as they were needed in France, every battalion under strength. I sat stupefied when I got the news. I could not believe it, yet there it was; back to France again. My God, I had thought I was finished this time, and had hopes of seeing Canada again, and home. Back to France? Twice I had missed it now, twice, two out of three, the third time meant death. I was positive it could mean nothing else. Back again! Oh God, oh God! I turned to the English chap and arranged a grin, though heaven knows how I did, and said, "Well, old scout, I go back to France. I've been boarded, and the doctor says they have orders to push me through. Back to France. This is the third time of asking."

"Third time is asking for it, as you people say, eh?"

"Yeah. If anybody knows of any reason why I shouldn't go back, the government tells them to hold their bloody tongues, and pushes me back again." I was still smiling, smiling at God. I heard the English Tommy's voice.

"I say, old chap, that is tough. Let's go out and have a drink."

We did, and I managed to be cheerful, but when I had my picture taken next day I felt as though I were being measured for my coffin.

Twenty-seven

I had my next affair of the heart, if you could dignify it so, at Epsom, another Canadian convalescent depot. I got leave for ten days and decided to take it in

Brighton, as I didn't want to go to London for fear I might meet relatives of my wife. I did not feel like bothering them, and again, it was all over now, and aside from imposing upon them, I would remind them of things.

For the first few days at Brighton all went "according to Hoyle." Then I met her. I had seen her several times in the dining room with someone whom I presumed was her mother, and in that curious way that knows no understanding, our eyes kept meeting. And as were trying to stare disinterestedly, our glances became all the more intimate.

I began to be interested because I was sure she couldn't be English, and thought she might be French, because her coloring, though nice, wasn't Nature's. She was dark with that dead whiteness of complexion which is characteristic of the American and the French, and her black eyes glinted, denoting, I thought, a devil of a temper. She was very evidently bored, and after carefully looking over the guests, had decided that I was the only person present likely to provide her with amusement. Such was the impression I gathered from her glances. When she stood up, she was tall and spare, a forerunner of the post-war type of women, yet she wasn't too thin, and she looked to be full of life. I didn't need to speak to her to know that she knew and thought one thing, and that one thing was men. Her business was to bring men to heel like spaniels. I wondered what opening she would give to aid me in making her acquaintance.

I did not have to wait long. I was sitting in the lounge when her mother or aunt or whatever she was, came over and addressed me. She gushed. There is nothing worse under heaven than a gushing woman, especially an American one. "I hope you will excuse my boldness, in addressing you," she said, "but I noticed that you are in the Canadians, and I wondered if you were an American, as I have heard that there are Americans in the Canadian Army."

I tried to be insulting, to see what would happen, and said politely, "No, Madam. I am afraid I am a Canuck. But we have Jews, Russians, Chinese, and negroes and every other nationality."

She gave me a very sharp look, but still managed to smile, and say, "Oh, you Canadians will always have your little joke. I once asked a Canadian in London the same thing, and he said, 'Madam, we are all from the continent of America, and there are very few Indians in our army.'" I couldn't help laughing at her words, and she laughed, and said, "Of course we can't say anything else but American, as you people have a distinctive name, and we haven't, except, 'Yankees,' and we Southerners don't accept that name."

Her argument was really in order so I said quickly, "If I resented the name American being applied, madam, I apologize."

"Oh, but I didn't come over to argue with you over national names. I noticed that you have served in France twice. Was it very exciting?" I admitted that it was. "It is really terrible war. My husband and I are over here on business, and it is really terrible how he is working himself to the bone for the cause of the Allies."

I managed a polite question. "Is he in munitions?"

"Oh, nothing so terrible as that. He is a broker, selling things for the manufacturers."

"Oh," I said, "that's what we call a commission broker, in Canada."

My remark must have touched a sore spot, for she broke out, "Oh, of course, he is making money, in fact we are quite wealthy now, but he is worked hard, and no one will ever appreciate the work he has done. And of course, he has bought British war bonds. He owns nearly a million dollars' worth, I believe." "Oh," I said. "Doesn't it look as if the Americans will have to come into the war? You know the Allies are becoming very anxious and pessimistic about winning, aren't they?" she queried.

I admitted the charge, looking down at my stripes. "But of course, if the Americans do come in, the Germans will surely lose."

I managed another "oh," and then as she rambled on, I grew very hot under the collar; in fact, words stumbled out of my mouth. I said, "Listen, Madam, I will grant that if the Americans come in, the war will be over sooner, but the Americans will never be able to say they won it. Did you ever see a boxing match?" She nodded. "Well, just imagine, two big heavyweights have been fighting for twenty rounds, one of them being a professional fighter and in training, the other someone picked out of the audience without warning. The pro starts out to knock the amateur out in one round, and beat the daylights out of him, but the amateur says to himself, 'If I can survive the first round, when he is fresh and steady, and I am not, I have him licked.' And behold, he does, so the rounds go on, and after each round the amateur seems stronger than the professional. They are still fighting, both getting weak, but the amateur having the other licked certainly, when a third man jumps into the ring and immediately the fight is over. Well, that's this war. It was won long before the Canucks, Aussies, or anyone else was in France, won when a little contemptible army of English stood up to that big pro, and survived the first round. You might as well say the Canucks won it at the battle of Ypres in '15 as to say that any new force could come in and win the war. The question you want to ask yourself is, if we had been licked, could you have come in and licked him alone?"

I stopped for breath, and noticed that her face was very red. There was silence for a minute, then her niece came over mincingly, and asked, "What are you people so interested in? You have been talking for the last fifteen minutes. I suppose Auntie has been holding forth on the Great American Nation?" I blushed. I had been a fool to talk like that.

"Now Luella," her aunt broke in, "for goodness' sake don't call me down again. This young man has given me such a dressing down that I feel positively naked. He is a Canadian. What did you say your name was?... Do you know, I almost took you for a Southerner?"

I admitted that my family came from Virginia a long, long time ago, and at once she inquired, "Surely you aren't a descendent of the Revolution?" I confessed, and they both laughed, "Oh, now I understand your animus against us poor Americans! Now I must leave you children to argue, all day if you like; but I warn you, Luella, he is dangerous."

Luella smiled. "That's the only way I like them, Auntie. I hope he is every bit as bad as you say!" So, she was looking for trouble, I thought.

I suggested a walk, and when we got outside she said, "I am sick and tired of Auntie and her perennial arguments. As for myself, I think there is a lot to be said on both sides." She was ready to be herself she tossed her head and I liked her, she seemed so like a Thoroughbred horse. But I said nothing, and she continued. "After all you Canadians and we Americans come from the same stock, but look at the difference. I have met everything from a Pole to an Irishman in your army, and our nation is like that. England reminds me of a grandmother, always looking with surprise at the children her daughters have."

I laughed. "Right on the head, Yankee, but let's talk of something else."

She changed to a coquette, languishing, demure, leading me on, then jumping away. The hunt was on. We went to the movies, the cinema—and she sat leaning close to me, arms touching, knees brushing. Then she would suddenly move away, to make it seem accidental. I admired her artistry, which was effective enough. I thanked heaven when it was over. She was a teaser.

We had supper, and it was while we sat there that an argument began. Equality of women. Did I believe in equality of women? Darn it, I saw an abstruse discussion before me. I assured her that I thought women should have the same rights as men, and not so many as they had now. She flushed, her chin went out, and she began, while I was trying to think of something I had read about the suffragettes, but all I could remember was that they had fought policemen. "You believe women have more freedom than men, then?"

I admitted I did, and illustrated my belief. "While Dad is out working all day, mother and the hired girl clean up the house in the morning and then go off shopping or to a tea-fight all afternoon. And we get tinned beans and fried potatoes for supper. What is that but freedom? Believe me, I wish I had been born a woman," I ended heartily.

"That's it, that's it," she almost shouted. "You men think a woman has nothing to do except to cook for you! What about getting the vote and having a say in the nation's affairs? After all, isn't it our children who are getting shot?" My soul clouded, my body grew stiff, but I said nothing. She continued. "All men seem to think of women, is that they are there for their satisfaction, and to have children by, and to slave and cook and slave."

I couldn't tell her what I knew about Dad, and all he had taken from his wife, his mother. Luella's insinuations amazed me coming from a girl, for we weren't used to sex being talked about by women, and I said, "I hate to start an argument with you about women, my Yankee friend, because I don't believe it does any good, anyway. Out of the talk of freedom, and it sounds big, of how women haven't the vote. Well, give them the vote, let them vote ten times a day, but I will bet this, that they will be as big fools when they vote as the men. Men don't vote for principles unless they get all worked up to it. They usually vote for a man who amuses them or panders to their prejudices. Women will do the same. As for war, they will likely encourage it. As for—"

"Oh—oh!"

"As for having children, did you ever see an old maid, or a childless couple? I never saw any that looked very happy. My uncle and aunt, who were childless, appeared to be really happy only when we kids were there. I heard our minister say once that when he wanted someone to do some really important job, that the only women who had time to do it were those who had at least six children. A woman who had none, or only one or two, never had time for anything, except to talk about her ailments and her doctors. I had a friend, a nurse, a very dear friend she was"—Luella didn't quite dare to grimace at this—"And she told me that the good Lord had so built women that their minds and bodily structures are different from men's. They were made to have children and if they kept healthy, they wouldn't suffer."

"I don't believe it," she snapped.

"Well," said I, "you don't have to. But let me tell you, a lot of stuff about the glory of motherhood and so forth is just bunk. Those self-indulgent women! Mothers by accident, I'll bet you. If women believe all the stuff they are talking nowadays, why do they tease men and draw them on? Do they rely on their intelligence to attract? Not on your life, they do as you do, rouse them, then turn around and say, 'Oh I'm not that kind of girl!' Bunk. Look here, my Dad worked steadily and uncomplainingly for us for years and years, but mother, after she brought us into the world, had a whale of a time. Dad kept us here. I knew one woman who was a woman, and she wasn't out on the street corners yelling for rights. The very fact that they are out yelling makes me figure that they must have freedom already. If someone tells me the cat is in the cage, and I see it in the street, what am I to think?"

"Oh, I didn't mean that, what I mean is, I want to be treated in the same way as a man."

"Then God help you, Yankee," I exclaimed piously. "You won't be able to get away with the stuff you do now."

"Oh, I can take care of myself, don't you worry."

"Well, there wasn't a man made whom some woman couldn't conquer, and never a woman that some man couldn't get. I accept your challenge. Let's go, and forget all about it."

We walked the promenade, and bewilderingly she changed her mood again; this time she was very much in need of a man to cling to, to lean upon, as she expressed it. Though a little doubtful, I saw no harm in playing up to her, and as a result she had me going again. It amused her to see me ardent.

But when I went to bed that night I thought long and carefully over the whole business, and decided that she had made me look and feel a fool, and it wasn't nice to have to admit it. The next thought that came to my mind was how pleasant it would be to beat her at her own game. That is, make her cry for, ask for, or at least want, the very thing she was teasing me about. The thought grew in my mind, and I began to believe it could be done. There was nothing like trying. But if I did, I must follow some definite method. Allen had said, "Play the same game with them. It never fails." So I mapped out my campaign. I had only a few days left, so I would have to work quickly. I would have to keep suggesting, but how?

Twenty-eight

Next day, the plan went into operation. We went for a walk, and I was careful to be impersonal, joking, careless, while all the time my joking planted seeds. I would say, "I'll let you hold my hand, if you are good." And she did not know just how far from or near to serious I was. Again, I would say, "No sir, I honestly don't want to make love to you, just enjoy myself and have a good time. You know a man and woman should be able to be friends and intellectual companions without love always creeping in." I never touched her, never attempted a caress, merely used suggestion.

We sat on a lonely part of the beach, but I kept my distance and smoked. She was puzzled, but not admitting defeat, she grew more attentive. Then more languishing, more careless in regard to her posture, and so forth. I grew so interested in the experiment that I grew forgetful of such things as passion and love, while she attempted to lead the conversation in their direction. Were women really like that, I wondered. The day passed, the night came, but still no difference manifested itself. She wanted to walk, and sit in a shelter on the promenade, but I grew nervous and suggested, almost insisted, on going to the theatre. There, I still kept my distance carefully.

We took another walk afterward, and she grew confidential, but I was waiting for her now. I was positive she was working on definite lines like myself, just to add another scalp to her collection. But I gathered that I was winning from certain words she dropped, a reference to "you cold-blooded Northerners." Before we started home, I put my arm around her once, but at her conventional gesture, I obediently withdrew it, saying brazenly, "Oh, I just did that as I thought you wanted it." That was turning the tables with a vengeance! I went onto say that girls usually expected you to do that, and get sore if you didn't. I heard her gasp, and grinned to myself. We walked home, she in silence, and I chattering like a magpie.

At the door, she looked at me sharply, smiled sweetly, and said, "Good night. See you in the morning."

And so that day passed, and the next, and the next. My leave was nearly up. We were together all of one day, and she had been mostly quiet and not inclined to be playful when I suggested that I must leave soon. Evening came, and she suggested a long walk in the country, to which I agreed. We took the tram to the end of the line and then walked. It was a beautiful night for walking. I took her arm as we sauntered along, and she was yielding and soft. I felt my victory. She made a misstep, and my arm went out to catch her. We did not feel that it was a game now.

When she suggested a rest, I was only too glad to fall in with her wish. We found a stile, and we hardly seated ourselves before we were in each other's arms. Hand, hands, groping, covetous hands. She was quiet, like one in a trance. But it was no good, I rose and said roughly "Come on, let's go home or we'll make damned fools of ourselves. Come on."

The sweat poured off me, and I walked on ahead quickly, cursing myself for being a blasted sentimental fool. Was I likely the first? And didn't she ask for it, by saying she could take care of herself? At least I waited for her, and she came to my side, took my arm, at which I said "Don't touch me, for God's sake. You have made me look damn fool enough." Her answer was a simple "Yes, Lionel." She had scarcely called me by my first name before. She had a hard time to keep up, but when we came to the end of the tram line, she didn't want to be rude, so we walked on into town.

She stopped at the last corner, so naturally I had to stop too. She took my hands while we stood there, not saying a word. At last she put my hand to her cheek. My hand was hot, but her cheek was soft and cool. Finally, she said, "You are a very funny man, Lionel. Do you think I am shameless?"

"Oh, well," I said, "Oh, well, what the hell does it matter? You'd better go home and forget all about it. For God's sake let me go." I tried to disengage myself, but she still held onto my hands. I tried to see her expression but it was too dark.

"You may go away tomorrow, back to France, and you may not. I may not see you again." This as though to herself. Then suddenly she asked "You aren't in love with me, are you Lionel?"

If I ever got out of this, I would leave these damn women alone! I was beginning to feel a revulsion against her. "Well," I began, when her hand closed over my mouth.

"Don't say it," she cried. "I would rather believe it." I stood silent. She took my arm and proposed "Let's walk a little more. Honestly, I am not tired and I want to walk."

So we walked in silence, while she held my arm tightly, and almost had her head on my shoulder. But I was so preoccupied that I did not appreciate the fact. After a while she said, "Do you forgive me Lionel, for trying to play with you?"

"Sure," I answered. "Oh, sure."

She laughed a funny little laugh, and repeated my words, as if they pleased her. Suddenly she had her arm around me, holding me tight. What in blazes was I supposed to do, I wondered. I found myself being gently but firmly pushed into the seat of a shelter while she plumped herself on my knee and put her arm around my neck, all the time chuckling softly to herself. "Seeing you won't love me, I must love you." Then her tone changed and became serious while she played with the buttons on my tunic.

She was heavy and strong for her build. Her voice was firm and quiet, and held my wandering attention.

"I suppose you don't know what to think of me. But I don't care. It is a night and a time for me to be honest. My dad always says 'Never let an opportunity slip.' Do you know what I found out when I was following you along that road? I found I had fallen in love with you. Oh, I know I shouldn't say it, but this is wartime and you—" She touched my wound stripes. "—are going to war again. Well, I want you to promise one thing, and that is, before you go, to see me, telephone, telegraph if you can't come, and I will be down myself. Do you promise?"

I promised.

"On your absolute word of honour?" Again, I promised. "Will you swear you will?" Again, I gave consent. "Well, then, hold up your hand and say 'I promise before God to let Luella know before I leave for France, to see her if possible, and if not, to let her know in time, so that she can see me!'" There I was, like a child, swearing solemnly.

Silence again, and then, very doubtfully for her: "Even now, I don't believe you will but I guess I'll have to take a chance." She put her cheek to mine, making my blood race and I clutched at her, held her passionately, growing fevered as I kissed and kissed her, and all the time, she clung to me.

I fought for control, and lit a cigarette. She stroked my head and murmured, "It's more that I can expect, but I want you, Lionel, I don't care how; I want you."

We stood up, and even in the semi-darkness I could see her eyes wide and shining. "Remember, Lionel, if you ever need me, anywhere, anytime, I will come, gladly. Do you understand? I don't care if you don't love me."

In silence, we walked home. Somehow my ideas of her were changed, and even of women in general. Beneath all of their frumpery trickery I saw a fierce primitive directness which I had to respect. We arrived at the hotel door. "I don't want to go in, but I suppose you are tired." Her mouth was held up appealingly, and I kissed her, feeling that there was something sacred in the kiss.

Twenty-nine

It was June when I was discharged from Convalescent and sent back to the reserve battalion. I stopped for an hour or so in Brighton on the way, and there met several men from my battalion in France. There were many reunions, and everyone told me the same story, of being boarded and pushed back into the units before they were fit. Of course, we had drinks, and I arrived at camp with a fighting jag on. Unluckily the only person in the orderly room to greet me on my arrival was the hapless Methodist who had won his name by being the angel child of the battalion, always clean and neat, and obedient to every order.

I had to soak him, just for old times' sake and the principle of the thing, and the little rat had the nerve to fight back, so I made a good job of it. I think I broke some of his ribs, or so I heard later, but anyway, I hadn't been back two hours before I was duly installed in clink, with some of my old friends who had celebrated in Brighton and fought some Military Police. There were enough of us, with some of the guards, to have a really good game of poker, and I finished the night with six pounds to the good.

The next morning, we were all hauled up to orderly room. The others, went in first, and were soaked fourteen days' pay each, and confined to camp until the next draft left for France. They were laughing as they came out, and winked at me as I stood there, hat off, waiting my turn, and one of them said, "Well, my debt to the blinking government is piling up. I owe them a year's pay now, and will owe them two years' before that draft."

"Prisoners, attention! Right turn, quick march, left turn! Halt, left turn!"

"Private Lionel Thor, #51934 (I pricked up my ears at the 'private') charged with disorderly conduct and breaking furniture in the orderly room, assaulting Sergeant Squire in the same orderly room, in contravention of the King's Rules and Orders, Chapter –, Paragraph –, sub-paragraph-x."

I looked at the officer. By Jove, they had changed O.C.s, and who should it be but my fat friend of the Machine Gun Section. Involuntarily I grinned, just as he grinned and held out his hand. "Hello, Thor, I thought you were a stiff. Where have you been?" I was delighted to see him, and started to tell him of all the chaps, when the sergeant coughed and said, "Pardon me, sir, we are in session."

The O.C. started. "Oh, yes, Sergeant, quite right, quite right. We must follow routine. Prisoner, what have you to say for yourself?"

I had been carefully primed by one of the others the night before, who had been going through for law, and had studied the Rules and Orders, and I said: "I must protest, sir, against being put under close arrest. I believe I am entitled to an escort consistent with my own rank, sir."

The O.C. looked startled. "When the devil did you get stripes?"

"I have been back to France since you saw me last, sir, and while there I have been confirmed in the rank of corporal by both Divisional and King's Orders."

The Sergeant let slip a "Goddam, a King's Corporal. He's the first I've ever seen!" And another officer standing behind the O.C. whispered something. The O.C. was grinning now, and he said, "Well, all I can see is we will have to adjourn court until we see what you can do with a King's Corporal. And, by the way, Thor, I have a little surprise for you. We have been trying to locate you for some time. Court adjourned! Prisoner, left turn, quick march, left turn, halt!"

I sat down on a bench outside, and smoked placidly. The sergeant looked thunderstruck for a minute, then said "Guard, dismissed," and "Corporal you come back, you are to act as escort for Corporal Thor." I was sitting on top of the world. Gosh, it was good to give the army one in the eye like that. I chuckled, "I'll bet a dollar they are sweating in there, trying to find out what the hell you do with a King's Corporal!"

It was one of my carefully cherished secrets, for when Daddy had promoted me in France, he had recommended that my rank be confirmed, for my work at Sanctuary. It was very seldom that such a recommendation ever went through, but it was given by the King, and though it only gave you one stripe, that one stripe had the protection of the King himself, and the owner could not be reduced except by the highest army court martial. But of course, one could be fined. However, even that had no effect in France, where you were paid only thirty francs a month field pay, and that by paymasters who visited the battalion at intervals, just gave out the money, whether you were in debt or not. Even the Sergeant had to laugh, and said, "By God, poor old Tubby will have one hell of a job trying to find out what he can do."

The door opened, and somebody said, "All right, Sergeant, show him in."

Tubby, as they called my old officer, was looking very solemn, but his eyes were twinkling. I stood at attention, and I was curious to know what solution he had found. "On looking over your papers from France, Corporal Thor, we find your statement verified, that you are a Corporal by Divisional Order, and not only that, but we also find that when this particular crime was committed that there is doubt as to whether you were actually on the strength of this unit, as your papers have not yet arrived from Epsom. Therefore, until this question is decided, it is not in our power to try you, as you may still he attached to Epsom for discipline and rations. Until this moot question, therefore, is settled, I find that you will he placed under open arrest until such time as we can give you your well-merited punishment. What would happen if every old C.M.R. who came back here should beat up the orderly room clerk, simply because he also is a C.M.R. but had not gone to France? There may be weighty reasons for his being kept in England. There is absolutely no justification for such an unprovoked attack. You yourself have offered none, but simply protest a technicality of the law about your detention. This can be immediately cleared up, however, if you will state your willingness to accept any decision I may make. Are you willing therefore to go ahead with this trial and accept any punishment that I may inflict? It will save a tremendous amount of letter writing, and your course is clear, you can either stay under open arrest indefinitely, or accept any punishment which. I may see fit to inflict."

"What the devil are you getting at?" I thought as he spoke. "You can only fine me anyway, and make me pay the damages, and I can't get to town if I accept open arrest." So, I said, "I may say, sir, that you have practically charged me with a crime without allowing me to make a defense, but, as you say I haven't any, I am willing to accept your sentence."

"I fine the prisoner seven days' pay," (good heavens, that's easy) "and order that any damages should be deducted from his pay. Prisoner, dismissed!"

I managed to keep solemn. Good heavens, it was worth a hundred dollars let alone ten, to sock the Methodist like that. Wouldn't he be sore when he heard how lightly I got off! The O.C. came out as I was chuckling over this and said, "Say, Thor, drop over to my hut this afternoon. I would like to see you." "I will try to be there, sir" And so ended the first twenty-four hours at Reserve.

I saw Tubby that afternoon in his hut, where he was waiting for me, alone. We had a drink, then seated ourselves comfortably. I could see that he had some question to decide, and was unable to do so. At last he said, "Well, Thor, I may as well break the news to you that I was referring to this morning. You are to receive a Military Medal, and a French medal of some kind. We are holding a review next week, when some big bug will inspect us, and you and others will be presented. I get the I.C.C. and D.S.O. myself, though what the devil for, I do not know."

"I-I- what do I get a medal for? I didn't do anything?" I stuttered. He grinned. "That's probably why you are going to get it. The doctor, you remember, who was in the dugout with you, recovered, in fact he is coming down next week to see you. He blabbed the whole works. You'd better have a drink, you look as if you need it. I suppose there aren't many fellows left of the old outfit, back in the battalion, are there?"

I shook my head gloomily. "The only ones, so far as I know, are the O.C. and some guys in the transport. Why even here I haven't seen an original yet. Even the bunch I came over with at Sanctuary seems to have all got it." There was a silence, then he sighed.

"I've got a real cushy job here. I'm only temporary rank of course, could resign any time and go back to France." He looked troubled, his fingers tapped the table, "I hear the machine gun section has broken up."

I nodded. A gloom seemed to have settled on us, the figures of the dead seemed to be in the room. All our friends, pushing up daisies now. At length, he spoke. "I suppose you don't care about going back? I can get you a job here, you know."

As easy as that, an opportunity for life, an escape open before me, I seemed to see Allen and Hartley, even my wife, in the room there, watching me, I stared into nothingness, as the O.C. too, watched me, tapping the table. And I talked with them all. "Listen," I pleaded, "here is a chance for me to live, have a good time, take it easy, and haven't learned. Twice now I have gone. There are lots of others, look at that damned orderly room rat. He could go. Maybe I could get back to Canada. It's only fair, isn't it? I've done my bit, why not take it easy?" I slumped in my chair, waiting, but they said never a word. "Oh, hell, sir, I guess I've got to go back. No hope for me, I'm an absolute damn fool. But I guess I've got to go back. May I have a drink?"

He watched me, his eyes clouded. "I know how you feel, Thor, and darned if I don't feel the same way. I guess I will just be bloody fool enough to give up this nice bomb-proof job and go back to France." We drank in silence. "I've got a wife and kids at home though. It's the very devil to know what to do. Well, anyway, how are you fixed for money? Got some?"

I thanked him, and was about to tell him how I had cleaned out the guard room, and then thought I had better not, so I just told him I had lots and we shook hands. His last words as I left were, "Aren't we a pair of damn fools to go back?" I heartily agreed with him.

Thirty

In due course I was presented with my medals by some high mucky-muck who fought the war in England, and hadn't even been in the Battle of Shorncliffe. He said it was a pleasure to meet a brave man, and I felt like saying, "You should change your company," but thought I had better not. I liked the doctor, on making his acquaintance in circumstances more normal than that of our buried dugout. I found he had lost his arm, and wondered if it was because I had pulled the scissors out wrong. He held my hand firmly for a second, dropped it and mumbled something about my having guts. He said he could get me a bomb-proof if I wanted it and watched me with a queer look while I answered. "Everyone seems to be making a point of giving me a bomb-proof. Why, my God, if I stayed in England I would be seducing all the women and drinking myself to death from boredom; so I'm going back."

"I thought you would," was all he said. He slipped me ten quid when he left, saying as he did so that he figured that was about what he was worth. I lost it and the French medal at poker the next night, so I thought I had better send the M.M. home to Mother, as a souvenir from her son.

The O.C. was not to be outdone, however, in making my last stay in England as comfortable as possible. I was made a military cop. I should explain a distinction. There were Military Police and Military Cops. The former were the ones commonly called Red Caps, and were permanent, that is to say, they were given special pay and allowances, to act in the same capacity in the army as the police did in civil life. They were owned body and soul by the Government, and as such were looked down upon by the soldiers. They never fought anybody except their own countrymen, in soldier riots, and they never interfered with Canadians unless they absolutely had to, to save their faces or in military hospitals where soldiers were sent. But please remember that one was a criminal in the army if one didn't shine one's buttons, or told one's sergeant to go to hell, and you were supposed to be shot if found asleep while on guard, in the line. Civil crimes, like theft, were taken care of by the soldiers themselves in their own way. Later, when there were so many disabled men that the Canadians did not know what to do with them, they had the bright idea of putting an armlet on them and saying, "Now you are a policeman," and rather vaguely leaving it at that. Nobody knew what they were supposed to do, and nobody cared. What did it matter? The poor blighter wasn't fit to go to France, and wasn't bad enough to send home. He couldn't attend drills, he wasn't fit enough to send to France, so they merely made him a 'cop and when he asked what he had to do, they waved their hands and said, "Keep order."

But as a policeman he could go where he liked, didn't attend drills, and otherwise led the life of a gentleman, and everybody was happy. And as for actually arresting anybody, well, it might have been done. A scene I shall never forget till the end of my days will explain the point.

In Brighton one night, some returned men of one battalion met members of another in a pub. The second battalion was the 42nd Black Watch, Scotchmen, with kilts and everything. It was rumored, though probably with exaggeration, that when they came out from a trip into the line with sadly diminished numbers, in fact about half strength, and had to receive a draft to fill up the blanks, this draft, duly arriving, proved to contain one company of fine upstanding blonde Russians, six feet every one of them, and a company of

Japanese. Well, there happened to be a real Scotchman in that battalion. They say he wept! However, both types of newcomers were wonderful fighters, but the kilts were too short for the Russians and too long for the Japs, and the whole thing became common gossip, so what was left of the 42nd couldn't enter a pub without hearing something about it. The fight usually would start in this way:

Two Canucks at the bar, not members of the 42nd. Enter two members of the 42nd. First Canuck: "Say, Bob, did you hear about the 42nd Battalion?"

Second C: "No, what about it?"

First C: "Well, they say those Scotchmen couldn't fight, so they put a lot of good blood into the battalion. Some Japs, some Chinks and Russians, and maybe a few Germans, but of course I ain't sure about the Germans."

Then things started.

I was watching one of these fights, where members of two battalions were trying to settle an argument. For if you interfered, both sides would turn on you. So, we watched, and of course it attracted civilians, the men looking on with interest as they saw the rest of us merely keeping a circle clear. But some woman screamed as she saw their noses bleeding, and called a military policeman, who was helping us keep the circle, to stop the fight. He had forgotten all about his precious armlet that gave him a permanent pass to Brighton, and looked thunderstruck. But the woman was determined, and screamed harder than ever, so that at last, reluctantly, he advanced and as we all stood there grinning, tapped one of the combatants meekly on the shoulder. The fighters stopped in sheer amazement, both highly indignant, and asked him, "What the hell are you trying to do?" He lost his nerve then, but the woman kept on screaming, so he said, "Listen, you guys, you better finish the scrap around the corner, that woman is yelling her head off." So, with mutual consent they both took the policeman gently but firmly and carried him to the side, where one of them took off his M.P. armband and put it on his own arm, whereupon they continued their labours, and the policeman was able to enjoy the fight in peace because he was not an emissary of the law. Finally, the knock-out came, with the Scotchman the winner. He happened to be a Canadian from Montreal. The badge of authority and license was duly restored, and everybody adjourned to the public house to discuss the fight and show the loser how he had lost. He had a very poor defense and tried to box, the policeman among them.

So, with such prerogatives, and free trips to Brighton and no drills, I thought it was really thoughtful of the O.C. to make me a military policeman.

Two weeks later we began to be examined for a draft.

I wrote to Luella.

W. Redvers Dent

Thirty-one

Three days later as I was busily trying to catch up with my mail, which was weeks behind, and telling them at home to begin to send parcels to my battalion in France again, she came. It was a sunny day, I remember, and a chap came and told me I was wanted in the orderly room, so I trotted up, and there she was, waiting for me. The O.C. was present too and he grinned when I came in and had been trying, very patiently, to vamp her. She looked so smart and cool that I hesitated. Could this be the same girl? Oh, well, there she was. Her eyes danced mischievously when she saw me, and I discovered she had dimples.

I motioned her outside, and we stood a moment viewing the scene before us. The orderly room was on a hill, and from it one could see row after row of huts. "I never knew there were so many soldiers in the world," were her first words. "Are you glad to see me?"

I stuttered. "Oh, sure I am, but honestly I don't know what to do with you. There is nowhere to go, and I'm afraid I can't leave Shoreham now. I'm booked out." She smiled queerly.

"Don't you worry about me. Can you walk to the village?"

I told her I could, so we started off, and as I still wore my M.P. badge we passed the guards all right. We exchanged only a few commonplaces until to my surprise she led me off the beaten track past the church, to a little grey cottage, outside of which stood a runabout car of some kind or other. Her car. She took my arm and almost danced as she got to them. "What do you think of that? You and your Brighton! Look what the famous American dollar has done!"

She took me inside the cottage, and I discovered a wonderful little place, with a clock ticking and quaint cupboards and tables about. I looked my amazement. "How in heaven's name did you get this?" I ejaculated.

She was greatly excited now, and talked so fast I scarcely could make it all out. "I arrived last night," she told me, "and found out about this place, and the owner's husband is off to war, so I rented it, lock, stock and barrel, and she has taken herself to London with her kiddies. My, they were cute, too. So here we are. How, you sit here, and smoke, while I get lunch. And for goodness sake take off that tunic and belt and be comfortable."

I did as she bade me, glad to note that I had on a Canadian fatigue shirt underneath, which was quite smart, for the army. I didn't realize how tired I was until I got my feet propped up and sank back to enjoy life. And by Jove, she had even thought of beer, so I had a mug. What bliss. I heard her working away in the kitchen, and I thought it seemed like a home away from home. Then, shameful to relate, I dropped off to sleep. It was the ticking of the clock that did it. What a glorious feeling it is when one wakes from a good sleep, drowsy, brain not yet working, but just as content as a purring cat! That was just how I was feeling when I awoke to find her standing over me, still smiling that queer smile.

"Oh, the romance of life!" she said, laughingly. "Where am I, considered a good-looking girl, alone with a man in the house, and a man I like at that, and what does he do? Does he act as they do in the movies, and take me madly to his arms, crush me to his manly breast, and shout, 'By all the gods, you are mine!' Does he? He does not. He takes a glass of beer and goes to sleep!"

I yawned, stood up and stretched myself. "By Jove, that was the best sleep I've had in years. Eh? What did you say?"

"Oh Lord, I give you up. Absolutely hopeless. Come on, lunch is ready."

And such a lunch as it was! I ate ravenously of pie, raisin pie, and strawberry jelly, mashed potatoes, chops, thick gravy, everything, with tea. I was prepared for coffee, as she was a Yankee, but she gave me tea, such watery tea as they make, and I am afraid I was very unmannerly in showing I didn't care for it. She asked me, "Can you make it?" And again, I erred and replied that I could. So she took me out into the kitchen and I made it properly. The meal was then perfect.

She pushed me out and cleared away the wreckage while I smoked. I thought afterward I should have thanked her, but I forgot to, and weakly justified myself by saying she wouldn't want me to anyway. I must confess I was nearly asleep again when she came back, it was so quiet and peaceful, and presently I found myself with my head in her lap, while she stroked my head. She liked to do it, she said, and we agreed it was nice. I began to talk, and told her of Hartley and Allen and my wife, and she just listened and stroked my head. I couldn't see her face as she was looking straight forward, but her chin seemed to stick out. I even told her about my feud with God, and how I had feared that I was a hoodoo, and she gathered me up to her breast, and I clung to her. I felt so peaceful with my cheek touching hers, and somehow a text came into my mind, "Come unto me, all ye that travail and are heavy laden, and I will give you rest." Jesus must have been like a woman, I thought.

The shadows fell and still I lay there, with my head in her lap, and told her how scared I was of going back, but when I got a chance of a bombproof I couldn't take it. I told her how frightened I had been in France, and how I got the medals, and what a hypocrite I felt receiving them when I was such a coward. Then her head came lower, and she kissed me not passionately but solemnly. And she laughed her queer laugh, and said "I am going to call you my little coward after this." Presently she said, "Well, shall we eat? I know you are hungry." I remembered that I had been there a long time and that she must be stiff from sitting in that position, and upbraided myself for selfishness.

When it got later I had to go back to camp to see if word had arrived about the draft, so she went with me and stood in the shadow of a hut while I enquired. But no word had come, thank heaven, so we went home. I showed myself willing to leave at the doorstep, but she would not let me, and said I was going to stay, come what might. I was dumb founded, and glad. I led her up to that quaint attic room, and finally I left her, uneasy in spirit, certain that she possessed the spirit of sacrifice, while no impulse of the sort moved me. But as I lay tossing on my bed she crept in and lying by my side, said, "Let me be the judge and master of that which I desire." And after a while I slept, to waken and find her sitting up in the bed, praying. I saw her silhouette. There was silence, while she looked off into the infinite vistas of womanhood. Then she kissed me lightly and snuggled like a child against me, and slept. It was my turn to pray, but I could not. Only make vows.

She was in high good spirits next morning, up long before me, and bringing my breakfast to me as soon as I awoke. She sat on the side of the bed and watched me eat, her eyes large and luminous. By Jove, she was good-looking. I almost stopped eating in sheer wonderment of it.

Then a gleam of mischief came into her eyes, and she attacked. "I suppose now you want to marry me?"

I gulped, tried to look serious, and then grinned. "Well, what about it? Isn't it the only thing to do?" I asked, and she laughed.

"You dear old muggins, as if I would marry you now! You are foolish." I looked as foolish as though she had turned me down cold. She went on meditatively, "I do hope it's a boy."

I did stop eating then, and my arm hung suspended in mid-air. "A boy? A boy!" I almost shouted. "Good heavens, oh my gosh, a boy did you say?" She laughed and laughed, and I had to too.

"Well, what do you expect, twins?" Good heavens, these Americans! She grew suddenly serious. "I will never marry you, never, until, well—until ..."

"Oh, yes you will."

"I suppose like every other man you are outraged, and made a vow as soon as you awoke that we were to be married. Well, we won't. Why, do you think I haven't almost forced you into this? So you think I would marry you after that? Not on your life—not until—well, we will know when. You are going to France, may never, never come back. Did you think I was going to forego everything then? Not if I can help it," she added defiantly. "I even want a baby. I don't care. I hope it's twins."

She was crying now, and I petted her and soothed her. She sobbed, "Oh, Lionel, I love you so. I don't know why I should, but I do. And you'll love me, won't you, Lionel?"

We lived there two days, going up to camp once in a while to see if news of the draft had come through, and each time she waited in the shadow of a hut while I enquired, and each time she would clutch my tunic when I came out, not asking, but just waiting for me to say which it was. And on the second night it came. We were leaving in the morning at eight.

It was that night I woke up again and saw her sitting at the window, just looking out, motionless. I went to sleep to find her still there, and near dawn she came and snuggled up to me, waking me, and after a while I found my head on her breast once more, and let it lie there content.

After breakfast, she helped me into my things, and had even polished my shoes and buttons while I ate, and she fussed around me, always on the move, flitting here and there, brushing my hair, standing off to look at me anxiously, until I said, "Can I go to school now, Mamma?" But she didn't laugh.

Six o'clock the bell of the church tolled. I had to go, must put on the mask again, and like all other men in the world, try and act once more like a man. She didn't cling to me when I left—I clung to her—then hurried away.

As we marched down to the station I saw her standing motionless beside her car, looking for me. She waved when she saw me, and the fellow next me asked, "Who's your lady friend, Thor?" I shoved the butt of my rifle in his stomach.

She was still standing by the car when the train pulled out.

Thirty-two

When we were embarking on the boat that night, the O.C., who was now just captain again, motioned me out of the line. I fell out, and he said, "Listen, Thor, you grab one of these bags of mine and follow me."

I took the bag, put it on my shoulder and gladly followed him, as I saw his game. He had a cabin, and wanted me to have a little easier trip than I would have had if I stayed with the others on the jammed deck which inevitably would be covered with moaning *mal de mer* cases before we reached the other side.

We pushed and jostled our way through, the captain with his tubby figure easily clearing the way for me to follow. He ultimately found his cabin, and to my surprise it was already occupied by two other officers. I had forgotten that they would be crammed in just as we were. Like all Englishmen, they watched with fishy eyes and dumb amazement, the phenomenon of a captain making an N.C.O. at home.

"Sorry, boys," the Captain said, "to pack you a bit tight, but this chap is really an old friend of mine. I hope you don't mind associating with a gentleman for a change."

They grinned, and the ice was broken. One, a fair-haired chap with the Flying Corps badge on said, "That's jolly well right, Canada. The question is, will he associate with us. If he will, tell him to forget all about officers."

My old O.C. friend's eyes twinkled as he replied, "Don't worry, Limey, he will."

We settled ourselves as conveniently as possible, and I glanced at the other "Limey" as the captain called them, and saw that he was a tall hawk-nosed chap, with a thin frame, and features that were almost gaunt. He wore a monocle, and was really the first Englishman I had seen whom a monocle really fitted in the general ensemble. He had, relevantly or not, a large mouth and grey eyes, I noticed.

Tubby fetched out a bottle, saying as he did so, "I don't know whether you chaps have ever tried 'Canadian Club?'" They both nodded solemnly, so with all due ceremony the bottle was opened, glasses found, and the usual 'Here's how' spoken. I noticed then that the tall one belonged to the Royal Engineers. As we set down our glasses the R.E dived into his kit and brought out a bottle of wine. "I don't know how you like port, Canada, but here's some real stuff my old man gave me before I left. Shall we?" "We shall."

I was beginning to get doubtful. Wine on top of whiskey! Gosh, these chaps could drink! Heavens, the Flying Corps chap was digging into his stuff. Brandy next! Would we? We would, and we did. The air was black with smoke and I wondered if the R.E. knew how damned strong that pipe of his was. "Well, Canada?" I woke with a start. "What the devil is that ribbon you've got beside the M.M. there?" "What, that?"

He grinned. "Yes, that." I looked at Tubby beseechingly. What the hell did they call the thing? "I think the chap said it was the *Croix de Guerre*. I think it means cross, doesn't it?"

"Have you got the medal with you?" he asked. I looked at Tubby.

"Well, to tell the truth, I lost the damn thing in a poker game." They all laughed. "If the French hear about that they will cluck for a week," somebody said. "Let's have another brandy."

Then Tubby's voice was heard suggesting poker, if they played it.

"Do we play it?" the flyer answered. "When half the blinking corps is Canadian? Say, I'm in debt for the duration, to some of your countrymen. Not for me! But I will play you Black Jack."

"I know damn well you would," said Tubby, "and all you people would leave us is our shirts. Oh, no. Say, Diggie," he added to the R.E., "were you ever at the Salient?"

"That's been my little grey home in the west for the last year. And by Jove, I guess Fritzie knows we have been working by now."

"Well sir, I am darn glad to meet you, but tell me this. How did Fritz ever slip it over you so well in June 1916 when he blew up those seven mines?"

"Do you know, I have puzzled over that myself for a long time," he answered. "We had all sorts of listening galleries, but we never heard a thing, in fact we lost quite a few men. In them when things blew. I suppose it was in the same way he missed us this time. Were you in that to-do?"

"Was I," said Tubby. "I'll bet I lost twenty pounds in that scrap, just with worry. Have another? Say, did you ever have any fun in your outfit Limey? I mean a real adventure? How us poor bloody grave pushers never get any real romance. How about you? Did you ever meet Fritz underground? I'll bet you fellows a lot of excitement."

"How by Jove," the R.E. grinned. "Here I am seriously thinking of transferring to the infantry to get a little romance, instead of just digging in the bowels of the bally earth. And then you tell me there is no romance or adventure in it."

The air corps man laughed. "By Jove, no romance in the infantry! Now look at the corporal there, who's nearly bosco right now. Look at his bloody medals. What did he get them for? Bunk. There must be real adventure in the infantry. Just think, you meet Jerry face to face, while the R.E. here never sees the light of day or the Jerrys either. And as for me, I've brought down two or three chaps, and suppose I killed them, I never met the gentlemen. All I do is hear the engine, see an iron cross and goggles peering at me, then, tap tap, and one of us goes down and the other goes home like a man after a drunk, in a taxi to breakfast. All over in ten minutes. Romance in the Flying Corps? Rot! The infantry have more romance in ten minutes than we do in a thousand years. Tell us your tale, corporal tell us the tale of dead men, of the Jerrys attacking while you stand up in the trench alone, facing the whole bloody German army! If infantry weren't there, the R.E. couldn't dig, and the flyers couldn't fly."

"Hear, hear!" said the Royal Engineer. "Let's have another. That's the best damn speech I've ever heard. You should be a parson, Angel." We all laughed except the flyer, who blushed and said simply, "I was." We drank again. "Well, now, Canada, tell us your tale."

"Well," I said, "I'm honestly more puzzled than anybody else about getting them. I guess it was pulling the scissors out of the doctor's shoulder," and let it go at that.

"Well, well," said Tubby, "it's the first time I ever saw a Canuck that could keep quiet. So you were going to be a parson, eh?" he asked the Angel. "Are you still going to be when you get back?" Tubby was a little drunk, but quite rational. "Well, you ought to know something about this religious stuff. Where is that God of yours? Does he hibernate in wartime?" Both Englishmen were distinctly shocked, for an Englishman to discuss God publicly was just about on a par with talking about holes in their woollen underwear in mixed company.

"Don't know, eh? Well, believe me, if I ever meet him I'll give him one sermon he never heard before." Tubby glowered.

His outburst had sobered me, and I coaxed him into a bunk, where he immediately began to snore.

There was silence for a minute or two, then they burst out laughing. "Canada, I do verily believe your fat friend will give him an earful, as he calls it."

The R.E. said, "When this war is over I am going to visit Canada. A country that produces men that aren't afraid of God or the devil, and who show ability like that General Currie who has risen by sheer genius to the command of an army corps, must be some country."

"Not only that," added the flyer, "but look at their airmen. Bishop, a prince of men, and a wonderful fighter, and all the other Canuck fighters, who have more planes to their credit, and when I say planes I don't mean cold meat like observation planes that that German Richthofen gets, but real fighting ones, than anybody I know of. I tell you I watched them go over at Vimy, and I hate to make our friend blush, but there is no other army that could have done it so quickly and neatly and expeditiously they arrived at Foley Farm only five minutes late and were throwing up their flares to show objective regularly as a clock. By Jove, that was a sight I shall never forget. But here we are talking shop. Did you see the *Bing Boys*, or *A Little Bit of Fluff*? You know they are the best shows I have seen for a long time. Even have *Flying Colors* beaten. Let's kill the bottle before they arrive shall we?"

We duly killed the bottle, and suddenly grew conscious of artillery fire and the heavy thud of shells and bombs. The ship stopped and I looked questioningly at the R.E. "Don't bother about that, Canada. Jerry's trying to lay eggs on Boulogne, and the Archies are receiving him with open arms. You'll have to wait till it's over, that's all," he reassured me. I sighed with relief, and noticed that the Flying Corps fellow looked brighter too. It was just like waiting to cross the street during heavy traffic.

We arrived at Etaples, staying there only twenty-four hours, as men were badly needed. Conscription was becoming a necessity.

It was July when we once more reached the battalion. There had been several more disastrous trips in the line since we had left, and many new faces where old faces used to be. My heart sank. Just as I thought. It was logically impossible for me to survive a third trip.

Daddy welcomed us as usual, but this time we saw a change in him. Grey hairs were prominent and lines of worry were appearing in his face. As soon as he saw me he congratulated me on my silver-grey hairs that were now plain to be seen. He told me cheerfully that I looked as old as he did, if not older, and said, "Have you had rheumatism yet?" I had to plead guilty. "That's a certain sign of dotage then. We old men are about done, Thor."

When I walked back to my billet I brought out my steel mirror and I had to admit that I looked old. Was I actually aged? I likened myself to an engine that had been set at a certain speed, and just built strong enough for that. Naturally it would wear out very quickly when run above that speed. I was no longer nineteen but forty, and it would be more merciful for me to die than to suddenly break. I knew I could hold myself under control for a while, hut the brakes were getting warm. Someday there would be a crash. I began to be afraid of shell shock. I knew my nerves were going, and I would catch myself tearing paper, chewing my nails, and fancied I saw other signs of an impending break. I wished that death would be at the nervous breakdown to the tape. I hated the idea of going out as a shock case.

That night an argument started in the billets regarding the ages of the men. One swore he could judge the age of every man within two years. He started, and finally came to me. He looked me over carefully, and said, "I guess the corporal at thirty-six." The others looked at me for confirmation, and as I was afraid to tell my age even for fear it would, sound too ridiculous, I admitted his guess. My God, thirty-six! And I was nineteen. The same chap came back later and said, "Do you know, you're the only one who nearly fooled me, because in some ways you look young for your age." I bought him a drink.

Later, orders came that I was promoted to sergeant, and second in command of my old platoon in D Company. There was no officer, as the last one had been killed a few days before, with the other sergeant, so I was in charge of the platoon when we went into the line at the beginning of August. Owing to unforeseen circumstances the trip had to be doubled in time, as there was no one to relieve us. I was ten days with about two hours sleep a day, and with the responsibility of looking after the lives of thirty to forty men. On the second night Fritz found us with whizz bangs, killed four, and wounded sixteen, and on the fourth night we had to act as covering support for some working parties who were digging a trench in No Man's Land, and he found us again and killed two more and wounded five. No matter how recklessly I exposed myself, I could not get hit and the joke seemed to be on me.

On the seventh day, my head and arms began to shake, so that I could not stop them. They trembled like that for twenty minutes and I couldn't even lift a drink of rum to my mouth. Luckily, I was alone when it happened.

We were relieved on the day of August 18th in the pouring rain, and several of our men were too tired to walk over the ridge. I stayed with them in the village of Petit Vimy overnight, and stood guard while they slept.

The joke was still on me. We climbed the ridge in daylight in full view of enemy observation balloons, but not a shell came over. The next day we were rushed by motor bus to Le Brebis to relieve the Second Division, who had fought the Battle of Hill 70, which was still raging. The First Division had captured the Hill, but there had been so many counter attacks that they had to be relieved by the Second, who were in turn relieved by the third. The Fourth was holding our old frontage at Vimy, three divisional fronts. After doing a double trip, we were back in line again with hardly any rest.

The strength of the battalion had never been lower, and there were no fresh men in sight in those dark days for Canada. Every one admitted that the war could not be stopped. It was too big for one man or group of men to halt. We went to try to hold, at the price of several hundred men, a few yards of chalk called Hill 70; the feeling had come at last for which I was hoping. That feeling of death made me calm again, and my nerves were steady. I looked forward with interest to death, and made a bet with myself that something especially cruel was being saved for me.

Thirty-three

Tubby was now captain of the company to which I belonged, and we had hardly got outside of the town of Le Brebis on our way to Loos, when he dropped back. I couldn't see his face in the dusk, but patently he was worried the men were not grousing as usual, and when Canadians don't grouse something is wrong. There was a note of the usual noise and cursing, with distracted N.C.O.s begging the men to keep quiet, but a dreadful ominous silence, broken, once in a while, by a sharp pettish curse. The men were tired, we could tell by the drag of their feet.

Tubby spoke up. "By the Lord, Sergeant, I don't like this, they are too bloody quiet. Poor beggars, twenty days now without a decent sleep, and now this! And by the sound of it, it is going to be hell. Can you sing?"

"I? Sing?" I stuttered it again. "S-sing? What the hell for?"

"We have to make those guys forget their troubles, by hook or crook." he replied, and suddenly he himself began to sing. He had an awful voice, like the bellow of a bull in pain. I grinned and slowly, very slowly, I heard the men in front of me begin to chuckle, one by one.

Mademoiselle of Armentieres,
Parlez vous,
Mademoiselle of Armentieres,
Parlez vous,
Mademoiselle, have you any wine
For the soldiers of the Line,
Inky-pinky, parlez vous.

I joined with him.

Keep your head down, Fritzie boy,
Keep your head down Fritzie boy,
Late last night in the pale moonlight

Cry Havoc

I saw you, I saa-aaaw you.
You were fixing your barb wire
when we opened up our rapid fire
If you want to see your mother or your brother anymore
Keep your head down Fritzie boy.

The chuckle ran through the line and picked up, and carried on, till soon the whole battalion was singing.

Tubby started another:

Goodbyeee.... Goodbyeeeee....
Wipe the tears, Baby dear from your eyee.
For it's hard to part I know
But I'll be tickled to death to go
Don't sigheeee, don't cryeee.
There's a silver lining in the skyeee.
Bye bye old time,
Cheerio, chin-chin.
Napoo, toodloo. Goodbyeeee.

The adjutant came running back to see who the hell was making the noise. The men roared with laughter, and sang louder than ever. I said, "If we make, enough noise, we can't hear him." The more he raved the louder we sang. Catcalls were heard here and there, they began to yell at the gun-limbers passing, and everyone started to grouse again right merrily. I saw Tubby in the light of a flare wiping his face.

If you were the only girl in the world broke out. Thank God, the men were back to normal. Tramp, tramp, tramp the feet were swinging now, not dragging.

Somebody broke out. "Say, I saw a couple of Yankees today. Officers going up to Loos." Another voice replied, "Yanks, what the hell are they doing in France? They might get hurt." Everybody laughed.

"You blockhead," number one replied, "don't you know the Yanks are in the war?" Number two, evidently a humorist, said, "What, have we got to fight the bloody Yanks too?" Number One grew sarcastic: "You damn fool, they are on our side." The same voice answered, "So are the Irish."

Another voice broke in now, "What are they doing here?" to be answered by another, "Trying to see what the water feels like before they take a dip. I'll bet a dollar to a doughnut that after this bloody war is over, the Yanks will start an argument as to who won it, and they will have to appeal to the Germans for judgment, and Jerry will say to the Frenchmen, 'You did it,' and to the British, 'You did,' till at last they will have to have another war to settle it."

"Well, who will be able to say they won it?" another voice enquired. The humorist answered, "The Portuguese!" The discussion ended amid bursts of laughter, for everyone remembered one night when one of the patrols heard strange voices, and a fight ensued but it wasn't till they got back in their own lines that they found it was a Portuguese working party. We hadn't even known that Portugal had declared war on the Germans, and had a division in France.

Plod, plod, plod, the boredom of war was upon us. We were in Loos now, and the soil was different than in any place where I had been before. It was chalky and hard. No sticking in the mud here, I thought. We were out of town now, and everyone became silent again, just plod, plod, plod. Shells began to arrive, and men fell here and there wounded.

I find it necessary to digress here, to explain the Battle of Hill 70, and the Canadian method of attack and defense. The plan of the Canadians was unique in itself, and contrasted with the orthodox plan, which was to attack in close formation, shoulder to shoulder, so that one man bolstered up the other's courage. And in defense it was the same, sitting in the trench, shoulder to shoulder waiting for Fritz to come and get you. If there were no trenches this plan proved unfortunate, as it made the individual soldier who had placed reliance on having the company of others, sometimes retreat or fall back to where he would have companionship. The Canadian idea, of Lord Byng and later General Currie, was to take into consideration, not the Germans or the defenses, but the kind and variety of troops at their disposal. A Canadian was not as good in a crowd, as he was in a group or acting individually. These generals utilized this fact.

When we went over, the first wave was usually weak in number with men at wide intervals. The second wave a little closer, and so on. Each wave would jump over the other, the first wave stopping and the second going on with a sort of leap-frog effect, which always left one wave to rest and lick its wounds. The whole idea depended absolutely on the individual who must fight as well alone as in a crowd. It would happen often that the first wave would never fight, but avoiding that, move onto its ultimate objective. It would be the second wave that would clean up the Germans as they advanced. Many a battle was waged between the lines of the first and second waves. Once on the Lens front, in an attack, the second wave advanced slowly fighting every yard of the way, only to come upon the first wave calmly digging in and even cooking its dinner, and catching the stray Germans who fell back into its open arms.

The method of defense was equally elastic. The new front line would really be only a support, and in front of that would be raiding parties, bombing, whose business was to keep attacking and raiding the German lines, to keep them so busy defending themselves that a counter attack would be disorganized before it was begun. It depended absolutely upon the fighting spirit of these lone groups under N.C.O.s and often private soldiers for its success. That the method was successful may be shown well enough by the fact that the Canadians never lost a trench after taking it, and that they always got their objective, and usually more.

At Hill 70, a hill that overlooked the city of Lens, a hill that the Germans had to have if they were to hold the city, these methods were used. The front-line trench would be lined with machine guns, so that if the small groups had to fall back to their real front, there was a warm reception waiting for the Germans.

We had heard that Fritz had made fourteen counter attacks in twenty-four hours, before we went in, and was still trying.

It was a moonlit night, we were in single file now, and Fritz had concentrated all his fire immediately on the hill and behind it, so that no shells were falling in our vicinity.

My mind was at peace. I was glad to have written to Luella and told her that I did love her, that I had found that out in my first trip in the line since my return to France, and that I was thinking of her always. I was glad because I had had my picture taken and had sent it home, which would please Mother. I even laughed to myself at a joke I had on the army. I owed them one year's pay because of my crimes, and when I died they couldn't get it out of me. There was only one regret. I should have beaten up that orderly room fellow more. However, it couldn't be helped. In preparation for death, I had pinched some blankets out of the company store and traded them for brandy. My water bottle was full and I carried two spares in my haversack, careful shielded by my shirt. My field dressing was ready to use, in my pocket, and I carried two spares of them besides. I felt at peace with the world, my nerves were steady too, that was good. I hadn't written home because I didn't know what to write.

We were in the C.T. (communication trench) at last, and I waited at the side until my platoon filed by. Twenty-four men I counted and there was only one man who was dragging very badly, leaving a gap that might be disastrous. I knew him, he was nervous, poor devil, so I called him out and when he came alongside of me I began talking to him gently. He came closer—time was short—and I pressed the end of my rifle as heavily as possible on his foot. I felt the bone give, he wilted and fell with a groan, I called the stretcher bearer and told him to look after him and keep his bloody mouth shut, then joined the end of my platoon. Well, that was one good turn. The poor devil was game enough, but just nervous, and it was better to save him the agony ahead and let him get out now while he could.

The trenches were in good shape, I noticed; chalky, too. The British must have been working at them before we relieved them to take the hill, I thought. A devil's own job working in that stuff. The trench grew deeper, the shell fire closer, the pace quicker. "Wire overhead" sounded more frequently, and I began to get ready for action. "Keep close up there ahead, don't lose touch, close up, close up!" We were in it now, smoke kept drifting in, the trench was broken here and there, and dead were lying in the bottom. The usual roar and whizz of bursting shells deafened us. "Close up, close up! Keep touch, keep moving." Shuffle, stumble. "Keep, up, don't lose touch. Close up. Shell hole to the right. Keep up. Who is that?" A figure was sitting in the side of the trench. He wasn't one of my platoon anyway. "Keep up, close up, keep touch, keep touch!" The men were cursing blindly but kept moving, on and on. I don't know how long it lasted, but we were out of the trench now, over on our old front line I surmised, going overland, with shrapnel breaking around.

Tubby was waiting and told us where to go. I was ahead now, and on we went again, making time. More shrapnel. I felt some rattle against my steel helmet. Halfway over I stopped, counted the men as they passed, and found twenty-three. Not bad, not bad, I thought. On again. I had to run to catch the front of the line. Then some figures rose before us shouting, "Who is this?"

"C.M.R's relief," I answered. One of them waved his hand and I spread out my men in shell holes, making my contact with the other platoons. As we went out the others didn't even seem to wait to say goodbye, but beat it. We didn't know where Fritz was, or even if this was our own line. Not a darn thing did they tell us, but just beat it. Tubby came along looking for me. Things were quiet just where we were, as the shrapnel was playing between the lines, and was supposed to cut us off. "Well, here we are again," he said. "Save any casualties?"

"Not one," I answered, "Except Howard, and he was wounded a long way back."

"Thank God for that, anyway. Everybody else has got some. For once your platoon is lucky."

"Do you know where Fritz is?" I asked.

"They said we would be able to tell by the flares, but he hasn't thrown up any. They said to put out a patrol from each section. So will you detail off a section, Thor?"

I agreed. I had two really good men as corporals, so I decided to take the patrol myself, and leave them in charge. I would be moving all the time, and at least that was better than sitting idle.

We quickly established ourselves and brigade machine guns also moved in. So, we were ready, in army parlance, to "establish touch with the enemy."

Cry Havoc

Thirty-four

It was nearly dawn when we started out. Judging by the Fritzie flares we were about eight hundred yards from his lines. My section was barely out of our own wire when figures loomed up and a voice shouted, "Who's that?" "Gosh," I thought, "I have forgotten the password. What will I do?" My hair stood on end, and I was expecting a hand grenade any second when a member of my own section answered truculently, "Who the hell wants to know?"

I grinned. If they were Canadians they wouldn't bother about passwords. After that they didn't, but merely said, "Well, why the devil can't you answer quicker?" and passed on. We held a consultation in a hole after that, but as each one of us thought the password was different we didn't get much farther ahead. Finally, one chap decided it by saying, "Look here, the only guys we got to worry about are those who try to answer politely. Any of our own patrol will cuss us, and if we cuss them back, all will be well, so if we answer them, 'Who the hell wants to know?' every time we are challenged, I think we will get through."

So, we started out again, and were challenged three times by different patrols. No Man's Land was simply crawling with Canadians. We gave the inevitable answer, "Who the hell wants to know," and it worked. Our limit of safety was about two hundred yards from the German front line, as our own machine guns and artillery would be firing in that area. So we proceeded cautiously.

We were now on our own about three hundred yards from our lines. We strung out in shell holes and waited, and as we were unable to smoke, there was nothing to do but just keep peering in all directions.

It came at last—a German flare thrown up showed me some queer figures about twenty yards in front, but I wasn't sure, so kept peering. The sudden darkness after the flare had died down blinded my eyes. I spoke to the man beside me: "Did you see anything?" He replied that he wasn't sure he had, so we waited, bombs ready in our hands, and figures loomed out of the darkness.

A man from another hole challenged, "Who is that?" and a voice answered, "Canadians" but they were coming, and none of our men would have. I pulled the pin, shouted "NOW!" and let her go.

God, it was just like throwing snowballs when we were kids. Pull the pin and let her go.... CRASH-crash-crash. Bang, bang, boom-flash-smoke. Bombs began to come back, but they were wild. A flare went up and showed a big German patrol right in the open—crash—crash—crash— "Now, fellows—ahead! Down the——! Come on!"

A wild rush ahead. We had been told to get prisoners if we could. I fired my rifle as I ran, then another flare went up. Neither front line dared fire because of their own men. At last, my rifle held by the barrel and swinging like a flail, I met something. Grunts, groans, curses, squeals, thuds. "Kamarad, Kamarad, mercy, Kamarad, mercy."

It was over. We counted them up. Five prisoners, new boys. "Beat it, before the damned machine guns find us." A breathless staggering run toward our own lines. Then, I saw the light of red flares thrown up! Germans. Too late. They had caught us! Damn them—damn them! Crash, crash—crash—smoke—glare of blinding lights. Our own wire now, I fell over it. A blinding flash of light, a searing flame of a thousand hells—I am finished.

Thirty-five

My first waking impression was of stabbing, burning pain, pain that throbbed at regular intervals through my left leg. My left eye seemed to be covered with plaster of Paris, for I could feel nothing except that, and I had absolutely no action from it at all. My face also felt queer on the left side and began to tingle with an indescribable agony. My right eye seemed all right, though I was afraid to try to open it. And I smelled abominably of chloroform.

My next impression, after my numbed faculties began to wake, was of surprise. I thanked God I was alive after all—alive. Good God, alive! I shouldn't be alive, I should be dead. How the hell had this happened? Had God relented after all? The idea of it filled me with joy. God lad changed his mind, had seen that he couldn't beat me. By Jove, I will see Luella after all, after all. I can marry her, have kids. Won't it be glorious! By Jove, isn't it wonderful? Damn that pain—ooooooooh!

I groaned in spite of myself then I heard someone speak to me, "If you are awake now, will you lift your right eyelid? You can, it is quite all right try."

I opened it very, very gently, but the light was too much, and my head began to throb. Again, a voice began to speak: "I am afraid you will have to try and stand that pain, will you try again?" I felt a hand, fingers, on my eyelid, which opened gently and again the burning pain. It was in my other eye. My head throbbed. I saw a kindly face bending over me, its eyes filled with anxiety. "Now will you try to open your mouth? Do it very slowly."

I closed my eyes and concentrated on opening my mouth. It opened slowly, the lips seeming not to want to part, but they did at last, giving like stretched elastic, "Well, well, that's not bad, not bad at all. You can close it again." I obeyed then I heard the same voice again speaking to someone else. "Now nurse, give him hot milk and a pill and let him sleep, in fact keep him sleeping." Then other voices, but I was too tired and pain wracked to pay any attention to them. My mouth was opened gently and some hot milk trickled in, which I found myself taking eagerly. A pill was given me, more milk, and then came sleep.

So, the days passed. The doctor, milk, pills, sleep.

At last I was ready to be moved, and was taken to England, with the pain in my leg gone now, and pains in my eye only at intervals. It was my third morning in England that I noticed it first, and the conviction slowly grew that the pain I had thought I had in my leg was a joke. I didn't have a leg. The next day I pumped the nurse. I said, "Say, nurse, I guess I will have to have a glass eye, won't I?" She thought I knew, and nodded her head.

My God my leg, my eye! Ha, ha! The joke's on you now, Slim, the joke's on you. Now you know, now you know why God wanted you to live! Ha, ha, ha, ha, no leg, no eye! I lapsed into unconsciousness.

No other thought filled my mind but that of self-pity. For days, I brooded, and once I even lowered my pride to pray for death, as a mercy. My old quarrel with God made me like an animal in a deep chasm against a thousand-foot wall of rock. But there were distractions. While the bandages were on I looked quite romantic, and many visitors would stop and talk in the two-bed ward which I shared with an Australian. He was a splendid-looking chap, and a fellow whom one easily liked. He had lost both hands at the wrists, and I pitied him as he pitied me.

Our relations as soldiers were curious. The Australians and Canadians behind the lines were deadly rivals, and usually whenever they met there would be a fight. But both united in fighting the British tommies or Red Caps. There were many riots of this kind behind the lines, and it was never decided which were the best men. Many people took these riots as signs of revolt, when nothing could be further from the truth. They were neither better nor worse than inter-college fights in Canada. After our efforts to find out who was the best man we usually bought each other beer. When the Australians relieved the Canadians at Ypres, they grinningly baited us by saying, "We came here to do what you couldn't do," and when the Canucks heard the Australians had lost the first Stokes gun, they didn't hesitate to rub the raw wound. But the war being over for us, my Australian roommate and I could be friends.

"Well, I see the Americans are in now, so I guess we Australians have got our hands full now, we will have to lick both Yanks and Canucks!"

"You're away off, Aussie, it will be more likely be the Canucks having to take care of you two, for the Yanks and us haven't both of you all right!"

He laughed. "Well, anyway, it will have to be decided before the end of the war, or there will be trouble. Are the Yanks really as boastful as they say?"

"Between me and you, Aussie, they aren't. But I couldn't tell a Yank that or he would get conceited. They are just like you and me. The Englishman takes it so much for granted that he is best, that it just provokes us into telling him how good we are. I don't think such questions will ever be really decided, though I know of course any Canuck could lick any three of you with his hands tied behind his back, but the trouble is you chaps won't admit it."

"Yes, that's the only way you could!"

Another time we talked of God.

"I suppose you, like all the rest of your Sunday School nation, believe in God, Canuck?" There was no offense in his tone, only a matter-of-factness. I was startled.

"Do you Aussies call us a nation of Sunday School boys?"

The familiar grin appeared. "We certainly do. You know, you Canucks are very quiet people, and it takes quite a bit to get your goat, but boys, when you do, the Sunday School veneer goes like snow in Australia. You know, when we came from the Dardanelles we wondered how the hell you got your reputation as fighters. You seemed more intent on looking like mamma's little pets and making a hit with the women than anything, so we thought at first you were afraid to fight us. But after a while, we came to the conclusion that the reason for it was that you didn't want to get your clothes dirty unless you had to. Gosh! I'll remember my first fight as long as I live. But you haven't answered my question yet, Canuck."

I didn't know exactly what to answer. After all, the poor blighter might have believed in God himself, and there was no use in hurting his feelings. Now the question was asked, and I had to answer, I hesitated, and then said, "Well, Aussie, your opinion of God and mine may not coincide. If you had asked, 'Do you believe in the Christian God,' I could easily answer 'No.' But I don't know, gosh, there has to be a cause for us being here."

There was silence for a minute, then he said, "You know, Canada, I am not a religious bloke at all, and maybe I am better, maybe not. But this I do know, that the God I found back beyond is not the same God as the Christian. But we can't help that, *c'est la guerre*."

My bandages were removed next day, and then came the shock. As I said before, they had made me look romantic. But when I shaved that morning, I began to comprehend dimly the joke. God, I was hideous! The left side of my face was a large livid scar, with a hole about an inch across, and a quarter of an inch deep in the cheek. With the black patch over my eye covering the empty socket, I looked fiendish, hellish, the spawn of Satan. The muscles had been hurt or disarranged, for I had no control over them at all. Whenever I opened my mouth one side of my face smiled, and the other—Oh, God, the other!

I fell on the bed and lay there. I think I wept. After hours of moody contemplation which the Aussie did his best to break, it dawned upon me in wondering what Luella would make of this, that I had not communicated with her. The question was, should I? Wasn't it best just to drop her altogether? I couldn't marry her, so why bother her? But in spite of this logic, I decided to write. I wanted to test her. I wanted to see what she would do. So, I wrote, telling her that I wanted to see her.

That afternoon two girls came to the door of our ward laughing, joking. Then they saw me, and there was silence, horror, repugnance. They did not come in.

I understood now why God had let me live.

She came next day. She looked splendid, poised there like a bird, her eyes darting around looking for me. My heart pumped. I lay on my left side with my face buried in the pillow. I called to her cheerfully: "Well, Luella, here I am, like a bad penny."

She saw which was I, and came over with a smothered cry, knelt beside the bed. It was our hands which met. She cooed over me as though I were her child, who had hurt himself.

"Oh, Lionel, my love, my love. Oh, Lionel." I felt that her explanations were absurd, and wanted to push her away, but in spite of myself the tears came into my own eyes. "Oh, Lionel, my love my heart. Oh, darling, darling, how I love you—my coward, my poor brave foolish little coward!"

It was hard. I pushed her back and seemed to be pushing my own heart away. Pushed her back, and managed to say, "Sit down, I want to talk to you."

She fell back in hurt amazement at my tone. "Why, what's the matter, Lionel?"

Again, I said, "Sit down, Lu. Listen, I am afraid it's all off, we can't go any further. I—I—I'm no longer in a fit condition for marriage so it's all off."

"But Lionel, it can't be. It won't be. I will never allow it to be all off, as you say. What has happened? Have you lost a leg? Why that's easily fixed. You will be better in a short time. You love me still, don't you?"

She started to approach me, but I moved her back, an inoperative weak gesture. "Listen, Luella, I have lost a leg, I have, lost an eye too, and other things. You haven't seen my face. You wouldn't marry me, only out of pity. See!" I raised myself up before she could interpose any more assurances. "See what you would have—."

She seemed to wither up. The true state of things had been borne in upon her at last. She moaned and fell beside the bed. She shook with weeping, but I was game, and would not give in. My hand stretched out toward her, but it did not touch her. Poor little girl, it was a coward's trick to strike her through me.

The nurse came in, I suppose the Australian had called her, and took Luella away. I waited and the nurse came back, alone.

Thirty-six

I lay, a sombre, sullen, snarling beast, for days after that, and though the nurse and doctors tried hard to cheer me up, it was of no avail. The days passed and in despair, the doctors booked me for an immediate transfer to Canada. They did their best to warn people not to show abhorrence when they saw me hobbling around the hospital, but I was too much for human nature, or so it seemed to my morbidly introspective mood.

The world was filled with eyes staring with pity and horror at me as I passed. Even that was not so bad, but no one, not even other Canadians, could get up nerve enough to sit and face the thing that had once been a face, I was lost, out of communication with the world as completely, in fact more completely, than if I had been dead.

Then I hit, in my completely bitter perversity, upon a bright idea. I saw a soldier one night saying his prayers, so every night before getting into bed I stood beside it and carefully, religiously, cursed God, feeling as comforted afterward as though I had said a prayer. One night the Australian spoke to me after lights out. "I get your idea, Canada, you are trying to make God so mad that he will kill you. You certainly have guts. I would never have the nerve to do that." I smiled for the first time in weeks. It wasn't nerve, it was fear, fear of living.

In December 1917, I started for Canada, and in spite of myself hopes began to arise, hopes that were encouraged even more on the boat, as there were several who were really worse than myself in some respects, though none so badly disfigured. And the doctor encouraged me even more by telling me that there were surgeons in Toronto who could fix my face so that it would be barely noticeable.

We arrived in Halifax on December 18th, after an uneventful trip. I was looking forward to home, to Dad, to Mother. I understood them both better now, I thought. I saw the end of the road. The trip to Toronto was a triumph. At every station, there were crowds, cheers, bands playing, gifts. The nurse in the car was a born mother to mankind, she disregarded my face and nursed and petted me. I talked of home, and one day she said, "How did you ever get overseas, a man of your age?"

I looked at her bewildered. "A man of my age," I repeated. "How old do you take me to be?"

"Oh," she said, "you are easily forty-five."

I paused, thunderstruck, and at last managed to gasp, "Forty-five, forty-five! Do you mean it?"

She nodded her head. "Why, are you older than that?"

I hunted for my steel mirror. Forty-five, forty-five! Good God, she is off her head. Then I looked at that hideous face in amazement, and had to admit it. My hair was quite grey now, and under my right eye were heavy wrinkles, and of course the wound distorted my face out of all reason. But—but—I forgot about the nurse, who left, and stared at my face stupidly. Forty-five!

I shall never forget the night we arrived at North Toronto Station. Looking out of the window I saw a veritable sea of faces. There was a roar of cheers, and a band was playing "See the conquering hero comes." My heart fluttered with excitement. I had telegraphed Dad and Mother about my arrival, and I knew they would be waiting. Every one of us who had a home in Toronto had been given ten days leave direct from the train, so we could go home again. Home. "See the conquering hero comes."

The nurse bustled through the car. "Sergeant Thor, you had better remain in your seat, your relatives will find you easier that way, and probably can have you carried out." I agreed.

The others filed out slowly, and as each one left the coach, a roar of cheers greeted them. The band played "The Maple Leaf Forever" and "O Canada." It was wonderful. I waited eagerly for Dad. There he was, towering over the others, looking for me. He made his way forward and I lost sight of him, but I knew what he was doing, he probably had entered the train farther up, and was even now pushing his way through the ears hunting for me. "O Canada, O Canada!" Home! Mother! Dad! At last he came—he entered the doorway, walked down the aisle, glanced at me and passed me by....

He didn't know me.... Oh, God, he didn't know me! I could have wept, or laughed. *Ha, ha,* the joke's on you! "Dad, Dad! Here I am, it's me, Lionel!"

Dad came back, stared at me, then, "God in heaven, my son!" I wept again, and he fell beside me, picked me up in his strong arms, crooned over me while tears from his eyes fell on my face. Through the doorway, out onto the platform, then that crowd of gaping fools saw him. A thunderous roar of cheers—the band. "See the conquering hero comes." And Dad marched straight through that crowd, cursing it.

In the car he held me in his arms still and crooned to me. After a little while he spoke: "Mother is waiting at home, son, with your favorite kind of pie and everything. Don't worry now, don't worry, you're home."

Mother was on the porch waiting, with the light on, and a banner strung across with "WELCOME HOME." Mrs. Braithwaite was there too, and many others, but Mother stood alone at the top of the stairs waiting. And once more I was going up that long path. The end of the road this time, true enough.

Dad marched on, up the path, up the steps. A glad cry from Mother, "Oh, my boy!" Dad said nothing, but looked at her with eyes that said, "Woman, behold your handiwork."

A scream that wrung my heart and made me rise out of Dad's arms to tell her not to worry. Then she saw that hideous horrible thing that was her son—saw that it was no one else—gave another cry, the cry of a damned soul, and fell.

W. Redvers Dent

Thirty-seven

I wakened in a strange room, dimly lit, in a bed that was most comfortable, and as my one eye blinked open my first thought was of Dad, poor Dad. Just more grief, more trouble for him. I rolled over and went to sleep. Again, I wakened to feel a hand on my head, a soft gentle hand that was cool to my head. I was afraid to open my eye for fear the hand would move, but at last curiosity compelled me. I smelt a most delightful perfume, and moved my head, and I couldn't see the face. At last, however, I stretched my neck back, and saw a chin, a woman's chin. I smiled and moved my head. With that movement, there came a startled gasp, and the chin came downward and a face came before my line of vision. A face not exactly beautiful, but piquant, with beautiful skin, a small tilted nose, nice mouth and bright brown eyes, wonderful eyes. I smiled she smiled, and we watched each other for the fraction of a moment. Then she realized her position, and moved. "I'm so sorry, so sorry, but I must have gone to sleep. Just a moment."

She disappeared, coming back in a moment with medicine which she gave me. Then she sat on a chair surveying me with those eyes, which, while they did not antagonize me, made me feel a resentment at being regarded as helpless. Yet I liked being helpless just then. The quizzical living eyes of a real woman. She spoke again: "I suppose it is permissible to call you Sobersides?" I started. Where had she found that name? The question must have shown in my eyes, for she said, "I am Allen's wife." Allen's wife! I began to ejaculate questions. "Where the—I mean, where did you come from? And where am I?" But she hushed me. "All in good time, Sobersides. But now you must sleep some more." I suppose my look must have been pleading, for she came over and put her hand once more on my head and sat beside me and once more I slept.

So, the days passed, sleeping, eating and petting. I wasn't in my home but in hers. Again, life began to come back to me. I wanted to sit up, and one day she allowed me. Dad visited me often, and my room was filled with flowers, until I said pettishly one day that I didn't like the overpowering perfume, so she quietly removed all but some blood-red roses. I wondered at this exception, and asked her about it. She said bluntly, "They are from an old lover of yours," and she smiled that curious smile again. "One of them?" I protested. "But Mrs. Allen, I haven't any old lovers." To that she answered merely, "I heard you talking in your sleep," and left me.

The next day Dad had a long talk with me. He told me that I had been given leave indefinitely on account of the illness. The loss of blood through my wounds had made me very weak, and this was not helped by my spiritual condition. Mother had died from shock and heart failure during my relapse, and had been buried without my knowing. Dad looked careworn, poor old

Dad, he had tried his best for all of us, and I was the net result.

At last I said to him, "Listen Dad, wasn't it Mrs. Braithwaite I saw on the veranda?" He nodded. "Well, where is she now?" I asked.

"She left her husband, Lionel, and obtained a divorce. Mother asked her to come and stay with us, for the sake of the children, when she came one day several months ago to ask about you. You know Mother changed a lot after you left. She became a wonderful woman, and I fell in love with her all over again."

"But how did I get there, Dad?"

He smiled, the first smile I had seen from him for a long time. "When you know her better, Lionel, you will find out that that young lady gets whatever she goes after. She came to the house one day just before you arrived, and enquired about you, said her husband had constantly talked of you. I am proud of you, Lionel. I met your other friend, the V.C., when the city welcomed him, and he said you were the finest, whitest chap he had seen." (I blushed.) "She wanted to know if you were the same man, and when she found out that you were, she said she would like to meet you when you came home. We were both delighted, and mother especially fell in love with her. So when things were the way they were when you got back, she insisted on taking you to her home, and I was so bewildered, I agreed. She brought you in an ambulance, and has nursed you ever since. In fact she has taken absolute charge of you and not let anybody see you except myself." He was silent a minute or two, then said, "You must have had a very trying time overseas, son."

I grinned, I couldn't help it, and said, "You cover it perfectly, Dad, it was very trying. In fact, almost painful at times!" We both laughed.

The door opened and my nurse peaked in. "Time's up, Mr. Thor, I'm afraid," she said with a smile. Dad left, and I was glad to go off to sleep again. I slept and dreamed of the rats and of Allen, and woke in a sweat of fear to find her sitting beside me, singing an old Irish lullaby, so softly and sweetly that I slept again, dreamlessly this time. But before I drifted off I wondered how many times she had done that very thing. What a woman she was.

Every morning she would bathe me and rub my body with alcohol, my body that was now just one mass of sears and holes, though apparently, they didn't bother her at all. Every other day her own doctor called, and every afternoon a specialist; but who had sent the latter I could never find out. I asked her one day when she was going to allow me to get up and have other visitors, but she only smiled and said, "You can get up tomorrow, for good, but as for visitors, not yet."

That made me mad, and I pouted like a spoiled child. Who the devil was she to boss me around like that? My mind filled with the grievance which finally extinguished all other thoughts, and the more I pouted the more delighted she appeared to be, and the more delighted she became. "Mrs.

Allen," I said "I certainly appreciate your kindness in looking after me, indeed I shall never forget it, but what right have you to forbid visitors? Remember I haven't seen these people for two years, and I would like to see them."

Her answer surprised me, to say the least. "You can have visitors or leave this house the day you stop pitying yourself and blaming everything on God, so put that in your pipe and smoke it."

I did. I was so dumfounded at the accusation that I gaped at her. She only smiled and left the room. I pity myself? Good God, no. And if I did, by Jove, didn't I have a right? Hadn't I gone through more than many able-bodied and older men? Why, what had got into her? Pity myself! I wonder, maybe I did sympathize with myself plenty. Look at Dad, hadn't he stood an awful lot? I wonder. She came into the room again, and I asked her, "Say, Mrs. Allen, were you honest then in what you said about pity?"

"I certainly was, and am," she returned. Wasn't she a terror, so blunt and honest! Well, after all, I did hate people who pitied themselves, too. What was it Dad had said to Gordon about playing the game?... And all the time she watched me with quizzical eyes. "Poor old Sobersides, he never was treated like this before by a nurse, was he? That's the trouble. You have brooded too much, and I am going to cure it. On second thoughts, you can get up this afternoon and come downstairs and make yourself useful. You have been lazy long enough!"

I started at her grimly. "I'll get up, but damned if I am going to do everything you tell me!"

She laughed indulgently and said, "We shall see. Get up." And I got up.

Reconstruction had begun.

There were many spirited arguments after that. I resented be interrogated like a small boy and it was not until long afterward that it dawned on me that her treatment of me was deliberately calculated to the end of arousing my temper, and by so doing, to occupy my mind. I began to take an increasing interest in life, even in trying to help her as much as possible.

Great portions of everyday were passed in reading. Allen's collection, philosophical and creative works rubbing shoulders haphazardly, suited my mood, and I found myself building new reason and faith in spite of my bitterness. A new house for myself. After all, it was a wonderful world in which so much had been done and thought. When I tried to unravel things, my mind would not hold to any course, much less its old too-sure one. But if I lay in a half-trance, my body forgotten, there was nothing too big for me to grasp. I came to the conclusion that God and I occupied the same boat. If I failed, so did he.

Not only that, but in this calm and secure harbor, cut off from the storms of the world and flesh, I could see Allen's arguments in clearer perspective, for after all, instead of being so ready to curse God, I had a lot to thank him for. Allen had said that these things were man-made, the war, the birth of myself and all the forces that pushed me against my will into the turmoil, man-made, every one of them, except, as I began to see more clearly, the friends I had gained, for at every period in my life there had been a friend at my side to help me through my troubles; Mrs. Braithwaite, Hartley, Dad, Allen, my Luella, even the German who had given me a drink in No Man's Land. There were two sides to the picture. I could curse God for the sufferings or thank Him for the friends, or neither. More and more did Allen's views come forward in their true light. I even saw God as I would my own father, who had created me, given me freedom to think and act, and by that very act of creation had curtailed His own freedom. God, Dad and I were together, and it was only by uniting our aim and ends that unified purpose could come out of it all, and until then, chaos, friction and languor that inevitable ensued through us all pulling in different directions. Endlessly on did my thoughts run, and all the time, God was at my shoulder, hoping and hoping.

As the days ran on, I fell in love with her kiddies. My disfigurement did not bother them for a minute, and we grew to be great friends. The eldest was a curly-headed boy, the image of his daddy. One afternoon as I drowsed in the den, he came in alone and stood looking at me very solemnly. "Mummy's crying." I felt embarrassed but also curious.

"And why is she crying, son?"

"Oh, just about you and Daddy," was his startling answer. "She cries nearly every night. Boys don't cry, do they?"

"No, son, boys and men shouldn't cry, just girls and women."

"But I don't like to see Mummy cry. I wish you could stop her. Daddy always could when he was here."

There was silence for a few moments, then I asked, "Where is your mummy?"

"Come on," he said. I took my crutches and he led me into another room, where she lay on a bed, her frame shaking. It was my turn now. I comforted her, and found a sweet relief in thinking of the sorrows of another.

Every night after the kiddies had gone to bed and the maid had gone for the evening, we met in Allen's den, a small cubbyhole of a room, but cozy and comfortable, with its walls lined with books of every sort. There was always a fire there, and she nestled in front of it like a kitten, while I lay on a couch and watched her. One evening shortly after I had found her crying, I asked her why she had cried about me.

For a minute, she said nothing, then: "Men are such queer creatures. I never believed the story of Don Quixote until I married. Then I found men were just like that.... It was a wonderful thing, your friendship. I was almost jealous of you until at last I understood that a woman could never have a lover like that. He had given you more than he gave me ... the passion men have for an idea or their work, or another man's friendship. But I heard you talking in delirium, and I understood. You went through so much together. I supposed, when Allen wrote about you, that you must be one of those men with a handsome appearance and a tremendously forceful personality, a man outstanding among men. You had to be, I thought, or Allen would never have worshipped you. I dreamed about you, and after Allen's death, or possibly before, I too began to worship you, love you from afar-off like a school girl. Oh, I dreamed dreams about you, and then, when I heard of your coming home, I could not resist it, I must see this man whom my husband loved. I had to beg your mother to let me wait and see you. Then, you came, broken, sobbing, and I took you home, gave you my bed, nursed you, and thought as I had never thought before. I had worshipped a god, to find that he was a man, or even sometimes a small boy." She smiled. "Then I began to see as I listened to your delirium, that if we would only see, every man is the prince of our dreams, if we could see. I saw your outward form, broken, but when I heard you cursing God, daring Him to do his worst, I saw you as you were, and could understand why Allen loved you.... I can understand any man far better."

I looked long at the fire, almost asleep, for her voice had soothed me, and when she stopped I waited a minute for her to continue. But as she did not I spoke of what was in my mind.

"I too have made my discoveries of men since I went overseas. I found good men, bad men, cowards, saints, heroes, villains. I have travelled a long way on the road, but even now I can't see the end. Shall I tell you about my discoveries?" She nodded, and I continued. "You may talk of heroes and think of men who have earned and received medals, or fabled beings who possess no fear, but I know what fear is. It has been with me a long, long time. See? It has turned my hair gray. I know fear, and I know men who possessed no fear, and every last one of them were bull-headed morons, ignorant, without brains to imagine either fear or bravery. Heroism is not an impulse, it isn't ignorance. I knew a man (not Allen) who was in my section when I was wounded, and fear possessed him, he was sick with it, his teeth chattered, his legs almost gave way under him, but he kept on, kept on. He had been one of these furtive pool room rats, a sort of guttersnipe in civil life, you see. But he kept on. Well, that was sheer stark heroism. I knew a saint; she was a harlot, who gave me what little self-respect I have. I knew a virtuous man, who kept sober, never smoked, and never broke any commandment, and yet I hated and despised him and the lowness of his aspirations. I have found beauty in rottenness, and rottenness in apparent beauty. I found myself loving blasphemers and rogues, heart-breakers, woman-breakers, and hating flat-chested, thin-lipped virgin maiden ladies as unnatural.

"I have found everything except God, and even then I begin to see the end of my quest for Him. I found a girl who loved me in one way, and I married her, and found a soul of beauty and even a new existence, and she died. She loved me as a mother loves her child. I had another who loved me, loved me for my body, physical passion, and it too was beautiful, but when that attraction was gone, the love wilted and died. Each love was true and perfect in its own perspective, and as for your love for me (I am old, old beyond my years, don't be offended), your love is not for me at all, it is your loyalty to a man that makes your love for me."

The fire flickered and almost died. She added two more logs, and we waited in silence, watching the flames burn up once more. I looked at the face of my nurse, her dark eyes seemed sad, and clear, and they turned to me unashamed; and they said, before I heard her lulling voice, "Does it matter?"

And I was content for that night.

Glossary

Archies: A slang term for German soldiers.

Battle of Hill 70: A Canadian battle on August 15, 1917 that was intended to act as a diversionary action to draw German attention away from the British offensive known as the Third Battle of Ypres. Located on a strategic high-ground outside the Belgian city of Lens, the action was a Canadian victory despite the predictions of British commander Sir Douglas Haig. The victory rendered Lens of little strategic importance to the Germans for the remainder of the war.

Battle of Ypres: The battle referred to by Dent was the Second Battle of Ypres, which took place over several weeks between the end of April and early May in 1915. The Canadian Corps, composed of relatively inexperienced troops, were exposed to poison gas from the Germans. The French Colonial Corps on the Canadians' flank broke and ran in the face of the chlorine gas. The Canadians managed to retake lost ground by mid-May and the battle did little to change the picture on the Western Front other than to instigate the use of a Canadian invention, the gas mask.

Blighty: A slang term for England as a place of rest and leave; also the term for a self-inflicted wound that would remove a soldier from the battlefield; or the term for a wound inflicted by soldiers on an unwanted comrade to remove the undesirable soldier from a troop.

Bosco: A slang term for losing one's mind.

Bing Boys or ***A Little Bit of Fluff*:** This is likely a reference to cheap music hall comedies that were playing in London, England, during the war, and the latter title may refer to London prostitutes who were frequented by soldiers on leave to "Blighty."

C.M.R.s: This is the abbreviation for the Canadian Mounted Rifles, originally a cavalry corps trained at Barriefield near Kingston. Dent's protagonist, Lionel Thor, and Thor's best friend, Hartley, join the mounted regiment in the hopes of wearing fancy cavalry uniforms and serving in a horseback brigade. On their arrival in France, the regiment was assigned to infantry duty. Dent remarks that the regiment of one thousand men was replaced eight times over by mid-1916, having suffered casualties at a number of major engagements such as Passchendaele and the Battle of the Somme.

W. Redvers Dent

Canon Scott and Woodbine Willie: Canon F. G. Scott, an Anglican churchman from Montreal, was an inspirational hero to Canadian troops during the First World War. His poetry and his memoir, *The Great War as I Saw It*, are important chronicles of the Canadian experience in the trenches of France and Belgium. Canon Scott was the father of F.R. Scott, the Canadian poet and one of the founders of the Cooperative Commonwealth Federation, the forerunner of today's New Democratic Party. **Woodbine Willie** was the British equivalent of the respected Canon Scott. Geoffrey Studdert Kennedy was an Anglican priest who wrote poems about his trench experiences. He was noted for giving spiritual guidance and cigarettes to dying British soldiers.

Colt/Vickers Machine Gun was the most frequently-used machine gun by British forces in World War 1. The 7.7 mm water-cooled gun could fire 450 to 550 rounds per minute. It required a crew of seven to eight men to haul, operate and set up. Known for its reliability in battle, the gun remained an active part of the British ordinance up to and including the Korean War.

Courcellette: The Battle of Courcellette took place from the 15th to the 22nd of September 1915 as a follow-up operation to the disastrous Battle of the Somme the previous July. The battle was the first major action for the Canadian forces in World War 1 in which they took an offensive strategy, and was also the first battle where the tank was introduced by the British forces as a weapon. During the action, the Canadian army captured the razed village and distinguished themselves for making a small yet significant gain, though at a high cost.

Croix de Guerre: The name of a medal given by the French Army for service in and to France in time of war.

Dugouts were reinforced caves in the earth dug beneath the trenches. They were used for shelter from enemy fire and for communications and command purposes. Some dugouts were sophisticated enough to have multiple rooms and rest facilities.

English Tommy: A slang name given to British soldiers.

G.A. Henty (1832–1902) was a Victorian historical novelist whose "ripping yarns" of adventure in the British Empire were widely read by the generation of schoolboys who fought in the First World War. Among his works were *With Clive in India*, *Bonnie Prince Charlie*, and *With Wolfe in Canada*.

General Currie: General Sir Arthur William Currie (1875–1933), the brilliant and innovative Canadian commander of Canadian troops in France during the latter part of the war, was the general in command of Canadian troops at Vimy, Hill 70, and later actions such as the Battles of Passchendaele and Mons.

Housie-housie was a card game played by the troops during World War I. The players would each draw a card off the top of the deck, and then bet on whether they had a matching card in their hand after the cards were dealt.

(The) King: George V of England, supreme commander of the British and British Empire forces, whose reign lasted from 1910 to 1936.

Limey: A slang term for an Englishman.

Lewis Guns: The American-made Lewis Machine Gun was a lighter, more portable machine gun that was limited in the quantity of ammunition that could be loaded into its unique circular canister mounted atop the gun. Though it took only two men to operate, its limitations for use as an extended rapid-firing weapon made it a secondary choice to the heavier and less portable Vickers Machine Gun. Lewis Machine guns were still in use during the Korean War.

Tommy Longboat (1887–1941) was a famous Canadian runner of Aboriginal origins who was known for his swiftness during the early years of the twentieth century. He served as a regimental dispatch runner in France during the First World War.

M.M.: Abbreviation for the Military Medal given for conspicuous gallantry and courage in the face of the enemy.

Mal de mere: A slang term for seasickness used by British and Allied troops. From the French.

The **Menin Gate** was built on the site of one of the original gates to the medieval Flemish city of Ypres in Belgium as a war memorial to the thousands of men listed as missing on the Western Front who have no known graves.

Mount Sorrell was a battle fought over a piece of ground near Ypres during the period from June 2 to 14, 1916. Canadian troops were assigned to take a particular piece of ground during the action, Hill 62. During the action, Lieutenant General Lord Byng assumed command of the British forces. Byng later became Governor General of Canada during the 1920s.

N.C.O.s: The abbreviation for non-commissioned officers—officers who were promoted from within the ranks of enlisted soldiers.

Passchendaele: One of the bloodiest and most prolonged actions of the First World War for Canadian forces, the battle took place between July and November of 1917 in an attempt to seize several pieces of high ground that were under German control around the city of Ypres in Flanders. The area where the Canadians fought was mostly flooded due to torrential rains, and numerous casualties occurred when men slipped off the "duck boards" (which looked much like today's wooden shipping skids) and drowned in the mud.

Parados: The name given to a firing step that enabled soldiers in trenches to stand above earth level and fire over the top of the trench. These were usually built of wood although surplus crates were often used for the purpose.

R.C.: Roman Catholic.

R.E.: Royal Engineers.

Red Caps: The name given to military police during World War One. They were distinguished from common soldiers by the fact that their khaki forage caps were replaced with red forage caps.

Richthofen: Baron Manfred von Richthofen, German fighter plane pilot and air ace credited with the highest number of kills (downed planes) in World War 1. His death, a matter of some debate, was credited to Captain Roy Brown, a Canadian pilot, though this has been disputed in recent years by Australian historians who claim that the infamous "Red Baron" was downed by an Australian anti-aircraft machine gun crew.

Royal Engineers' Dump K: An ammunition dump established and managed by the Royal Engineers, who were responsible for creating trenches and communication lines and who handled and stored quantities of explosives for the purpose of creating major earthwork projects such as tunnels under No Man's Land and enemy lines.

R.S.M.: Regimental Sergeant Major.

Sanctuary Wood: The Battle of Sanctuary Wood was part of the broader Canadian operations begining in June 1916 and continuing through to August of that year. Sanctuary Wood is a broad term that embraces the separate actions at Courcellette, Mount St. Eloi, Mount Sorrell, in and around the razed city of Ypres in Flanders. One of the seven Canadian memorials to the fallen soldiers of the First World War stands at Sanctuary Wood just outside Ypres.

Sam Browne belt: The belt, named for its inventor, a former Victoria Cross recipient who served in India during the nineteenth century, consists of a regular belt around the waist and a diagonal shoulder strap running from the right shoulder to the top of the waist belt on the left side. It was originally designed to keep a cavalry scabbard from shifting from side to side during battle. During the First World War, the belt was issued to all officers and to Red Caps as a symbol of authority, and as a means of keeping small side-arms at the ready.

Stokes Gun: The Stokes Gun, designed by Sir Frederick Stokes in 1915, was essentially a portable mortar used to fire light-calibre shells in the trenches. It is also known as a "trench mortar."

Tea-fight: A slang term for a tea party. Also a slang soldier's term for a light action with few casualties.

V.C. (Victoria Cross): The Victoria Cross is the highest decoration for gallantry and bravery in the face of the enemy given in the British and later Commonwealth armies. The medal was created by Queen Victoria in 1856 during the Crimean War, and is cast from bronze taken from cannon seized at the Battle of Sevastopol.

Vimy Ridge: The Battle of Vimy Ridge took place between April 9 and April 14, 1917 as part of the extended British campaign known as the Battle of Arras. The Canadian Forces led by General Arthur Currie took the ridge after French, British, and Australian troops had all suffered heavy casualties in previous failed attempts. The major Canadian War Memorial in France now stands atop Vimy Ridge. In taking the ridge during the three-day action, Canadian forces suffered heavy casualties of over 7,000 dead.

Whizz-bangs: A type of shell that was set to explode in the air after making a whirring or whizzing noise.

Ypres: Situated just inside the southern border of Belgium in the Flanders area, Ypres (pronounced "i-e-per") was considered strategic to holding the northern portion of the thousand-mile Western Front. The medieval town, known as one of the "cloth towns of Belgium," was razed early in the war by German artillery. Several battles were fought for control of the city (the Battle of Vimy Ridge is often called the Third Battle of Ypres because the Vimy

Heights provided a broad, panoramic view of troop movements and deployments in and around the city). The first Battle of Ypres took place from the 19th to 22nd of October in 1914, when British and French troops captured the city from the Germans. The Second Battle of Ypres involved Canadian troops in their first significant action of World War One when, from April 22 to May 15, 1915, Canadians held the town despite being outnumbered by the Germans. It was at this battle that poison gas was first used in the war by the Germans. The Third Battle of Ypres in 1917 involved Canadians in actions at Passchendaele, Vimy, and surrounding areas in an effort to repulse the Germans from the northern side of the hilly country to the north of the city. By the end of the war the entire medieval city and its famous Cloth Hall were reduced to rubble.

Zeps: Abbreviated form of "Zeppelins," dirigible German airships used for reconnaissance and for bombing cities such as London and Paris.

Zillebecke was a village about 1½ miles south of the city Ypres in Belgium. The village, which was quickly razed during the First Battle of Ypres in 1915, was situated on Lake Zillebecke, and provided the only crossing point over flooded ground between Ypres, held by British forces, and the front lines. Considered a portal in the rite of passage into battle by Canadian troops in the First World War, it was held at great cost in order to maintain access to the front.

9's: A term for artillery pieces that fired shells that were nine inches in diameter.

Acknowledgements

I am grateful to a number of individuals who made the reclamation of W. Redvers Dent's *Cry Havoc* possible. Thank you to Bruce Whiteman, formerly of McMaster University's Mills Library, for pointing out this book to me over 30 years ago as a bibliographic anomaly; to Steven Temple, formerly of Steven Temple Books in Toronto, for obtaining an autographed first edition copy of the 1930 edition of *Show Me Death* more than twenty-five years ago when I began my pursuit of Canada's lost trench literature; and to Barry Callaghan, my co-editor of *We Wasn't Pals: Canadian Poetry and Prose of the First World*, who saw the merit in what I had found in my relentless search of various archives, barn-sales, and second-hand bookstores as I sought to unearth a missing era of Canadian literature, and who assisted me in bringing authors such as W. Redvers Dent back to public attention. A very special thanks is owed to Karen Wetmore of Grenville Printing at Georgian College in Barrie without whose technical brilliance the electronic text could not have been transformed from a carbon typescript to a workable document. Her patience and perseverance are very much appreciated. I wish to thank Peter Redvers for forwarding a copy of the original typed manuscript of *Cry Havoc*, his wonderful work in obtaining various family records from W. Redvers Dent's descendants, and in obtaining his family's permission for this book to be reborn in this edition; Daniel Dent, who met with me in Barrie and provided the first concrete information about the author; Madeline Dent, for sharing detailed information about Walter Dent's life; Mark Dent, who saw the excerpt of this novel in *We Wasn't Pals* and contacted me to see if the original manuscript could be brought to light—Mark's diligence in protecting the legacy of W. Redvers Dent was a key factor in the germination of this project; and members of the Dent family, including Tassillie Dent, Steven Dent, Robert Dent, Cameron Dent, Mardi Getty, Rhonda Dent, and Adam Dent, for all their support, enthusiasm, patience, and excellent input throughout this project. This book would not have been possible without your belief that the project would come to a fitting conclusion. The children of W. Redvers Dent must also be acknowledged: Gilbert (killed in the Second World War), Ronald, Hartley, Norman, and particularly Carol, who kept the original typescript of this book for many years and preserved it in the belief that it would one day be appreciated in its original voice and form. A special acknowledgement is owed to Edith Olive Dent, the wife of W. Redvers Dent, who prepared the typescript from handwritten copy provided to her by her husband; it is because of her dedication to this work that the typescript of the book survives. A heartfelt thank you to Jen Rubio of Rock's Mills Press for her critical eye in the preparation of this book; to my wife, Kerry Johnston, for her wonderful feedback and support; and last though certainly not least a very special thanks to David Stover, publisher and president of Rock's Mills Press for his belief in this project through all its manifestations, challenges, setbacks, and rejuvenations. I would ask that readers of this book remember Walter Dent, the trials he endured while serving Canada in the First World War, and the tribulations he experienced in attempting to share the truth of his story with his fellow Canadians. He was a hero in both war and peace.

B.M.

www.ingramcontent.com/pod-product-compliance
Lightning Source LLC
Chambersburg PA
CBHW030907080526
44589CB00010B/185